The Spanking Writers
The best of the blog
2006-2007

Abel and Haron

The Spanking Writers
Abel and Haron

First published in Great Britain in 2009 by
Abelard Books

This paperback edition published in 2010
by Abelard Books
www.abelardbooks.co.uk

Copyright © Abel and Haron

The Martha Papers © Martha

A catalogue record for this book is available from the British Library

ISBN: 978-0-9558483-1-5

The moral rights of the authors have been asserted. All rights reserved. No part of this publication may be reproduced, stored in a retrieval system or transmitted in any form or by any means, electronic, mechanical or otherwise without the written permission of the Publisher.

2006

Welcome to our spanking blog!

By Abel and Haron on 22 March 2006

Hi! (Wonder how you've found us? Do tell...!)
 Here goes... Putting on posh voices, in unison: "We name this blog..."
 Really looking forward to meeting you, whoever you may be.

Time for serious punishments

By Abel on 25 March 2006

Wandering round Greenwich this afternoon, being silly at the Royal Observatory, jumping back and forth across the prime meridian line ("now I'm in the east, now I'm in the west, now I'm straddling the whole world").

We wandered into their wonderful souvenir store. I always adore unusual shops like this – and they usually throw up something that can be misused for fetish purposes!

This time, my gaze fell on a display of egg timers and hourglasses. Now three minutes may be long enough to soft-boil an egg, but one can hardly make an impression on a girl in three minutes – and an hour might be deemed excessive.

But they had a device called a sermon timer – the grains slide through in exactly fifteen minutes. I had to buy one, of course: a visual tormentor to support "you may wait for fifteen minutes to think about your misbehaviour before I administer your whipping", or a quarter-hour with hands on head to "reflect on what you've just learnt".

Or, of course, to time a fifteen-minute punishment: an unusual form of 'sermon' to correct a girl's misguided approach. Haron was horrified at the thought, of course.

And what a nice image of a demure maid in some Victorian rectory being called before the parson for a carefully timed punishment, using his sermon timer...

Punishing cheating students

By Abel on 28 March 2006

According to a survey in the Guardian yesterday, one in six undergraduates at British universities "admitted copying from friends' work". Apparently "students caught cheating are far more likely to feel a sense of irritation at being caught out than to feel a sense of shame, humiliation or remorse".

You can imagine where this took me on a flight of fancy over the breakfast table: would our local University appreciate my help to ensure that future punishments are more apposite?

I'd expect suitable recompense, of course: it would be demanding work. I don't know how many university students we have locally, but let's guess 10,000. Fifty per cent female (others could deal with the boys!)? Let's assume they'd only cheat once in a four-year University career (and believe me, if I were dealing with them, they *would* only cheat once). Thirty weeks in an academic year?

That's one young lady a day needing to be disciplined, making well over a thousand strokes per year to be administered (at the usual tariff of six per time, which some readers may deem lenient for an offence of this magnitude). You can just imagine the risk of repetitive strain injury.

A girl's first caning

By Abel on 2 April 2006

The headline in Time Out, the London listings magazine, made me stop in my tracks: "The First Cut is the Deepest".

I'm sure songwriter Cat Stevens wasn't writing about canings. But in our little world, of course, it's the final 'cut' that's traditionally the most severe.

I'm guessing, though, that for a lass being caned for the very first time, it would indeed be the first stroke that went deepest. Deepest into her psyche: no longer an always-good-girl but now a has-been-caned-pupil; now shamed. Deepest in terms of the surprise, horror at the intensity of the pain. Can any subsequent cut ever compare?

The uber-cool 80s German dance act Propaganda (where are they now???) were also confused, albeit I found their song Duel incredibly thought-provoking at the time:

> "The first cut won't hurt at all. The second only makes you wonder. The third will have you on your knees."

What on earth were they using as an implement?

My birched girl: a real-life story

By Abel on 5 April 2006

If you go down to the woods today...

...you'll find that spring is sprung. So Haron was dragged off into the local forest at lunchtime, scissors in hand, to cut the first switches of the year from the birch trees. It took about eight of them to make a robust birch rod (a couple of firm rods to give it backbone, the rest lighter and more whippy), neatly trimmed then tied firmly with string.

She was Violet. Her parents were working abroad, so she'd been sent to stay with her father's best friend (now a schoolmaster) for the Easter holiday. Her behaviour since she'd arrived had been typical of stroppy teenager: at turns argumentative and sulky. Breaking a vase, on purpose, was the final straw.

We talked: I was disappointed. It was a shame, I said, that such a lovely young girl was growing up so defiant; I reflected on how sweet she'd been when she'd been little. I asked how her father dealt with her when she misbehaved (knowing all too well that the slipper was his implement of choice); there was even a confession of being caned at school. I used the birch on students in my house at school, I explained, and that was how I was going to deal with her now – with her father's full permission.

Her trousers and panties came down, and up she went over the pillows on the middle of the bed. And then she was birched. Slowly, firmly. A birching breaks her very easily: by the third or fourth stripe, the young lady's insubordination is long gone.

I'd awarded her ten strokes. If the girl starts to struggle by the fourth, "six of the best" allows her solace from the fact that her whipping is almost complete; with ten, on the other hand, her punishment has hardly started. A meek, apologetic Violet struggled her way through the flogging: yelping, shamed. Brave, very brave.

We talked before the final blow: she assured me that she would be the proverbial "good girl" in future. And then the last stroke was laid, and Violet was climbing up from the bed, wincing as she pulled up her clothing, obediently returning the birch to its home in my study.

And then Haron was back, and we could cuddle...

Whackings with the tawse

By Abel on 7 April 2006

Couldn't help but giggle at the description of a tawse on eBay, from one of my favourite sellers there. He's describing a school tawse which came from a London school, and which dates from the 1930s. It's '17" long x 1 1/4 x 1/8" thick' and he bought it from someone who thought it came from Highgate School.

The section that made me laugh: "on the reverse someone has written "bastard" in ink".

Cue stern, outraged, booming voice: "Who was responsible for this?"

Silence amongst the assembled masses, pupils staring down at their desks. The author sitting still as a statue, maintaining an air of innocence. Some glancing around, seeking out the guilty party. Some blushing despite their lack of involvement.

"I shall thrash each of you unless the culprit owns up."

Silence. But furious glances now being thrown around the room.

I wonder what would have happened. A mass whacking?

Or a sheepish student owning up? My goodness, what a whacking that would have been...

Judicial whippings

By Abel on 8 April 2006

I love waking up with Haron and whispering fantasies into her sleepy ears. This morning, I imagined the whippings across the road in Edinburgh castle: the magistrate, sentencing a girl to a 'private whipping'.

Everyone assumes that a 'private whipping' was a lesser sentence than one in public. I imagined the magistrate deciding that he would administer the punishment himself. In private. Deep in the bowels of the castle's prison wing. Where no-one could hear a girl scream, and no-one would bat an eyelid even if they did.

Where a gentleman could make a girl strip, then whip her to his heart's content. And then punish her in more intimate ways...

He might even decide that to prevent her falling back into a life of crime, he'd take her back to his country estate. Clean her up. Keep a close eye on her...

Aren't lazy Saturday mornings great?

On the good ship...

By Abel on 9 April 2006

Thank you, Your Majesty.

Really. I mean, I know I'm not the biggest fan of the monarchy. But us mere 'subjects' can now tour your Royal Yacht, Britannia, moored in Edinburgh. Below decks is an old handwritten notice regulating the sailors' lives.

Item ten inevitably caught our eyes: "Any transgression of these rules will be punished severely." How nice. Not 'all', presuming that transgressions would occur. But 'any': in the very unlikely event...

Then the audio-commentary in the dining room described how the place settings had to be just so. Everything laid out precisely. To the centimetre. And how the settings would be measured with a ruler before dinner. Guess what Haron's going to have to do the next time we have pervy friends for dinner? Guess what's gonna happen to her with the ruler for any inaccuracies???

And then there was Your Majesty's souvenir shop. Resisting the temptation to purchase the pseudo-naval memorabilia (there being a distinct absence of cat o'nine tails), we found ourselves in front of a leather fly swat. A very nice leather fly swat indeed.

My mum arrived: "Oh, they come in really handy in the summer. Do you need one?" I assented, as Haron shook her head frantically. What a kind mother: the implement was whisked out of my hands into her shopping basket.

I'm pretty confident (despite some suspicions about my father's probably-unfulfilled kinky inclinations, of which more anon) that her definition of 'handiness' is different to mine… Three hours later, Haron was bent tightly over the armchair back in our hotel to appreciate her mother-in-law's generosity. Most enjoyable. And at least any Buddhist readers can rest assured that no flies will be harmed with our new swatter.

Later in the evening, over dinner, my father asked Haron how girls were punished at school in Ukraine. He seemed quite disappointed that they were merely made to stand in the corner. I was quite disappointed that she didn't invent birchings in front of the school, or solitary canings in Headmasters' offices.

Two weeks' worth of birching

By Haron on 12 April 2006

This morning I was steeling myself for two vanilla weeks: I was flying off for a stay with my parents in Kiev.* The taxi was due at 4:14 am, the alarm was set for 3:45.

There was a birch rod next to the bed - still more or less functional after our scene last week.

Last night Abel said that he would birch me just before I left, but this morning, seeing me on edge with flying nerves,** he offered to scrap it.

"No, I want a birching," I said.

I didn't want the pain, I never do, but I needed the intimate connection we develop through the pain, and I needed some stripes to take onto the plane with me. I lay over the pillows he stacked in the middle of the bed, and clutched the covers. The strokes were sharp, precise, and each one hurt more than I can easily cope with, but that was what I needed this morning.

I got twelve in all: a mass of red in the middle of my cheeks, runaway twig marks on the edges.

We kissed, and held each other, and then I left.

*Of course, my time there won't be completely devoid of kink, because a) my dear friend t'Larien is there, and he's kinky as they come, b) I'm actually going for the science fiction convention Eurocon. Writers are sick bastards on the whole.
** Hate flying; hate flying anywhere without him.

The Wind in the Switches

By Haron on 14 April 2006

Today I walked home past a row of beautiful weeping willows, fresh and green. I thought of Abel, and of the switches he would cut before he dragged me up the hill by the ear.

Or maybe he wouldn't bother taking me home. Maybe he would whip me right there in the street. I mean, maybe I was particularly bad, you know?

Wooden spoon spankings

By Abel on 15 April 2006

To Germany – having conveniently scheduled a business trip there for the day prior to the Easter holiday weekend, giving me the excuse to stay over with a similarly-minded friend for a few days.

We returned to the hotel one afternoon to find my brand new wooden spoon ever-so-neatly placed on the bedside table: so thoughtful of the hotel to leave it in easy reach! I do wonder what our room maid thought when she saw it – whether it was "I wonder what they were eating" or "I wonder whether it hurt"?

No wonder the hotel staff were being so polite to us for the remainder of our stay.

Curtain of Dark Passions, My Ass

By Haron on 16 April 2006

Today, over a cup of coffee to ~~celebrate~~ mourn the end of Eurocon, a friend shared with me a great piece of salacious gossip about one of the grand-masters of Ukrainian fantasy. (Remember when I said that writers were sick bastards? Well.)

The ~~gentleman~~ guy in question spent part of last year's convention trying to convince my friend to - quote - lift the curtain of dark passions - unquote. At the end of the conversation, says my friend, the two of them were surrounded by a group of this writer's fans, to whom he preached about the joys of (reading) de Sade.

This friend's taste in men doesn't include either drunk middle-aged fantasy writers who lack in muscles, or de Sade. Thus, she declined.*

"Did you ask what passions he meant, though?" I'd always found the guy interesting in a "he sends me kinky vibes" way; there are plenty of tasty references in his novels.

"Not really. I wasn't interested either way."

"Damn. If he ever tries it on again, can you say 'no, but my friend wants to know what passions exactly you mean to lift the curtains off'?"

So, I probably wouldn't have taken him up on it either - kink and talent is all very well, but a pleasant personality helps, too, and he doesn't have one of those - still I've spent the rest of the day wondering what he'd meant to do.

* For those who are wondering: I do like middle-aged fantasy writers. Muscles are optional. Inebriation is out of question.

Serious punishment pending

By Abel on 17 April 2006

I got home last night. Easter Sunday. Plenty of chocolate waiting to be demolished. And no heating.

You may have noticed by now that from time-to-time Haron discusses those occasions on which she is on the receiving end of real-life discipline. She's a good girl: really, she is. Absolutely decent, honest, hard-working – but occasionally she has lapses that need correcting. Never anything malicious; she's just a little prone to letting herself down.

These particular punishment scenes aren't usually kinky, or hot, or fun when they take place. But they're an important strand of the twine that binds the two of us so tightly together.

One of her responsibilities is keeping the gas meter topped up with cash. (I'm away for work so often that I'm not around enough to keep a regular eye on it). She forgot once, as one might: that met with a scolding but no more. She forgot again – and, as I was feeling generous, she was given a final warning rather than the spanking that she probably deserved.

The third time (for inevitably there was a third time), she was caned. However, the poor girl was so mortified at her mistake that I was convinced that even a light punishment would resolve the issue. Four gentle strokes, plenty of cuddles, and it was dealt with – problem solved, once and for all.

And then, last night. Back home, to an icily cold house, the gas meter flashing away at "£0.00".

Haron's not here, which makes it worse: she knows she's in serious trouble, yet has a week to wait before facing the consequences. My mind keeps debating how to deal with it: I so want to be lenient, especially as we'll have been apart for a couple of weeks. Lines? Corner time? Yet I've been very far from severe on three occasions now and it's simply not worked.

I don't think leniency is what she needs. Nor do I really feel that it's the most compassionate option.

My butt is doomed

By Haron on 18 April 2006

Eeeek. That's all I have to say in relation to Abel's previous entry. Eeeeek!

Happy St. George's Day!

By Abel on 23 April 2006

I always think it's a shame that we're not given a public holiday to celebrate our national saint. Although I am not religious, and therefore don't believe in saints with special properties or powers, I do believe in holidays... Perhaps I should give Haron a good English caning to mark the festivities. Shame she's away.

Indeed, we could start a cycle of the saints of Great Britain: a belated caning when she gets home for St. George, then a tawsing on 30 November celebrating St. Andrew, followed presumably by a good daffodilling for St. David next 1 March.

Interior decoration, spanking style

By Haron on 24 April 2006

My friends took me to a new eatery in Kiev, a place called "Trali-Vali" on the Shevchenko Boulevard. The walls are painted to look like a child's drawings (a very artistically gifted child's drawings), with captions: "This is my brother. He wants to be a professional footballer." And so on.

Guess what I kept imagining on the walls.

"This is my teacher. He keeps a tawse in his desk. It really hurts."

"This is my mum. When I'm naughty, she smacks me with a brush."

Honestly, can't take me anywhere.

One of the ones in which my wife gets caned

By Abel on 26 April 2006

It's been a very English day: a few hours watching a cricket match locally, and then home to administer a caning.

Haron's home: time to deal with the gas meter incident. A few words from the safe end of the cane might interest some.

The lecture, first, as I held her very tight. How she'd been given chances; how I'd been lenient; how that hadn't worked and the time for leniency was behind us. We talked about trust: promises made after her previous caning, subsequently breached. How I would be punishing her severely.

She was sent to the spare bedroom, to stand in front of our school desk waiting for me. I selected a cane: one that I knew would imprint my messages effectively. She didn't turn when I entered the room. I made her lower her trousers and knickers to her ankles, and lean forward: the desk is at just the right height to position her perfectly.

And then I caned her. Twelve hard strokes, marking her: each white stripe transmuting chameleon-like into red to match its predecessors. Plenty of time between each blow. The occasional stroke of her hair or back, to help her through it. Hard strokes. Very hard.

She was brave. She always is. A good girl at heart.

How I love her.

Strictly come spanking

By Haron on 30 April 2006

Tuning in to watch "Doctor Who" last night, I caught the end of the amateur dancing competition "Strictly Come Dancing". I never watch it, but maybe I should: before my very eyes a guy contestant threw the girl contestant over his shoulder and mimicked spanking her sparkly-dressed bottom. That's right, spanking: it wasn't just one smack, but a rather extended - if somewhat over-acted - piece of pervery.

The best part was the reaction of the audience: they broke out in loud cheers. As soon as his hand landed the first time.

I should be going into a feminist rage, but I can't summon up the fury.

The hardware shop

By Abel on 1 May 2006

I just wandered past an old-fashioned hardware shop, one of a dying breed. A carefully-hung selection of mops and brushes fluttered in the breeze; peering inside, I spied a veritable treasure-trove of household essentials.

The friendly proprietor of a neighbourhood store such as this would know everyone, be at the heart of the community.

Children would be despatched by their parents on errands; smiling down at them, he'd check their order, wrap their goods with brown paper and string, and teach the youngest how to count out their change.

He'd have a special drawer, of course. I imagined one young lady, in her smart school blazer, nervously perusing the shelves inside as I walked past, sniffing the shop's distinctively clean air, waiting for the coast to clear of other shoppers. He'd welcome her warmly: he would have known her since she'd been a little girl. He'd have heard of her successes - the scholarship to the Grammar School, the prize-winning poems.

And now she'd be telling him, under her breath, that her daddy had sent her to buy a strap from the special drawer. He wouldn't hear the first time: she'd have to repeat herself louder, glancing over her shoulder lest anyone had entered the shop.

And he'd shake his head sadly. He'd know that she was an only child: there could be no confusion as to her imminent fate. And he'd reach into his drawer, and rummage around for the lightest strap he had left, and parcel it up carefully as a tear trickled down her cheek.

Waiting for my punishment

By Haron on 1 May 2006 in The Punishment Book

The punishment I got the other day was marked by the longest wait I've had to endure between finding out I was going to be punished and finally getting it over with.

Do you know that in Tyrer v. the UK, the European Human Rights Court case that screwed judicial birching of juveniles forever, the Court was swayed, among other things, because the lad had to wait 3 days for his birching? Yup, the Court thought things like that made a punishment inhuman.* Well, I had to wait for 9 full days for my comeuppance, and it nearly killed me.

It so happened that earlier this month Abel and I left home on the same day to go in different directions: I was going to spend a couple of weeks with my parents in Kiev, and he was doing his usual flitting-about all business-like thing. He was coming home a week before my return.

"I wonder," he said on the phone just after getting home, "is there a good reason why the indicator on the gas boiler should be flashing red?"

I have a history with the gas boiler, documented for posterity, and rather unpleasant. "Um," I said, feeling slightly ill. "It's, um. I think it might be out of credit."

Silence was my answer. And then a few bad words, as my poor husband discovered that he'd returned to the house that had no heating on.

This is where I felt really bad. It was a cold night, and quite late at that; there was a good chance nowhere would be open for Abel to put money on the card, and what if he had to freeze all night just because I hadn't checked the credit before leaving? I didn't even think about being punished at that point: the thought of Abel having to spend all night in a cold house was tearing through me like a hooked claw.

Eventually he called back to say that he found an open shop, and that the heating was now on. And told me that I was going to be punished when I got home, though honestly, he didn't even have to tell me that: I'd figured it out by then.

For the most part, over the next week I was able to shove all thoughts of the impending whipping to the darkest, dustiest corner of my mind, though sometimes it felt like somebody had walked into that corner with a lamp, lighting up all the things I didn't want to look at. From time to time, all through the week, I would get a jab of "Oh damn, I'm getting a thrashing" feeling, which I would hurry to forget, but never for long.

The morning after my arrival home, Abel announced that after dinner that night he would cane me. I could have howled. After dinner? Why not before dinner? Why not mid-afternoon? Why not right then, for that matter - so OK, I had work to do, and he had a cricket game to go to,** but surely it could all wait half an hour? All these rather annoyed thoughts have found expression in one squeak:

"After dinner?"

"Yes," said Abel.

Seeing how I was in the doghouse to start with, and quite deservedly so, I chose to leave it and practise some more compartmentalisation.

It was a wise choice. In the end, Abel must have been as tired of waiting as I was, because, as soon as he was back from his game, he asked whether I wanted to get it over with now. Yes, yes, yes, I very much did. Funny how the fear of the cane got completely overshadowed by the need to get rid of the hulking great boulder of anticipation hanging over my head.

He lectured me, even though he didn't need to: I was sorry enough without it. He held me all through the lecture, which was nice. Then he told me to go to the spare room, and wait for him while he selected the cane. I didn't care to see what he'd chosen, and he didn't insist. He told me I would get 12.

The first of these felt like I'd never been caned before; like I'd never so much as felt the slightest tap before. I couldn't imagine ever having liked this sort of treatment, or having been into it. I think I howled. My memory about the rest of the punishment gets slightly fuzzy here, as though the remaining 11 strokes were one long stretch of pain. I didn't cry, but I did jump around a fair bit. Abel might have lightened up after the first one, or he might have gone on as hard as he'd started, I really couldn't tell. All I know is that it was a hell of a hard caning.

Maybe next time I'll just choose to wait for my punishment indefinitely.

* Just saying.
** Yes, really, he's just that boring; thank God it's not golf, or I never would have married him.

The best way to make strokes count?
By Abel on 2 May 2006

I should work in advertising.

I'm in the departure area at Heathrow earlier this afternoon, off on another dreary business trip. I find myself standing in front of an advert for Philips' new electric shaver. Their slogan: "Make every stroke count."

The illustration? A boat crew rowing up a river.

Here's my alternative suggestion. A blazered schoolgirl is bent tight over the Headmaster's desk. Wearing a gown, he administers a hard stroke with his crook-handled cane. The photographer snaps at the precise moment of the rod's excruciating impact across her pleated grey skirt.

It would get the ad noticed more, right?

Testing a tyre paddle
By Haron on 2 May 2006

I got paddled last night for no other reason than to try out a new implement Abel bought for us a few weeks ago.*

It's an enormous tyre paddle from a company called *Burning Rubber*.

More specifically, it's a large piece of tyre rubber (complete with tracks) on a pretty metal handle. It looks very industrial, something out of a steampunk novel, or perhaps a post-apocalyptic movie. In fact, if Judge Dredd dispatched judicial paddlings, this would be exactly the sort of implement that would be used to deliver them.

Anyway, we felt like playing last night, but I was too tired to come up with a role-play, so it was going to be a good old just-because paddling with a gigantic chunk of rubber.

My impressions of this beautiful implement? It hurts like nobody's business. With the first stroke Abel must have intended to imprint tyre tracks on my butt, because he whacked so hard I couldn't even scream for about three seconds. He didn't get the tracks, just some redness (as he informed me), so he decided to hit even harder. This time I screamed alright, and also danced about the room, saying nasty things about the paddle, its wielder, its maker, and the postman who'd delivered it. After this Abel lightened up - not by much - and I got the rest of my six swats with just about bearable strength.

Man... it was horrible. The burning feeling afterwards was really nice, though.

Abel spent the rest of the night being quite pensive, and in the end declared that, perhaps, to get those tyre marks he'd have to get another of these paddles, only smaller.

Do you think this would be a good time to call a spousal veto over how our budget is spent? Or maybe I should bribe the postman?

* Yes, weeks. What can I say? We've been busy.

Singing in morning assembly

By Haron on 3 May 2006

Last night was "That'll Teach'em" night: modern teenagers made to go through a term in a 1950s school. They don't use corporal punishment in the programme, obviously, but there is usually still a lot to sink my pervy teeth into.

Yesterday, for instance, one girl was goofing off in choir practice, and so the music teacher made her sing solo in the morning assembly, in front of the whole school. She was visibly worried beforehand, though she did try to brazen it out that morning in the dorm. When the time came to sing, she quickly found her voice, and in the end managed to give as reasonable a performance as her vocal talent allowed.

I was watching this, and imagining a story I would write. The main character is a frustrated musician, whiling away his still-not-famous days teaching music in a school. He can't find a way to approach his pupils; whatever he does, they seem to mock him.

There is one girl in particular who spends the entire lessons whistling the tunes instead of singing them. The teacher would love to send her to the Headmaster, but he wants to make her submit to his will without external help. And so, he makes her sing the school song in assembly, expecting that embarrassment will subdue her, and he would come out on top.

Far from it: the girl is enjoying her time on the stage, and proves quite a performer. She makes the whole school sing the chorus with her, and gets a standing ovation from the pupils.

The Headmaster is now aware that this teacher has no control over his pupils, and is not impressed at having been kept in the dark.

The girl gets caned after all, for not treating her punishment with the seriousness it deserved. The teacher gets fired. The end.

Spanked 16?

By Abel on 6 May 2006

Hotel chain Hyatt have just launched their hideously-named "HyaTTeen Suite 16 program". The prettily-illustrated press release tells us that "this new package empowers teens to assert their independence and celebrate their birthdays by indulging in a range of fun activities with their best friends."

The package includes a suite for the night, limo transportation, popcorn, dinner for eight and a "Trained Hotel Disciplinary Officer on hand to administer paddlings to young ladies whose behaviour disturbs other guests".

OK, I made the last part up.

The Shah's pleasure house

By Haron on 9 May 2006

Abel is reading a travel book about Iran and emailing me quotes. The following conversation ensues.

From: Abel

To: Haron

"The Pleasure House stood nearby; its walls and ceilings were made of mirrors, and in its centre was a sunken chamber, down whose sloping sides the Shah would slide, and frolic naked with fifty of his favourites."

From: Haron

To: Abel

1. Fifty?

2. How did he get out?

From: Abel

To: Haron

1. You don't think 50 is enough?

2. Floated, I should imagine.

A good honest spanking article?

By Abel on 10 May 2006

Sitting in a pub with a decidedly vanilla friend on Monday night. She disappears to powder her nose, and I pick up the Evening Standard, abandoned by a previous drinker.

I glimpse my friend returning from the far side of the bar, and fold away the paper. Fold the paper, in all innocence, in such a way that the headline on the top of the page reads: "Taking the danger out of a spot of good honest spanking".

I nearly choked, and only just composed myself before said young lady reappeared at my side. Yes, dear readers, the Standard did it again. Said paper accidentally found its way into my briefcase for the journey back to my hotel.

"One of the more peculiar experiences I had recently was attending a two-hour 'spanking skills' seminar in Soho House in order to write it up for a glossy magazine". (I'm not into it myself, see? Let's just make sure that the denial gets into paragraph one. I was only doing it for the money. Really. After all, my friends might read this).

Topics included "Where to spank?" (People paid money to be enlightened on this? I am missing a business opportunity) then "How to spank? And with what?" (oooo, onto the tough questions now).

People get paid to write this stuff?

Bamboo, boo hoo

By Abel on 12 May 2006

Poor Haron.

You see, she's not very good at watering house plants. Even cacti and Joshua Trees - survivors in the most arid desert conditions - perish at her hands if I head off on a long business trip.

Now, I'm too generous to whack her for failing to water plants that she probably dislikes in the first place. That would be cruel. And I'm not a cruel man.

But when she was away recently, I decided it was time for a selection of our more recently-expired plants to find their way to the great garden centre in the sky. I happened to notice that one particular orchid (or, perhaps, 'ex-orchid') has been propped up by a rather nice cane. Thin, not hugely flexible.

Said orchid disappeared to the waste bin; said cane was hidden away for future application.

So, Haron finds herself at 11pm last night with a good few hours of work still ahead of her to finish off an important paper. She wanders upstairs, and I happen to notice the by-now-forgotten length of bamboo. I whacked her with it across her jeans, as one would. "Doesn't hurt," she grinned, with a trademark 'I want to be smacked' wiggle.

A girl underestimates a cane at her peril. Apparently it did hurt, a lot, when it was applied more forcefully, the young lady positioned face down on the bed, backside in the air, jeans and panties removed. Hurt enough that a firm hand was needed on her back to hold her down for the whacking.

And then she went off to complete her work. She always seems to study more diligently when her backside is striped; I have a theory that it reminds her of the impact of slacking. See, I was only helping.

Gentlemen spankers invariably head towards rattan for their cane collections; I'm beginning to think that the qualities of bamboo need further research.

I want to be an academic

By Abel on 16 May 2006

I've just found that Google has a "Scholar" site that searches academic papers. A search on "corporal punishment" serves up more than 10,000 papers.

Whilst I suspect that the majority of these aren't in the least bit kinky, the idea of turning up in the office in the morning and researching spanking has a certain appeal. (NOT that these days I ever go into my office in the morning and research spanking rather than doing the work I'm supposed to be doing. Honestly).

I do so love unearthing learned reports on the web that explore historical corporal punishment. This, for example, was published on a Canadian government site:

"Punishments were meted out frequently for simple disciplinary offences, often of the most innocuous kind, and whippings were administered before an assembly of the inmates.... In the prison's female quarters young girls experienced similar treatment. The records show that one 14 year-old was whipped seven times in four months."

Haron, c'm here. Role play ahead...

Camel whips

By Abel on 18 May 2006

We're going to a wedding on Saturday. The friends concerned are decidedly vanilla. His parents are certainly not. Let me explain.

Said parents were away when we first visited their house. Son sits us down, disappears to fetch drinks. And our eyes simultaneously come to rest on the huge plant pot in the corner of the living room.

We wandered over, as if in shock: yes, it *was* stashed with the most impressive collection of crook-handled school canes that I have ever seen: junior, senior, in every conceivable degree of whippiness.

Our friend came back in. "Camel whips," he explained. "Dad collected them when he lived in the Middle East."

We - just - managed to suppress our giggles. Later research confirmed that camel whips don't come with crook handles. Not that either of us is likely to mistake the traditional school rattan, in any case.

I'm just looking forward to the speeches at the wedding reception at the weekend: "We'd like to thank my parents for their kind gift of a camel whip from their priceless collection." I promise not to laugh out loud.

Newspaper delivery girl

By Abel on 20 May 2006

I'm used to seeing newspaper *boys* pounding the streets in the early hours. Heading to the railway station at some ungodly hour on a surprisingly-cold morning yesterday, I saw my first ever newspaper *girl*.

Oh, how cute. How adorably cute. Wrapped in a big, colourful woolly jumper. Trudging along, straining to drag a trolley of heavy papers. Looking cold. Downright miserable.

My mind wandered, as it is wont to do. Mr. Hawkes at number 43, telephoning to complain of yet another delivery of The Guardian rather than The Telegraph: Julie (for that was the name I imagined), trembling hands outstretched, taking her whacks with the strap that Mr. Borthwick the newsagent kept for the purposes in the back room of his shop.

Mr. Finch, her father's friend, in the big house next to the park. His four papers as usual, tearing as she pushed them through his letterbox. The door opening, and the gentleman appearing, fierce, formidable. A time being agreed for her to return after school to be punished, lest he tell her employer ("again") or her father. Her nervous day at school. The grand drawing room in the fading early-evening light. The switches, freshly cut from his garden.

Rushing through the streets, cursing her heavy load, glances at her watch confirming her worst fears. Dashing into the classroom, just as her teacher closed the register. The master re-opening it, picking his pen back up, inscribing: "That will class as 'late' again, young lady." A plaintive "Please, sir..." Please, sir: that's my fourth 'late' of the term; that's an automatic caning.... The classroom door swinging open during the second lesson of the morning; the Headmaster's secretary escorting her to meet her fate. Three strokes - "because you're one of our best girls, but the rules are plain for all to see, and I can't make exceptions now, can I?"

Her father. Seated at the dining room table, as she cleared the dishes after dinner. Mumbling her story, hoping he might not mind: "I've finished at the newsagents." His lecture, instructions that she had to go back. Her terrified explanation - that she couldn't, that Mr. Borthwick didn't want her back. That he'd had one complaint too many. That she'd been fired. The long, lonely, familiar walk upstairs. The wait in her bedroom - always a wait. Father unbuckling his thick belt as he entered. Face nestling in her soft duvet, as she took the thrashing. Tears afterwards. Hugs.

Poor girl. I hope she wasn't actually as miserable as she looked in the early hours of yesterday.

The spanking reflex

By Abel on 21 May 2006

Sitting in a café with Haron one morning last week, eating breakfast.

Pretty young lady, late 20s, standing at the counter waiting to pay her bill, her elderly mother next to her. Daughter makes a cheeky comment in a broad Scottish accent; mother whacks her shoulder; we look up.

Daughter to waitress: "She may only be wee, but she's always had a hard smack on her."

Old lady: "Aye. I think it's biological: when you become a mother, your hand just develops the reflex."

Any scientists out there able to point us towards the relevant research?

DC: District of correction?

By Abel on 28 May 2006

Location: Washington Dulles Airport, Domestic Arrivals, Luggage Carousel 3. Time: 9pm Friday night, the start of the US holiday weekend

Assorted happy teens, released from the confines of their flight, rush round manically, giggling loudly.

Stern female teacher shouts over the crowds: "[School name deleted!] over here. Now!". Miss Jean Brodie, with an American lilt. Even the adults in the area stand up straighter, fall quiet.

The group gathers in a flash, suddenly silent. There are 15 of them: a dozen girls, three (lucky?!) boys.

Their teacher lectures the assembled semi-circle, her voice quiet enough to command their absolute attention (and, sadly, to ensure that nearby pervs like me are unable to hear quite what she says). Chastened young students nod their promises of impeccable behaviour.

One girl mutters a comment under her breath. Dark hair, tied back. Sixteen? Braces, too-tight orange top, designer-looking jeans, red Gap rucksack. ('Allie', I later overhear).

Second teacher, male. 40ish, joins the lecture. Finger is wagged at Allie. Scolding continues. Finger wags some more. Allie looks satisfyingly downcast.

"You will be soundly paddled for that comment when we get to the hostel, young lady. We will not tolerate insolence on this trip."

At least, that's what I imagine he was saying.

The group has since claimed their bags, and have been lined up in pairs to walk out to their transport.

Poor Allie. I hope the other girls look after her afterwards.

My kinda shop

By Abel on 29 May 2006

My final Washingtonian startle was a shop sign: "Correctional Shoe Repairs". I know a fair few fans of the slipper and plimsoll; how nice that they can get them patched up professionally after serious use.

The Caning World Cup

By Abel on 31 May 2006

The chap in front of me coming through immigration at Heathrow yesterday was wearing a sweatshirt emblazoned with the slogan:

"Cane VIII 2001"

He was in the queue for British citizens, naturally.

I'm fascinated. Who are the Cane Eight? Were they wielding or receiving?

Did they perhaps compete against other nations in a Caning World Cup tournament, each country sending teams of four caners and four canees, points being awarded for style and stoicism respectively as they thrashed it out live on primetime TV to carry off the coveted Golden Rattan.

I wonder who selects the team? Abel for England?! All those training sessions would doubtless be tough, but if my country calls...

A licking for a licking

By Haron on 4 June 2006

We had a friend with us over the weekend, a sassy girl with quite an appetite for being spanked. The three of us didn't just stay home all the time, swinging implements (or having implements swung at us): we went to see how the Duchess of

Northumberland was getting on with her new garden in Alnwick.

The garden is looking great: it has lots of fun things in it, like the world's biggest treehouse, a poison garden (we were particularly impressed by healthy-looking cannabis plants growing in their own individual cages), and the most fabulous fountains and water sculptures.

Obviously, our friend and I couldn't help speculating whether Abel could be improved by being dropped into a fountain. We didn't exactly discuss it out loud, but winked and gestured at each other behind his back, and reached the decision that he could definitely use a dip. Alas, Abel - in an uncharacteristic flash of insightfulness - crushed our scheme.

He turned around, took us by the shoulders - a shoulder each - and said: "If you make me get even a little bit wet, you will both get the cane when we're home." Our friend gave him a bright, innocent smile, then poked out her tongue and gave him a long, wet lick on the arm. Abel stayed serious for long enough to say: "You're getting a caning." After that we collapsed in giggles.

I congratulated myself for being out of the line of fire - because surely, nothing I did would live up to the licking our friend gave Abel, and the one she was going to get at home - but it wasn't all over for me. In the wooded part of the garden, we wandered upon a secluded clearing with a handy seat in it. The benches there are all very pretty, and are begging to be sat on. So, Abel did that. Characteristically, instead of letting me sit next to him, he pulled me over his lap and set about spanking me - quite hard, I'll have you know. I had been careless enough to wear a skirt; Abel reached underneath it and tugged down my panties.

Our friend, a very shy girl, looked more horrified than I felt. She helpfully stood guard on the path while I got my first bare-bottom spanking in a public garden. It was short, stingy, a little scary and very tasty. A few smacks later Abel pulled my panties back up, smoothed down my skirt, and we continued our walk. (And if you're wondering how outrageous Abel's behaviour was, bear in mind that this garden gets over a hundred thousand visitors a year, and many of them appeared to be there on the day.)

When we got home, our friend's licking turned out to consist of 24-of-the-best with three different canes, but we shall keep from posting details of that to spare her modesty.

If you go down to the museum today...

By Abel on 8 June 2006

You can tell how often I tidy my office at home by the fact that the latest near-archaeological dig through my paperwork unearthed a newspaper clipping from 31 January:

> "Secret papers released under the Freedom of Information Act revealed how two schoolboys once damaged one of the disputed Parthenon marbles figures when they began fighting in the British Museum in 1961. Apparently one of the boys fell and knocked off part of a centaur's leg."

It doesn't take a huge feat of imagination to picture the consequences, does it?

Ragged School

By Abel on 10 June 2006

The current Time Out magazine has a feature on London's more unusual museums, one of which surely merits a visit. The Ragged School Museum in the East End comprises an 1886 classroom, founded by the famous Dr Barnardo:

> ...the only difference now being the room has electricity. It is used by visiting school children (nearly 15,000 a year). They are given a class in the style of a Victorian school, using chalk and slate and a dunce's hat. Luckily for visitors, canes did not feature much in Dr Barnardo's methods.

It's the "much" in that final sentence that stood out when I read the article. Not that the cane didn't feature. It simply didn't feature "much". So maybe, just maybe, if a visitor misbehaved especially badly...? (Haron? We're going on a trip!). Even the school's website is ambiguous: in the Victorian lessons, "Discipline is strict, although punishment is not over-emphasised." (Emphasised. Just not overly so).

A quick glance at their website shows that they even hire it out in the evenings and at weekends for events, photo shoots and "private art & crafts activities". I somehow doubt that Eleanor in their events office would approve of the type of activities that I have in mind.

The British elite: setting a spanking example?

By Abel on 11 June 2006

The Evening Standard maintained its reputation as the kinkily-disposed reader's evening newspaper of choice, with Friday's delightful report of Eton College's annual Fourth of June celebrations of King George III's birthday. Posh diarist Leonie Frieda bemoans the decline of the event, which takes place in a field called Aggars Plough:

> What used to be a happy saunter from picnic to picnic has now degenerated into a teenage booze fest. Were a Martian to land in the middle of Aggars, he might well conclude that Eton is a college for girls not boys, since the former far outnumber the latter on the late king's birthday....
>
> Not only has this once-pleasant, typically English day... become a 'drinkathon' for underage girls, this year a gang of streakers struck a new low at Eton's high day.

This is an outrage: they should restore standards at once. I picture gown-clad masters patrolling the fields next year; young ladies being escorted to Housemaster's offices; the thwack of the birch and the shrieks of the miscreants echoing across Aggars.

I must check what we're doing next June 4. Sounds like an interesting day out.

On belts and hotel rooms
By Haron on 12 June 2006

On Friday night I found myself standing naked in front of a glass-top table in a London hotel room, wondering how I would lean over it without freezing my chest and tummy right off. Behind me, my husband was unbuckling his belt.

"Cold," I complained when my skin touched the icy glass surface.

"I'll warm you up," Abel promised with a carnivorous grin, folding the belt into a loop. I'd guessed he might say that.

Why was I about to get a whipping? The simple answer would be "just because", or even "why not?" - which in many cases is good enough.

The more extended answer is that we had just returned from a gig by our favourite band Keane. We had agreed beforehand that for every song they played, I would get two strokes of the belt. Admittedly, Keane - bless their little public school socks - were very generous with their set list, so that in the middle of the concert Abel put his lips to my ear and shouted over the noise of the crowd belting out their favourite songs: "I think I'll have to use discretion over those strokes!" I would have been the last person to object.

Thus, the glass table in the hotel room, a chair in front of it for me to grip, and Abel's voice behind me:

"I think twenty is a fair number. You can count them."

Before we started, I had decided to try and take this whipping as stoically as I could. Normally I don't bother, but Abel likes spanking ~~motionless sacks of flour~~ stoic girls, so I gritted my teeth, and gripped the back of the chair really hard.

I think my resolve lasted until about the eighth stroke. The pain had been building - not gradually, like with a hand-spanking or even a caning, but in great jumps. It grew manifold with every lash. I remember the eighth one particularly, because my mouth refused to wrap around the count, and when number nine came, I suddenly found myself upright, clutching my behind, with Abel's arm around me. I honestly don't remember how I got there.

"Shhh, good girl," he was saying. "You're very brave. Come on now, it will be over soon."

I allowed him to help me back over the desk. Funnily enough, I didn't object its coolness any more.

It wasn't over all that soon: each of the following strokes was memorable for its particular little ways of hurting me more. Finally, Abel ended my suffering by delivering the last five strokes so fast that I didn't have time to freak out about them separately - I just howled the place down from their cumulative effect.

I don't know if I'm still into being whipped with belts - maybe it's just that particular belt that should be urgently shredded and recycled. I'm definitely into going to gigs, though.

Being stoic and stuff? Forget it.

A new and painful implement?

By Haron on 18 June 2006

So, I'm watching a western here called "Outlaw Josie Wales",* and Clint Eastwood threatens a young lad who rides with him:

"I'm going to whomp you with a knotted plow-line."

1. Ouch! Ouch, ouch, that sounds *painful*. Who on earth has come up with that? Has anybody tried it, seen it done, read about it, heard about it at all? A *plow-line*? Knotted, too? Ouch.

2. Mr. Eastwood? Yes, please.

* My first one ever, actually. My education has been very deficient where westerns are concerned.

Butlers, maids and hot email

By Haron on 19 June 2006

Hot spanking email is so nice to wake up to when your husband has been away overnight. Here's what Abel sent me this morning ~~to try and distract me from hard work~~ to inspire me for the day ahead.

The Morning Line-Up.

An imposing country house. The servant girls are lined up each morning, before starting work. The butler walks down the line-up, inspecting every girl. Is their hair neatly brushed? Is their uniform perfect?

Before checking the first girl, he takes a thin, whippy cane from its hook on the wall. The girls tremble slightly as he draws near, knowing that the slightest deviation from perfection will lead to a punishment: "Hold out your hand", for two strokes, always one on the left, one on the right. Two? Sometimes more, if the butler feels that the girl is too poorly turned-out.

Sometimes he'll walk to the end of the line, adjusting uniforms as he goes, and then turn: "Elizabeth, Alice, step forward" for their canings.

Occasionally, he'll turn with thunder in his face. "Your standards of appearance this morning insult his lordship. You will all be punished." He'd patrol from one end to another, a stroke for each outstretched hand, then instruct them to swap hands and walk back, dealing with the girls in reverse order.

Or the girls will be dismissed to start their daily duties, "Except for Sally" - a repeat offender, particularly untidy that morning, who'd be ordered to follow him along the narrow maze of corridors to his office, where she'd be bent over to be thrashed on the bare with his heavy cane.

See you tonight (hands outstretched?).

Given that we'll have a guy from his work staying over, this promises to be a particularly interesting and *quiet* scene.

Recipe: Toasted Hands

By Abel on 20 June 2006

As created last night...

Ingredients:

One young lady

One cane

One tube Deep Heat muscle cream

———

Instructions:

Several hours in advance, warn young lady of impending scene.

Remove cane from packaging.

Instruct young lady to hold out left hand. Administer three sharp whacks with cane.

Repeat previous step with right hand.

Check hands display stripes. Repeat previous steps if not.

Open tube of Deep Heat.

Rub into caned hands.

Watch as girl squirms.

Cuddle girl.

(Poor Haron! Or lucky Haron, depending on your perspective. Lucky me, either way)

A return to the Victorian schoolroom
By Abel on 22 June 2006

I sat opposite a lively six-year-old on the train yesterday, as I returned from a meeting. He was chatting merrily to his father:

> "I was the captain in football last week. I wasn't very strict though. Not like the Victorians. Do you know they used the cane? We were told all about it on our school trip today: we went to a Victorian school in Reading."

Father changed the subject; son stared out of the window, lost in thought. Ten minutes later: "The boys got the cane on the bottom, so they couldn't sit down and had to stand up to write. But the girls," gleam in eye, "got caned on the hands, so they couldn't write at all. That was even worse: they couldn't even hold their pens."

My eyes nearly popped out of my head. Had their teachers been reading my post about the Ragged School? A quick google on my return home revealed that the boy must have visited Katesgrove School – is the whole country full of these potentially-kinky venues, corrupting the youth of today in the nicest way possible? I wondered how many of the girls on his trip had gone home dreaming about being caned on their hands!

As for Katesgrove, its website is a mine of wonderful information: visiting girls are made to wear authentic Victorian schoolwear (pinafores, knee length socks, no jewellery). Their reconstructed lessons even start with a "hand inspection". And the suggested follow-up activities include a selection of topics for writing assignments and class discussions that could fill entire evenings for kinky dinner parties.

It's a relief for us spankos to see that the education system is keeping the flame alive...

Bathtime spanking

By Haron on 27 June 2006

What is it about baths that makes some spankers' hands itch? I was filling my bath this morning, and was just about to submerge myself in the bubbles, when Abel appeared - a fly swat in hand. (The one his mother bought for us, bless her innocent soul.)

He made me bend over with my hands in the tub - yep, right in the water - and swatted me all sore and hot and pink. Because he could. After which, mightily pleased with himself, he departed, while I got into my bath, first sighing with pleasure when my stinging butt touched the cool bubbles, then hissing when it touched the hot water.

At least the water didn't have time to grow cold.

The Horrors of Bridewell

By Haron on 29 June 2006

Have you ever been to the Bridewell Museum in Norwich? If not, don't bother going for the sake of pervery: the museum is almost entirely dedicated to the history of local trade, with any mentions of its more exciting days as a house of correction and then prison banished to a hand-out in the introductory room. So, I copied out everything that looked remotely pervy, to save you a trip.

> In 1585 part of (the house) became a "brydewell to keep and stay idle persons to some honest worke and labour", that is a kind of workhouse to correct as well as punish. Vagrant women and girls were trained for domestic service or as apprentices in crafts such as millinery. Tramps and beggars were taken off the street and put to work cutting wood and grinding malt.

No, it doesn't specifically say what happened to these folks if they didn't apply themselves to their work, but I have no trouble filling in the blanks.

Apparently, they had a real problem with vagrants in Norwich back then, but they knew how to deal with this:

> Vagrants were arrested, whipped and sent back to their place of origin.

Those would be the vagrants that didn't end up in Bridewell instead, I suppose.

Then the house became a proper prison. In 1622 its Keeper produced an inventory of items found there. Among other things, like sheets, pillows and benches, there were:

> One paire of stockes, two whipping postes, one chaire for unruly p(er)sones, two paire of manicles, two paire of shackles.

A chair for unruly persons? OMG, they gave them time-outs!

Anyway, this is it for kink potential in the Bridewell Museum. All the rest is Norfolk shawls, wrought iron gate latches, recreated workshops and stuff like this.

Back to school

By Abel on 4 July 2006

Me. With my reputation. Running an event in a former school?

Had the organisers of a session I ran at work today known of my extra-curricula interests, I doubt they would have booked the team into a recently-converted school building that now operates as a small conference centre.

Did I really tell one of the female delegates that, "If you don't behave I'll send you to the headmaster's study"?

Did I honestly question another: "I hope I didn't see you smoking in the playground during break"?

Lest anyone accuse me of gender bias in the workplace. I did scold one of the male participants for coming back into the building through the staff entrance, not via the 'Boys' door.

They hire the place out for private functions, apparently. I wonder if they kept the old furniture? Or the canes? Haron called into the venue at the end of the day, "to help me pack up": sadly, there were too many staff around for me to thrash her.

Doctor Who: the (should have been a) spanking episode

By Abel on 6 July 2006

Last night's episode of "Doctor Who" featured a werewolf trying to kill Queen Victoria, in a spooky Scottish country mansion. (Where on earth is this going, I sense you wondering? Queen Victoria spanking the Doctor's scantily-clad young assistant Rose, over her regal knee? That wasn't the idea that occurred to me at the time, but now I think of it...).

Early in the episode, Rose is trying to choose a dress. She flings open a wardrobe, to find a terrified maid cowering in the corner. My mind immediately transported said maid to another Victorian country house, still hiding away, terrified of the whipping she was due to receive from the butler for breaking valuable porcelain. Much commotion, as the staff hunted high and low for her.

The lord of the house was disturbed by the noise: "When you find her, bring her to me." And so it was that, not long after, the trembling girl was dragged into the great hall. Like most servants, she would never have been spoken to by the master. Now he was asking her name, and explaining calmly why Meissen porcelain needs to be handled with such care, and asking why she ran and hid.

She was almost too nervous to speak, her words when they came quiet and hesitant: "Because I didn't want to be punished, sir."

"And causing all of this disturbance makes you *less* likely to be flogged?"

"No, sir."

"You strike me as a good girl. But such behaviour in this household has inevitable consequences. You will be whipped." He turned to the butler. "Please go and fetch your crop: I would like to observe the punishment."

Scottish howls

By Abel on 9 July 2006

We were in Scotland recently, visiting a dear friend. Whilst investigating places to visit, I noticed a flyer advertising the following attraction: www.scottishowlcentre.tk

I like the idea of a "howl centre". The owls turned out to be pretty impressive, too.

Haron's howling came later that afternoon, as she was upended for a bare-bottomed, open-air, OTK spanking on the Mull of Kintyre. I think I'm always going to giggle in future whenever I hear the relevant Paul McCartney song.

Spanking at t'mill

By Abel on 14 July 2006

We visited wonderful New Lanark recently, a World Heritage site near Glasgow. At the start of the nineteenth century, enlightened mill owner Robert Owen's pioneering initiatives here included the world's first nursery school, and the first shop run on co-operative principles.

Haron and I could hardly keep up with the number of kinky ideas sparked by the fabulous restored mill buildings. Our fantasies were totally inauthentic – Owen opposed corporal punishment, and was a hugely benevolent employer. That didn't stop us wondering what might have been.

We visited Owen's house, where he lived with his wife Caroline and her three younger sisters, who joined them after their father's death. As we stood in his study, in front of the mill owner's imposing desk, we imagined the three trembling newcomers being called in to see him, glancing nervously at the cane on his wall:

"I know from Caroline that your father was a good man, and a strict one at that. Now that you are in my care, I want you to understand that I will be taking on all of his responsibilities. New Lanark is built on the principles of hard work and honesty, and the behaviour of my own family must be exemplary. I do not wish to see any of you in here again, for you will only visit me in my study if your behaviour has fallen short of those high standards to which we must adhere. And should you give me occasion, then I shall have no hesitation in whipping you, and whipping you hard. Do I make myself clear?"

Thence to an audio-visual display, told through the eyes of a young mill worker. We imagined a bright girl being told by her father that it was time to leave school and start earning money. She argued, not wanting to forsake the comfort and safety of the classroom, and was duly bent over and flogged with his doubled-up belt.

Another of our make-believe girls reported to the mill manager for her first day at work – only to be told that her school records showed her to be ill-behaved, and that she could not start until the schoolmaster reported an improvement. Her father, too, thrashed her severely.

Hygiene was deemed hugely important at New Lanark. We pictured a girl arriving for the morning shift, dishevelled. Being taken to the supervisor's quarters. Being made to strip; being washed; being whipped, being sent on her way back to the mill.

And this was *New* Lanark. What of *Old* Lanark, presumably down the road, where the owners were less enlightened: the dark, satanic type of mill that inspired Owen to his good works?

Do visit, if you are ever anywhere near. On a vanilla level, it's a truly moving and inspiring experience. For sparking kinky dreams, there are few places to rival it. Haron would have been spanked vigorously that evening, were it not for the fact that we stayed in Gretna Green, and other fantasies inevitably took over.

Spanking on Evening TV

By Haron on 15 July 2006

Last night on the chat-show The Kumars at No. 42 they had an interview with Gordon Ramsay, the incredibly bad-mouthed celebrity chef. Meera Syal (as always, suitably nutty in her role as Granny Kumar) told him:

> You're a grown man, but you're also like a naughty little boy. I'd love to put you over my knee... but it needs replacing.

Now, there's a problem that's easy to solve. Why not tawse him instead?

Kinky eateries?

By Abel on 20 July 2006

A surprising entry in a restaurant guide, which recommended a London eatery intriguingly called "S&M Cafe".

Shame it merely serves "Sausages & Mash". One must wonder whether the owners have certain interests, though... If they're reading this, how about a free lunch?!

Of course, if you're after the real thing in terms of friendly, safe, welcoming, reputable pervy places to eat in London, the only place to go is the absolutely fabulous Coffee, Cake and Kink near Covent Garden. All three elements of the title are catered for admirably. (Haron and I have one of their fabulous black and white photos - of a chained, naked girl - framed on our bedroom wall).

Any wealthy business angels out there? How about a chain of kinky cafes worldwide: a Spanko Starbucks, if you like? (Send me the money: I'll set them up for you for a very reasonable percentage. I make a mean cappuccino, bake pretty well, and the kink can be taken for granted).

The spanko menu

By Abel on 22 July 2006

Congratulations to Hull Council, on the east coast of England, for making school lessons more interesting by loaning out interesting memorabilia from the archives.

Browsing their online catalogue, I think I'll order an E33, an E48 and an E127 for starters.

That'll give me a "Girl's School Smock: c1900" in which to dress Haron, their selection entitled "Corporal Punishment: cane, mortarboard and punishment book, 1900-1928, from Clifton Street Girls' School, Hull", and a "Teacher's Adjustable High Desk, c1900" over which she could bend.

Shame they only lend this stuff to schools. If only someone could hack into their site and add links to eBay for every item... Or maybe there's a schoolteacher in Hull amongst our readers, who might borrow a few of these curiosities and sneak them out for a weekend of kinky fun?

Of cheeky schoolgirls

By Haron on 24 July 2006

I wish I could resist the fits of giggles that sometimes overpower me during scenes. Say, yesterday I arrived for my detention. Abel placed in front of me the book I had to copy from. It was the Economist Style Guide; in the middle of the page there was a cartoon that illustrated the difference between "distinctive" and "distinct".

And suddenly, there they were, the giggles. "Do I have to copy the picture too, sir?" I asked, choking on laughter and horrified at the same time. Ouch. I paid for that one.

Three with a dragon cane, in case you were wondering.

The last girl in the book?
By Abel on 25 July 2006

Satirical magazine Private Eye writes this week about Bedgebury School. It notes that governors have just written to parents with "the shock announcement of the imminent closure of this 80-year-old day/boarding girls' school set in 200 acres of Kentish parkland.".

The school, with over 300 students, occupies a "six-storey 'French chateau with Versailles-style gardens", surrounded by "rolling pastures, lakes and forests". Its reputation "was founded on its ability to turn less able girls into high achievers."

Naturally, I'm picturing the lasses that must have been caught 'out of bounds' over the years, and their painful consequential punishments. I'm day-dreaming about the upper floors of the mansion full of dormitories, patrolled by strict masters, home to tearful girls lying face down on their beds.

And I'm imaging a world in which one of the current batch of young ladies would earn the dubious distinction of being the very last to be taken into the Head's office for a caning: the final entry on the final page of a punishment book documenting the shameful history of so many miscreants from the past eight decades.

Actually, I wonder if they did ever use corporal punishment at Bedgebury? I must do some research on "Friends Reunited", that wonderful resource for the scholarly spanko. And I wonder if the school might dispose of its assets - might I put in an early bid for any canes, or for the dusty leather-bound punishment books from olden times, or even a few desks?!

A spanking interlude

By Haron on 26 July 2006

"Are you behaving down there?" Abel shouted to me from upstairs.

He often does that during the day, when each of us is glued to our own workstation. Not because there's a wealth of room for misbehaviour, you understand, but because when both of us are working from home, it's nice to remind each other that this is no lousy corporate office, and we can do whatever we like.

"No!" I shouted, as usual. And then: "I need a spanking!" I don't know what made me say it; an instant before, I was unaware that I needed a spanking, or that I was going to request one - but as soon as I said it, it was true, and I knew it. If I had my bottom smacked now, my work would go so much better.

"OK," he called down. "Come here."

I jogged up the stairs, to where he was waiting for me on the landing. He unclipped my fancy belt, yanked down my trousers and bent me down, with his arm around my waist. I could see our cat where she was stretched out on the carpet: a figure of feline bliss. She didn't even deign to open her eyes as the spanks started echoing around the hallway. Thus, holding me under his arm-pit, Abel gave my bottom a dozen crisp, heavy slaps. I owwwed and squealed in appreciation, and wriggled about a little when it started to really hurt.

"There," he said, helping me upright. "Better now?"

"Immeasurably." We hugged. The cat opened one golden eye: it was obviously missing the slapping sounds and the cries.

This is no corporate office, alright.

Furniture fetish?

By Abel on 27 July 2006

Next table to me in a restaurant. Mother turns to restless daughter and comments, "If you take your bottom off that chair, I'll spank it."

Pedantically, I wondered whether the chair was into being spanked or not.

Prince William the spanko?

By Abel on 29 July 2006

Remarkably, it's 25 years to the day since the "fairytale wedding" of Lady Diana Spencer and HRH Charles Philip Arthur George Windsor, Prince Of Wales, Duke Of Cornwall, Duke Of Rothsay, Count Of Chester, Count of Carick, Baron Of Renfrew, Great Steward Of Scotland, Lord Of the Isles. (Yes, really).

One of Diana's qualifications for a royal marriage was supposedly that she could arrive at the altar in pristine virginal state. I'm given to wonder whether the same criteria are being applied to Prince William's apparent beloved, Kate Middleton.

Miss Middleton is rather cute. If sex is not an option, the heir-to-the-heir-to- the-throne presumably has to find alternative ways of 'entertaining' her on their holidays together, without actually doing the deed that might debar her from a role as a future Queen.

Now I don't want to start any scurrilous rumours, but I can't therefore help but wonder whether spanking forms part of William's must-not-have-sex repertoire? Now there's a image to bring to mind the next time you see a tabloid snap of the young lady in question.

PS if you hear tell of a spanking writer thrown into The Tower for High Treason in the next day or two, that'll probably be me.

School detention
By Abel on 31 July 2006

A thought-provoking entry on a school message board I was browsing earlier:

> "How many times did we copy out the school rules in detention only to go and break them all again within a few days?"

What a nice concept: I've always thought of girls copying out Latin tracts, or writing lines, or neatly reproducing pages from a heavy encyclopaedia. Copying the school rules would re-enforce correct behaviour, and allow no excuse were future offences to be committed.

One could imagine that some girls in detention would have committed more serious offences. Their hands would shake as they copied out the relevant section from the rules, documenting how these particular misdemeanours "would additionally result in a caning at the end of Detention".

Alternatively, they might be made to copy out the school history, a chapter per detention. A note would be taken of how many chapters each girl had copied during a year: once they had written out the whole book, their next detention would be replaced by a caning.

Travel spanking
By Abel on 4 August 2006

Every journal, every newspaper is a source of potential kinky ideas.

Take a travel magazine I read on a plane last week. Good thing parents have articles on "how to deal with your kids on vacation": without the insights of this particular journal's erudite contributors, children everywhere would no doubt have been abandoned at the edge of the hotel pool in the blazing sun without protective cream, left to wander the streets of the city alone late at night, and fed leftovers from the dodgiest food stalls in town. I mean, really.

One section of the feature did catch my attention, though. "HELP! My daughter's formed an unsuitable relationship with a local youth." The advisers opt for the cool advice: "invite him on a family day out" and encourage them to keep in touch afterwards via MySpace. I jumped instead to mental images of the young lady bent over the end of her hotel-room bed, as daddy's belt punished her for disappearing without permission and drove home the importance of chaste behaviour.

And then they recommended a new hotel in Boston – the city in which I administered my first-ever real-life spanking back in 1999. (Oh, what wonderful memories!). I travel there on a not-too-infrequent basis for work, and this establishment sounds like my sort of place: "rooms are immaculate, modern and bright", yet it's relatively central and cheap.

The publication then qualifies its recommendation:

> "The only thing guests might object to is the YWCA downstairs, which brings a touch of 'youth hostel' to the lobby."

Object? To the presence of lots of cute young American lasses – away from home; needing guidance and discipline? My goodness, that sounds like the best thing about the hotel. Guess where I'm going to stay next time I'm in town.

Hello, spank

By Abel on 15 August 2006

Grrrrrr: back at work, swapping sun, sand, sea and spanking for the same-old manic lifestyle.

Holiday startles? Perhaps the best was flicking through the local TV channels, and catching a marvellous ditty entitled 'Hello Spank', the theme music for a cartoon of the same name. If anyone knows where to download the tune as a ringtone, I would love it on my phone.

And then there was the fascinating conversation with one of the lasses working in our hotel's executive lounge, discussing low crime rates in the area. Misbehaviour is rarely reported to the police, it seems, but rather to their fathers, to be dealt with at home. You can doubtless imagine the whispered fantasies that *that* provoked every time we walked past one of the local cuties...

Left (kinky) luggage

By Abel on 17 August 2006

Checking a couple of bags into storage at a railway station en route home from holiday, I was reminded of my previous experience of said facilities.

They scan every bag these days using airline-style X-ray machines; I'd just returned from a weekend with a spanko friend.

"Do you have any electrical items in your bag, sir?"

"Yes, an alarm clock and shaver."

And then the guy behind the counter looked extremely puzzled as he studied the silhouettes of my belongings on his screen.

"What are these items, then?" (pointing to X-ray).

Politely: "That one's a cane, and that one's a whip" (OMG I can just imagine having said *that* a few years ago. Not).

Shock on his face: "Can you open your bag for me to have a look, please?" (Was he asking out of sheer disbelief, or rigid adherence to company policy – 'all spanking implements must be inspected'?).

"Sure," I smiled back.

Cue very embarrassed-looking left-luggage attendant, especially as I took out the large paddle to get to the other two items and laid it on his counter.

Honestly, these vanillas...

Still, he accepted the bags into his store; it's good to know that – in the words of their notice – spanking implements don't class as "dangerous weapons".

The reform school

By Abel on 18 August 2006

"So," I asked of the team I was working with in their grand corporate headquarters today, "what's the history of the building?'

"It was a reform school."

Cue difficulty in concentrating for the next few minutes. We were working in what must have been the old reception: I pictured girls driven up the long, tree-lined drive; marched in by the scruff of their necks, their details recorded by the severe orderly behind an imposing desk.

Then on into the ornate circular hallway. That first room on the right must have been where they were taken to strip off their civilian clothes - and to shower, or be showered.

Thence, presumably, next door, to be kitted out in their reformatory uniform. Made to wait in the hallway, perhaps.

Then called in to the large room opposite, where the birching block was set up, for their court-determined whipping to be inflicted.

I'm sure I saw one of the lasses at the back of the room squirm knowingly.

Festival fancies

By Abel on 19 August 2006

Lazing in the open-air at a music festival recently, Haron and I indulged in the "reverse Clinton" approach to naughty substances – we don't smoke, but boy can one have a good time inhaling if one stands next to the right people!

During a gap between performances, we pondered the punishment tariff should the naughty young ladies around us transfer their festival smoking habits to their (presumably strict) scholastic environments.

We decided that the cigarette smokers would be best dealt with on a sliding scale: two strokes for the first offence, four for the second, six should they dare to return a third time.

And the young ladies smoking more fragrant substances? An automatic six with the senior cane, kept for the most serious offences, before a week's suspension. Their daddies would not be best pleased with them on their return, either, one would assume...

Then we realised that the cigarette debate was slightly more complicated. Festival goers were wearing colour-coded wristbands, and some of those with tobacco in hand were duly marked out as being under sixteen (and thus too young to purchase cigarettes). So questions of legality crept in: should a fifteen-year-old receive additional strokes for her criminality?

We agreed that the fairest solution would be to punish whichever girl had purchased the tobacco. An additional four strokes (also to be meted out to any young lady who refused to disclose the source of her supplies) might act as a suitable deterrent, especially should said young lady already be qualifying under the tariff for consumption.

My kinda wine bar
By Abel on 21 August 2006

Wandering round central London earlier, killing time before a meeting, I stumbled on my new favourite wine bar: "The City Flogger".

Honestly. It's in Fen Court, if you don't believe me. It describes itself as a 'traditional' place, which sounds about right.

Cut me a switch, young lady
By Haron on 25 August 2006

I was walking home from the library today - it was closing time, and only the most dedicated (or desperate) aspiring academics were still there - when I had to step off the path to avoid getting run over by a cyclist. I found myself standing in the branches of a weeping willow.

Well, I know what weeping willows are for: you send a girl out with a knife, and make her fetch a few switches - one for now, and a couple more in case the first one breaks. Then you peel down her panties, and make her bend over the arm of the old sofa in the living-room, and you cover her bottom with even pink stripes. That's what whipping willows are for.

I parted the hanging branches to look on the ground under the tree, and I found a switch, just lying there, as though discarded by somebody who'd just stopped for a minute to deliver a quick whipping. I picked it up and headed for the bus home.

"Hey," I said to Abel when I walked into the house. "I brought you a stick to beat me with." I held up the switch like a flower.

I think he liked it.

On not getting caught

By Abel on 30 August 2006

My parents are coming to stay at the weekend, and Haron and I have already started checking every nook and cranny for long-lost implements - and for books that might be hard to explain. (I don't think I could find *any* legitimate reason for owning the guide to being an effective Headmaster that's perched behind me on the bookshelf, for example).

It'd be so much easier to ban non-spankos from entering the house.... We go so far as being the only house on the street not to use the services of the local window cleaner, lest he peer in and see anything that might make him fall off his ladder.

In search of votes…

By Abel on 1 September 2006

The UK government intends to legislate to ban pornography that is (1) violent, or about (2) necrophilia or (3) bestiality.

Anyone who accuses them of flogging a dead horse in their search for votes would be entirely unjustified.

Naughty Father-in-Law

By Haron on 4 September 2006

I'm not saying Abel's dad is a total and utter brat. No, I'm not saying that. But visiting of the weekend, he looked out at the clothes drying on our line outside - and suggested that we hang the colours out using the semaphore code to send rude messages to the neighbours.

"Sod off, you silly old bat!" - spelled out in t-shirts and towels.

The origins of the cane
By Abel on 10 September 2006

I read recently about a company manufacturing polo sticks, whose staff make an annual pilgrimage to remote areas to hunt down the rattan harvest. It made me ponder the origins of the use of this particular material for corporal punishment purposes.

I wonder who first looked at a length of rattan and decided, "*That's* the material I've been looking for all this time. I must purchase some forthwith from the local farmers, and export it to the finest schools in the Empire."

Perhaps tales were told of a few villages, deep in the forest , where the local girls were unusually well-behaved? "Head forty miles up river, old chap, hire a donkey, trek for two days - and you'll come to the region in question."

Or was it perhaps some marketing ploy in the mid-1800s by the farmers concerned: sitting round at their annual sales conference, brainstorming ways in which they could diversify away from an over-dependence on the furniture market?

Then again... I'm reading a book at the moment about leisure in the Victorian era ("Consuming Passions" by Judith Flanders - very highly recommended). The opening chapter deals at length with the Great Exhibition of 1851 - that landmark event in the development of society and enterprise. Perhaps *that* was the moment at which the cane became popular: "Stand 498. A length of rattan from the east, designed for the discipline of young ladies." Maybe the Prince Consort noticed it on one of his many visits to the Crystal Palace, and his patronage led to the gentlemen of the day placing large orders?

Speaking of the Victorians, and meandering aimlessly in my kinky thoughts, I'm reminded that I read a review of a CD by a new band the other day. They're called "The Victorian English Gentlemen's Club". I can just imagine such an august body, gathering weekly in their splendid Pall Mall premises to try out the latest batch of canes purchased from the

Exhibition. Their constitution would require them to bring with them any of their servant girls who may have misbehaved in the previous week, for discipline in front of the assembled group. Learned discussions on caning technique would follow, with proceedings written up into leather-bound tomes.

All this talk of caning is making me want to fetch Haron. A rare bout of tidying up last weekend before my parents came to stay means that our spare bedroom - usually impenetrably untidy - is completely clear. Acres of cane-swinging space. Seems a shame to waste it...

Bloggers and punishment

By Haron on 15 September 2006

I was searching for some statistics on life expectancy of an average blog, when instead I came across this:

> Discipline and Punish
>
> Of all the new genres facilitated by digital technology, the blog is the one that brings the loudest calls for discipline and punishment.

Goodness, yes. I mean, there are *whole blogs* about discipline and punishment. Fancy somebody noticing.

OK, the author actually meant young people who get punished for what they write online:

> One indicator of the impact that blogs are having on our communication practices is the growing number of bloggers who get in trouble for what they write. As the examples above suggest, many bloggers are teenagers, and just as school principals have always tried to control what students write in the school paper or the literary magazine, administrators are starting to take action against bloggers who aren't sufficiently true to their school.

I can just picture it. A high-school principal in an old jacked with leather elbow patches. A broad wooden paddle on the desk in front of him. In front of the desk, a nervous girl squirms, her hands instinctively stuck into the back pockets of her bluejeans for protection. "So, Miss Kelly, do you care to repeat in my presence the words you used to describe me in your LiveJournal?"

Here comes the tawse man

By Abel on 18 September 2006

I spotted a fantastic item on eBay recently from one of our favourite sellers – a bag containing a collection of tawses, that were used as "samples":

> My friend bought them from the daughter of the original owner and was told he had all sorts of different design patterns and took them to customers of whom many were schools in the late 1970s early 80s... he transported them in his gladstone bag (which is much older) along with leather samples, so customers could choose style colour of leather and thickness etc as well as stamps or hanging holes/loops etc...

One ponders the discussion on the morning of his visit:

"Remember, Headmaster: the tawse man is visiting today."

"Of course, Mrs Benham. Line up four girls for me, would you, in case he has anything interesting that I need to try out? And could you speak to Mr. Price, please? I have a suspicion that he may have worn out his XH on the Upper Fourth last week."

Shame that finances are too tight right now for me to bid!

The seller's final caveat is worth noting lest any of you had started formulating perverted plans:

> ***please note this is NOT A FETISH ITEM... IT IS A HISTORICAL/ COLLECTORS ITEM FROM OUR SOCIAL HISTORY AND IS NOT INTENDED FOR USE***

But of course.

Switching my bottom on

By Haron on 19 September 2006

Recently my life has been centred around - or reduced to - one thing: finishing off my thesis. Every morning I crawl to my desk (upright walking being impossible after so many hours hunched over the blanket of papers that covers every surface in the house) and begin typing inspiring things like "See mutatis mutandis *Smith v. Iceland* (2010) 1009 EHRR 12 at 17". Gripping stuff.

It takes a while to convince my head to start functioning every morning. This morning at breakfast I was cuddling my cup of coffee, convinced I would never, ever be able to type one more word again. Even thinking about going back to work made my eyes water a little bit.

"I can't switch my brain on," I complained to Abel.

He looked with me with due sympathy. And then he suggested:

"Maybe you need your bottom switching on? Would that help?"

Oh, I thought, a spanking! Why, that would take me out of the thesis misery for at least 10 minutes! It might even wake me up! I nodded several times with great enthusiasm.

He led me upstairs - by the hand, holding it gently, comfortingly. He sat on the bed and drew me over his lap. I hadn't got as far as wearing any panties yet (panties at 8am don't really happen), so he swept up my house dress and started smacking my bottom. It was a light spanking - as comforting as a long hug first thing in the morning. There was just enough sting to create a little cloud of warmth, but not enough to make me regret accepting his offer with so much enthusiasm. Little by little, my bottom was switching on.

In the end I got a proper long hug. I think it helped to switch on my brain in the end, too.

German beer: spankings all round

By Abel on 20 September 2006

Munich's famous beer festival is underway; nearly two million pints were downed during last weekend's opening ceremonies alone. Scenes behind the beer tents are apparently "Hogarthian" with "couples who were strangers a few hours earlier groping each other."

What particularly caught my eye, though, in the report in The Times yesterday was the comment that young Bavarian women are "enlisted from farms to serve as waitresses". They have to be trained to carry up to eight tankards of beer at once.

Given that the festival dates from 1810, I'm imagining 'Hogarthian' scenes of a different nature in the earlier days of its existence - with delectable Bavarian village girls being soundly whipped for spilling beer over clients. One complaint would lead to a warning; a second would inevitably lead to a thrashing before the waitress returned straight to work, wiping away the tears.

The paddling principal

By Haron on 21 September 2006

The Dallas Morning News reports that Principal Anthony Price has reinstated paddling in his junior high school, which has apparently helped to turn it around completely.

Paddles were hard to come by, so he ordered a load of them from a local cabinet maker. I wonder whether he'd first done any price checks at some of the Texan BDSM toy-making outfits. He might have got a bargain. Or maybe a wholesale paddle order from a furniture-maker is cheaper?

Though honestly, I wish he stopped beating kids, and came over to beat me instead. What a waste of a good-looking man with a great big board...

Flog a Fresher week

By Abel on 22 September 2006

The north-east of England, where we live, has a multitude of Universities – five, if I count correctly: Newcastle, Northumbria, Durham, Sunderland, Teesside. The students must be arriving shortly for the new academic year, and a comment on the Yahoo Traditional Mentoring and Discipline group fired my imagination:

> You sound so much like my wife and myself. We are life coaches for a few local college students. We even have one that travels to us from several hours away as needed.

This could bring a whole new perspective to Freshers' Week: sign up for classes, meet new friends, buy textbooks, register with a local disciplinarian. Oh, what fun could be had – and all whilst helping a student to adjust to the demands of university life. Long conversations first, setting the ground rules. A misdemeanour a few weeks into term: a first, nervous trip over the knee. Later, a serious transgression, and that first sharp taste of the cane.

The best mentors might even take on two students. I picture the young ladies, passing outside our front door, one arriving, one departing have had her work reviewed and correction applied. Knowing that they must surely visit the house for the same reason, they would avert their eyes shyly from one another.

One imagines them meeting subsequently in more conventional surroundings, in some student bar. A mutual friend would introduce them: "Have you met?" "No, we haven't," they'd both respond, just a fraction too quickly.

Haron wouldn't join in, of course. She'd be too busy reflecting ruefully on some of the 'motivation' that's come her way during her studies in the past few years…

Spanking in academia

By Abel on 23 September 2006

I feel like addressing a conference. Not just any conference, you understand, but the ever-so-eminent-sounding 42nd International Congress on Medieval Studies, from 10-13 May 2007 at Western Michigan University.

The sub-title explains why: 'Capital and Corporal Punishment in Anglo-Saxon England'. I could focus on the interesting stuff, and play truant for the other half of the sessions.

I've just missed the 15 September deadline for the call for papers, but perhaps I could sweet talk the organiser (who's at Cornell) into letting me submit late:

> We are looking for papers that deal with the various forms of, concerns with, and issues surrounding both corporal and capital punishment in the Anglo-Saxon period. Papers may address secular, ecclesiastical or combined interests. Legal, historical, and literary treatments are all welcome.

They want twenty-minute presentations, but I'd rather drag Haron along for a practical workshop. After-dinner entertainment, maybe?

I wonder if they'll publish an anthology of the papers?

The punishment book, once more (a spanking story – sort of)

By Abel on 27 September 2006

Browsing Hansard (the official record of UK parliamentary proceedings) last night, as one does, I uncovered an interesting debate from 1998 about corporal punishment in schools. One phrase sparked a kinky bedtime conversation with Haron last night, what with her being a lawyer. Much of the debate had focused around human rights legislation; Baroness Warnock then commented that: "I am not much enamoured of the concept of human rights."

My mind wandered... Their Lordships were debating abolition from the standpoint of the pupils: of course, it would infringe their human rights were they to be caned.

But what, I asked, about the human rights of the teachers? I pictured the test case that would be taken before the courts. A schoolmaster with a group of misbehaving young ladies, who are supposed to be studying in silence for some test. One flings a heavy textbook across the classroom, missing her target and clattering across the teacher's desk at the front of the classroom. The book catches him a glancing blow; the red ink he'd been using to mark exams floods across his suit. Pray, what of his human rights?

The case would proceed, of course, to the European Court. Learned lawyers would debate at length and at cost. The judges would make their pronouncement: where two sets of rights conflict in this way, they would of course defer to the gentleman in the position of authority.

Meanwhile, such cases taking not a little time to be resolved, the young lady would have escaped to the relative safety of a good University. Its Vice Chancellor would have followed the case with interest. On hearing of the judicial decision, the culprit would be invited before him. He'd reach for the university's rules and regulations.

"When you entered the University, you went through a formal process called Matriculation. In it, you confirmed that there were no outstanding issues with your former place of education that might prevent you from taking your place here. I now find that to be untrue."

"Please, sir..."

"Whilst, strictly speaking, I should send you down immediately, there is another option. I have spoken to your former Headmaster at length this morning, and we believe that we have found an acceptable solution."

She wouldn't sleep that night before catching the early-morning train, dressed in her smart interview suit. She'd avoid the eyes of the other passengers lest they recognise her from the now-dated photograph of her in school uniform, clipped from an old house photo and used in so many of that morning's newspapers to illustrate the reports of the case.

She'd change onto the local train, rattling through the countryside to the small stop a mile down the road from her old school. Never would the walk through the village, up the hill, have seemed so long. She'd hesitate in front of the grand school building: to use the front door, or walk to the back and go in through the pupils' entrance? The latter, of course.

She'd find herself almost bowled over as she entered, by a group of giggling fourteen-year-olds rushing out to the hockey field. Along the corridors, with their familiar musty smell; up the stairs, someone answering her prayers as she crept past the staff common room unnoticed.

The Headmaster's Secretary would expecting her, but, "Mr. Jenkins is engaged at present." Would she mind awfully taking a seat? Ten-minutes-that-felt-like-an-hour, before he would emerge, smiling his farewells to a distinguished couple – potential parents, maybe, their eyes alighting momentarily on her as they wondered where they'd seen this familiar face.

He'd be surprisingly welcoming. Thank you for travelling all this way so promptly. How nice it was to see her back, albeit not in such unfortunate circumstances. Had she had a good journey? How was she finding University life? Were her studies going well? A postgraduate degree afterwards, my dear? How very interesting. "And shall we move on and deal with the matter which brought you back to St. Christina's?"

The cane would be hanging on its old hook on the back of the study door. She'd wince at the thought that his previous visitors would have seen it there, must have guessed. "I had to ask the porter to dig this out from the storeroom, to be honest, and get him to give it a good soaking overnight. We wouldn't want it breaking, now, would we?"

"We'd better do this the conventional way, I suppose. Knickers down, skirt up, touching your toes. And I agreed with the Vice Chancellor that the traditional six would be appropriate."

Her tears would drip onto the carpet before he even started; the undeniable, shocking pain of the first stroke seemed almost incidental in the context of her overall nightmare. Almost. By the third, the burning stripes would be all-consuming, despite the Headmaster's best attempts to re-assure. By the sixth, she'd – just – have managed to regain some degree of composure: mustn't let myself down....

She would dress painfully, as he filled in one last entry in the long-neglected punishment book. He would hand the leather tome to her, a calming hand briefly resting on her arm. "If you give this to Mrs. Burton on the way out, she'll take the photocopy that the Vice Chancellor will need to file away." And then she'd was free, the gravel crunching under her feet as she walked away from the school as quickly as she could, the autumnal air chill on her burning face. Trying to forget.

Trying to forget. Despite every bump of the train on the narrow branch line, every glance from passers-by, every newspaper stand trying to remind her.

Punishment choices

By Abel on 28 September 2006

The history of a distinguished public school includes an extract from the school rules of 1965; by then, "the cane was rarely used", replaced instead by the following options:

- Extra duties in School House

- Handwriting tests with the copying of extracts.

- Essay writing - approved titles only

- Reporting at various times in different clothes – smartly

- Gating - boarders only

- Early bed-time and getting-up

- Running

- Cleaning of corridors etc.

- Gardening

- Rolling (the lawn and cricket field)

- Detentions

- Half-Term detention

- End of Term detention

- Send to H.M

- Removal of privileges

- Public works.

I'm guessing that "Send to H.M." might explain the "rarely" in the phrase "the cane was rarely used."

A celebratory caning

By Haron on 29 September 2006

At 4pm yesterday afternoon I submitted my PhD thesis. At 4pm today I was setting out plates for celebratory dinner, anticipating the caning I was going to get to mark my last evening as a student.

Two of our friends were coming over, one of whom happened to have been the first person to cane me after I arrived in England for grad school. Abel thought it was fitting that should also deliver the last strokes of my student life. At first I was appalled by this idea: Mr Friend canes hard, and this dinner was supposed to be a *celebration*, for goodness sake. However, as I cleared piles of my papers off every surface in the house, and set out place mats and shiny cutlery, I gradually began to see the ultimate fairness of this suggestion. I believe in marking milestones in an appropriate way.* A caning to round off fifteen years of full-time education (and I do count the primary school) would give me the sense of closure. I still dreaded it, but I was beginning to accept it.

Abel cooked a beautiful dinner; the four of us polished off two bottles of wine and got started on champagne and cherry liquors, and I started to think that maybe the caning wouldn't happen today after all. Nobody mentioned it, and we were sitting on the sofa, chatting about pervy things when Mr Friend's wife (who has expressed a wish to be known as K.) leaned close and whispered: "I want to cane you." If either of the men had initiated it, I might have made a great show of protest and fear, but here I was disarmed: she wasn't suggesting that I somehow *deserved* it - just that she want to cane me, and who would refuse a beautiful girl who wants to paint tramlines on your bottom? I didn't.

I went upstairs and fetched a cane. Abel and Mr Friend were happy to wait for their turn. K squeezed my shoulder in encouragement, and guided me over the arm of the sofa, where Abel could hold my hands and stroke my hair to help me get through it.

K is excellent in warming you up with the cane: sharp taps over my jeans which bit, but didn't burn me. An occasional harder slash made me kick up my foot, but I tried to be stoic. Something about being caned by people who are nice to me throughout, brings out in me a need to be brave for them.** The strength of the cuts grew; even my jeans were beginning to heat up. K pressed her hands against my bottom, and only then did I feel the ridges rising on my flesh; she ran her nails across them, and I felt like screaming. But I wanted to be brave, too. Abel stroked the side of my face, and K said she wanted to see how much damage she was doing. I pushed down my jeans and settled down over the arm of the couch again.

K leaned to me, put her lips against my ear and whispered: "Can you take 6 hard ones?"

I *wanted* to take six hard strokes from her, even though I knew that when she was finished, Abel would take up the cane, and after him Mr Friend would step up to deliver his share. I braced myself, digging my nails into the upholstery.

They hurt, every one of them, and I couldn't keep count for anything, though I could probably tell you where each stroke landed. Yet, every rush of pain made me stronger. By the time those six were over, I knew I could take my licks from the men.

It was Abel's turn. K took his place on the sofa, holding my hands. I don't think there was an unmarked spot on my bottom by this time, so every time the cane touched my skin - even when Abel was addressing it with light taps - I felt it as a separate, stingy stroke. Again, I lost count. And again, I tried my best to be brave. I failed only once, when instead of delivering the stroke he slashed the cane through the air; if K wasn't holding my hands, I would have leapt up halfway to the ceiling. Abel gave me his six, alternating reassurance with painful squeezes of my bottom. K offered me my glass of champagne while the cane changed hands.*** "You're such a good girl," she whispered. I squeezed her hands in gratitude.

Finally, Mr Friend came to deliver his strokes. I'm sure he would have liked me to be apprehensive, but I was flying. Despite struggling to cope with each stroke - I couldn't help kicking out and yelping any more - I needed this last caning of my student life to be hard. I had been 21 when I started grad school; I had been frightened and often sad, and, because people often told me that I was wise for my age, I had thought I was done growing up. At 26, I know better.**** I often wish I had a way to tell that sad girl far away from home that it would all turn out well; that at the end of that rainbow there were rewards she couldn't imagine. Tonight we had the pain in common. There's no going back to the girl I used to be (and thank goodness for that), but there was closure for me, which meant more than I could have imagined when I was setting out the dinner plates a few hours before.

When it was done, I had a hug and a kiss from all three, and I pulled my jeans back on. I couldn't - and still can't - comprehend not being a student any more. It's true, though: it's done, I'm done. There is still a defence to go through before I'm allowed to graduate, but in about ten minutes I forever lose my claim to discounted movie tickets, and that means it's real: it's finished.

I mean, the tax man says I'm an adult. The tax man and about 35 cane strokes make for a very convincing argument whenever I'm tempted to think otherwise.

* You should *see* what a big deal I make out of my birthday
** Whereas if a top shows a tiniest bit of meanness, I kick and thrash around, and generally show zero intent to cooperate.
*** It was my first sip of alcohol while bending over. I should do it again; it's quite nice.
**** Not being a virgin any more also helps.

Caned and re-caned

By Abel on 30 September 2006

Inspired by Haron's thesis-submitting caning, I had naughty, naughty dreams last night as my young lady slept next to me, face down, wincing every time my mischievous hands reached out for her bottom...

A Housemaster at a prestigious girls' school had a son at University, who had formed a relationship with one of his father's sixth-formers.

Said young lady was part of a group of the girls who found themselves before the Housemaster for the whack; her strokes – whilst painful - were administered noticeably more gently than those inflicted on her contemporaries.

Her punished friends considered this unfair. Word of their grievance percolated up to the Headmaster, who therefore re-administered the girl's caning later that evening.

It's not unknown for us to re-enact such kinky dreams when we whisper them to each other in the morning. Yet today, Haron's safe. After all, last night's caning was to be her last dose of discipline as a student. Her backside is therefore an implement-free zone - for another five hours and thirteen minutes, at least, until the clock strikes midnight and she formally leaves academia. And then she's mine. My own. My preciousssssssss...

A collection of domestic brushes
By Haron on 1 October 2006

We were just watching the "Antiques Roadshow",* and this little girl comes on, probably about 10 years old.

> The specialist: So, what have you got here?

> The Little Girl: It's Gran's collection of domestic brushes.

And what do you know? Twenty or so antique brushes of every possible kind and shape. Brushes for hair, and clothes, and carpets; polished wooden backs (some with inscriptions), pristine bristles, the sort of things that we would snap up for one purpose, and one purpose only: the smacking of bottoms. (Usually mine, obviously.)

> The specialist: What's so special about brushes?

> The Little Girl: I like their texture and weight and bristles and...

Yes, I quite understand. It's hard to explain to an antiques seller, but there is nothing quite as enticing as an old wooden brush with its years of imaginary disciplinary history. How can you not want to buy one the second you see it, even if you have ten others back at home?

The pride of the girl's collection was this enormous square-backed brush the size of a paperback novel, which was supposedly meant for brushing fur coats. Guess what we'll be looking out for on eBay.

(Abel's really pleased. She had exactly the same carpet beater as he uses to punish me.)

* In case you don't know: a TV show wherein people who have stuff in the house they think might be old and valuable

(as opposed to just old), bring it to specialists to value. The entertainment value is in a) looking at antiques b) marvelling at how a garish painted pot can be valued at 3000 pounds.

One of us?

By Abel on 2 October 2006

We were browsing with a kinky friend in a tiny second-hand bookstore. We're deep into the old children's storybooks, biographies, history texts – anything that might turn up anecdotes with kink potential.

In walks a new customer. "Do you have any old school textbooks?" he asks the bookseller – before looking surprised, and not a little embarrassed, when we three burst simultaneously into fits of giggles!

On the discipline of valuable housemaids

By Haron on 7 October 2006

Why have I never before heard of the British drama series "Upstairs, Downstairs"? Seriously, what sort of a spanko am I, completely ignorant of a whole five seasons' worth of masters, maids, butlers and their very fabulous costumed interactions?

Well, that's been remedied this week, when I switched the TV on at an unusual for me hour, to find a girl in a housemaid's dress having a royal tantrum in the kitchen, with an older maid and a butler frowning at her.

A bit of research online has disclosed that the maid is Daisy Peel, that there is a war on, which is why, although she's doing a proper petulant foot-stomping routine, she isn't getting sacked.

Daisy is unhappy about her workload, you see, and she whinges that she should have gone off to work in a munitions factory where they have rules against slavery. Throughout the episode she makes various blunders, like repeating in the kitchen what she'd heard discussed in the parlour, and letting in a guest when the mistress is not at home.

The butler, Mr. Hudson, complains that were these the ordinary times, he wouldn't hesitate to see that she is thrown out without a reference.

"But these are not the ordinary times," Rose, the older maid says. "Housemaids are worth their weight in gold!"

I know what to do if the girl can't be fired! I know! Do you?

London birching

By Abel on 10 October 2006

In a black cab crossing London en route to a meeting. We're chatting about allergies. A colleague comments:

> "My daughter R—— is extremely allergic to birch pollen."

Damned good excuse, for a naughty girl, if you ask me…

Coincidentally, the cab then swung into a narrow side street to take a short cut. Its name? Birchin Lane. Honestly. I couldn't wait to get to the Internet to look up stories of the ancient whipping posts that must have lined the route (albeit it seemed a little too narrow for a good flogging). I was fascinated by the real origins, albeit a little disappointed:

> The name means "lane of the barbers," from an unrecorded Old English word, beardceorfere. He points out that the Middle English cherven (from OE ceorfan), meaning "to cut," was used specifically for the cutting of hair

Wrong type of cuts, sadly.

The master of the house

By Abel on 13 October 2006

Ever since the first time Haron and I toured a grand country house together some years ago, lost in reveries about servant girls being whipped, I've had endless fantasies about aristocratic birchings.

I wrestled with two scenarios in my dreams last night, each competing as if to be selected for a future story. In the first, the young Duke (for the lord of the manor is always young, single and kindly, albeit strictly concerned about the well-being and survival of his estate) would insist that any girl requiring thrashing would be sent to his study. He would issue any such miscreants with a cane, to be taken to the Head Butler who would administer the punishment. The tearful servant would be made to return the cane immediately afterwards to his Lordship.

Scenario number two saw the Head Gardener plant a row of birch trees outside the window of the Duke's study. Girls would be sent to cut switches for their floggings, whilst their employer watched from within.

Interestingly, in neither case was the Duke administering the punishments himself; he left that to his staff. Yet in both cases, his favourite girl (a recurring and some might say clichéd theme of mine) would end up in trouble, and he would cross the class boundaries to console her afterwards – albeit in a most chaste manner.

Spanking in space

By Abel on 14 October 2006

It seems that Virgin Galactic, who are planning on launching the world's first space-tourism service in a couple of years' time, have decided to exclude three groups of customers: those under 16, anyone with heart problems... and women with breast implants.

Apparently the silicon could explode. I am *so* glad they thought of that before they fired their first 'enhanced' porn star into space...

Makes me wonder about spankings in zero gravity. How: it would be tough to catch one's girl to spank her. If: a spanking in space could hurt. Whether: any astronauts have ever succumbed to kinky temptation and experimented.

If any of you are rich enough to afford a ticket, please can you report back on your findings?

Ten strokes to test the cane

By Haron on 15 October 2006

I wish other bloggers stopped giving Abel wicked ideas. For example, Lily's husband has a habit of testing new implements by giving her 10 strokes. Luckily for her, the most recent one was a silicone spatula.

Unluckily for me, Abel has just bought a particularly ferocious antique knotted Malacca cane. He had, in fact, already tested it (one stroke over my jeans, which sent me howling to the ceiling). Except then he read Lily's blog, and decided that it was necessary to adopt what he now sees as best practice.

So, onto the bed I went, conveniently bare after my bath, and he duly delivered ten fast, biting licks of the cane. The pain from that thing is indescribable, and the inherent unfairness of the test (did I mention he'd already tested it?) made me say some things to him that might have swiftly turned this into a punishment if he hadn't been in a good mood. (Or if I hadn't shut up on time: I know what's good for me.)

I'm going to lobby for the idea that new implements actually have to be tested on the spanker first.

St. Trinian's: screen spankings on the way?

By Abel on 18 October 2006

So, there's a new St. Trinian's movie on the way. Most "Spanking Writers" readers will doubtless share our affection for the series, described as "nostalgic hymns to a golden age of juvenile delinquency".

I've just drafted my job application:

> English gentleman, experienced in many of the more old-fashioned educational techniques necessary for the film. Open to offers for acting (housemaster or similar), script development or wardrobe work.

That should do the trick.

Actually, perhaps they should cast the film via one of these reality TV shows, in which girls have to convince the public of their suitability. I want to see the episode in which applicants are tested for their reaction to a sound caning of the sort that must surely be a feature of the film.

Sweet dreams are made of this

By Abel on 20 October 2006

A remarkably detailed spanking dream last night, inspired by my lovely new cane and an even lovelier new friend!

Said friend – "one of us", you must understand – had come to stay with us. (I'd been typing a note to her with dates for just such a visit immediately before going to bed; the cane's hanging next to my desk. Oh how strange the sleepy sub-conscious can be!). We'd just finished eating dinner – a dinner throughout which she and Haron had misbehaved; a stern final warning had been issued, but to no avail. Whether something got broken or spilt I can't tell you, but the switch flicked: two giggling girls were suddenly still, silent.

"Go to your rooms."

Serious, worried now as they walked upstairs.

I let them wait. Gave them time to contemplate. Knew that each of my belated footsteps on the stairs would make their heart beat a little faster.

To the study, first, to pick up the cane. Malacca; incredibly flexible; incredibly effective. Then I opened the door to the spare room. Our friend stood up, biting her lip, eyeing the cane. "I shall deal with you in a few minutes. Put on your pyjamas and get ready for bed."

Next I headed into the main bedroom, where Haron was waiting. She's often quite contrary when she knows a spanking is in store. Quick-witted, as if her arguments might find a chink in the case for the prosecution.

Not tonight.

I scolded. At length. Knew that the tone of my voice would carry to the next room, if not the words themselves.

Twelve strokes. Hard. Hard enough for a brave girl to struggle, for the tears to flow.

Knew that the sound of the strokes would carry to the next room too. That someone there would be counting, Haron's tally inevitably her own.

And then hugged my tearful girl; told her to get into bed.

I headed along the corridor. Discussed a girl's misbehaviour. Considered how it had fallen short of the standards that I would expect. Explained to a girl that she was now to be punished: not some play spanking, but for real. Watched the tears well up as I told her to bend over and touch her toes. Pulled down her pyjama bottoms.

Twelve strokes. Hard. Hard enough for a brave girl to struggle, for the tears to flow.

Knew that the sound of the strokes would carry to the next room too. That someone there would be counting, recalling her own thrashing, feeling her own stripes, willing her friend through.

I held her afterwards; let her snuggle close. Comforted, re-assured.

Here endeth the dream. I wonder when she'll be able to come to stay?!

Reporting for punishment

By Haron on 20 October 2006 in The Punishment Book

'I hope you'll dress smartly for your appointment,' said Abel as I curled up in my bath robe at half past 10 in the morning.

'What do you want, a ball gown?' I said. Nevertheless, I dragged myself upstairs to put some clothes on. At 11am exactly I was supposed to knock on his office door, reporting for my punishment.

This used to be a fantasy of mine: hours of anticipation, self-conscious squirming, minutes ticking away - walking up the stairs with enough time to spare that I can take a few deep breaths at the door to calm my nerves. We sometimes role-play with scenes like that, and I love it. Reality has shown that I'm just so good at compartmentalisation, that the first time I thought about the punishment that morning when Abel reminded me to get dressed for it. Not that I wasn't happy to get over with it: the punishment had been hanging over me for more than a day.

We Punishment Book babes get spanked for a variety of reasons, and some times our misdeeds are pretty contradictory. We simply can't use each other's experience for guidance. One day I'll be spanked for working too hard, and then Mija will be spanked for not working hard enough. One day Sparkle is in trouble for not locking the front door - and guess what I get strapped for next.

Abel arrived home the other night to find the front door latched. He doesn't like this. I always have the latch on, particularly when it's almost midnight, and I'm alone in the house, but when he's due to come home from a trip, I unlatch it before he comes back.

Or anyway, I'm *supposed* to unlatch it. Unless I forget. Or put the latch back on automatically. When this happens, I usually hear a crash as Abel tries to open the door, and then some very bad words when he fails.

Only this time, there was a crash - and complete silence. Bad words were mentally provided by me, because I'd suddenly remembered that last time this happened he'd promised me retribution. I wondered whether it would be safer just to leave him outside, but then figured that at some point I'd have to leave the house to get food and stuff, and by that time he'd be really unhappy, so I sighed and trotted to the door.

'You'll be spanked for this,' were his first words.

'Hello to you too,' I said. I really wanted to explain to him about serial killers, monsters from the outer space, and maniacs who get into your house *just* as you're about to have a shower, but thankfully I was too tired to say anything witty, so we just hugged and went to bed.

The next day he didn't mention it at all. All day.

Until that night, when he suddenly remembered. But then it was quite late, and we'd had a glass of wine, and I reasoned that maybe he should put off my punishment to some time when I'm not comatose. I have this thing where I prefer not to be spanked when I'm too tired to understand what's happening. Although, if you think about it, maybe it would be better to sleep through the punishment, and wake up pleasantly refreshed in the morning, wondering why my bottom is sore and striped...

Anyway, my spanking was put off again. Only this time Abel told me to report to him the following morning.

At exactly two minutes past eleven I was touching my toes in the spare bedroom, in the middle of a vast space he had just cleared for his swinging needs.

He had picked out a strap - not the scariest we own, but one of the pretty scary ones, with a nasty wooden handle and a nasty black leather tongue, and announced that I was getting six strokes.

Well, that's not too bad, I said to myself, I can take six; I've had six before - I've had many more; no big deal, I though: it's only six.

When you need to tell yourself something so many times, it's because deep inside you know that it's a lie.

I knew it was bad after the second stroke, which bit so heavily into my skin that my ears rang before I could even feel anything. I couldn't stay in position for anything. After each stroke I shot straight up, hollering and clutching my bottom. I went straight back to touching my toes, though, because I wanted to get through this, and I didn't want any extra strokes: it was hard enough to get through the strokes I'd had.

I didn't cry, but I came close to tears, particularly after the last stroke, when I crouched on the floor, thankful I didn't need to present my bottom to the strap again. I had a band of fire across my cheeks, so sore that I didn't even look at it in the mirror. I just didn't want to see it.

Abel gave me a hug - a really long and warm one - and I gingerly pulled my trousers back on.

I'm still going to keep the door locked, thankyouverymuch, but maybe I'll put a big sign on the inside of it, saying something like *Husband Alert, Take Off Latch*.

The flogging experience. (No, sorry: "Flogging the experience")

By Abel on 21 October 2006

I missed what sounds like a rather fascinating Radio 4 programme last week. According to The Observer, "Selling the Old School Tie" reported on British public schools such as Harrow and Dulwich College...

> ...setting up in Beijing and Shanghai, where there is a keen market for boaters and Blighty.

Despite the BBC's own caption for the story ("Flogging the public school experience to the Chinese"), I'm left wondering quite how traditional an experience they recreate in such foreign climes. I'm guessing that authenticity may have been sacrificed to an extent, but it won't stop me speculating...

In the head teacher's office
By Haron on 22 October 2006

There's an piece in yesterday's Times about the head of St Paul's school. Written by two journalists, the article begins thus:

> Not for the first time in either of our lives, we are keen to get out of the head teacher's office.

I can't help shuddering in sympathy. I know what they mean, I really do.

The article goes on to describe the Head's campaign to go back to the policies the school had when it was founded nearly 500 years ago. He says:

> 'What we are primarily doing is deciding to turn the clock back to 1509.'

What he means is that he wants the school to be able to sponsor the education of poor – but bright – kids, which is what it had been founded for. But it's not the image I get when thinking about schools turning their clocks back. Somehow, my images involve lengths of rattan with crooked handles. Or, for still greater historical accuracy that far back, bundles of birch rods.

Dickensian Playground
By Haron on 23 October 2006

I first became aware of the cane as a punishment implement while reading "David Copperfield". I read the caning scenes over and over, until first I knew them by heart, and then the words began losing their meaning, becoming a collection of sounds. I owe a great deal of my kinky make-up to Charles Dickens.

That said, I don't think I'm going to visit the upcoming Dickens theme park. I don't think its creators are quite getting the meaning of the word 'dickensian'. They have planned to build –

> "old curiosity shoppes" in mock-Victorian squares, a "haunted-house ride", a "naughty burlesque show" to entertain adults in the evening, and a children's play area called Fagin's Den.

I'm all in favour of naughty burlesque shows, but it isn't exactly the first thing that comes to mind when you think about Dickens. Mucky orphans, debtors' gaols and really, really sleazy lawyers are a little bit more *it,* don't you think? I suppose, the problem is that making people pay to visit artificial slums might prove problematic.

Tell you what, Dickens World people: lay on some authentic Dickensian canings, and I could be persuaded to visit.

Spankers' Bible

By Haron on 25 October 2006

There's been an online poll to distil top ten funniest typos in church magazines, and the second funniest entry was this:

> The advent of the computer spellchecker has ensured that the church secretary doesn't need to proofread the service sheets any more - or does he? In one church, the word "speaking" was spelt wrongly, so the spellchecker gave the nearest equivalent. As a result, puzzled worshippers sang...

"Teach us, Lord, the art of... spanking."

It didn't help that the next verse in the hymn begins with the words, "You release us from our bondage..."

Actually, I'm sure there are enough spankers out there who could benefit from divine instructions. Not implying anything about anyone here you know. (Cough.)

"Bend over, Miss Bennet"

By Abel on 26 October 2006

So, we went shopping for fancy dress. A local theatrical costumier hires out its stock.

"We're after Regency era outfits for a party."

"Pride and Prejudice?"

"No, spanking, actually."

I didn't say that, of course. Sometimes the truth can be just a little too truthful. But the young lady who helped us was so adorably cute, and so enthusiastic about our preparations, that I teased: "You'll be wanting to come to the party yourself, next."

Fortunately, we'd already given her the dates for the hire, and she'll be at work. Just as well, really: much as I would have enjoyed her participation, I think she might have been just a tad taken aback.

A shower moment

By Abel on 30 October 2006

I've just installed a new shower curtain. (Don't laugh - that's as advanced as I get when it comes to home maintenance). It's covered in relevant words: "cleanse", "purify", "energise", "refresh", "invigorate", "revive".

I was reflecting that they'd missed a couple of the obvious phrases such as "wash", "water", "soap", "clean the bath after you've used it, Haron, or else". And it occurred to me that it's not without precedent for girls to find themselves being showered during scenes in our house. So I started reflect on the words that I want to add, for pre-punishment showers:

"Tremble"

"Flinch"

"Worry"

"Squirm"

"Cover"

"Blush"

...that sort of thing. I should go into shower curtain manufacturing: I could make a fortune.

'I write this sitting at a school desk'
By Haron on 31 October 2006

I've been enviously reading about a company that's placed its employees' offices in a pirate ship, a fake cave (with a fake waterfall in it), and hell knows where else, to give their creativity a boost. I hope it's working for them, and they don't just end up playing with bits of office scenery on company time, the lucky monkeys.

I can just imagine a zap of creative energy I would get from stationing myself in a kink-inspiring location every time I was writing a spanking story.

> Is it time to spank a schoolgirl? Welcome to our well-stocked classroom (with a power socket for your laptop, or freshly filled ink pots if you're in favour of full immersion).
>
> Are Navy floggings calling your name? Here's your ship, the 'gunner's daughter' to tie your sailors to, and the cat o'nine tails; off you go.
>
> Our country house welcomes spanking writers. The kitchen is ready to be populated with imaginary maids; feel free to examine our collection of corsets for dressing up your characters.

In reality, Abel and I often end up in inspiring locations, where my notebook fills to bursting with plot ideas, but most of our actual writing happens at prosaic cafes, hotel rooms and the good old office at home. Our real school desk is a good start, but it's not much help when I need to whip harem girls or mermaids.

Clearly, we need a wealthy benefactor with spare pervertible premises.

Spoil the rod, spare the child?

By Haron on 2 November 2006

We've just had our oven professionally cleaned by a nice man with lots of clever chemicals. Honestly, we needed it. It was seriously, seriously icky, and now the cat uses the oven to play with the funny-looking kitty reflected in its shiny door.

Anyway, as I chatted away to the cleaner guy, I imagined a service provided by a professional implement-maintenance service. They will polish your paddles, soak your old canes back to suppleness, and re-tie your birch rods as you wait.

I'm rather glad they don't exist, actually. I'd rather all those toys went unmaintained.

Thou shalt not touch thy students

By Abel on 5 November 2006

Obviously, the idea that physical contact between schoolmasters and the poor innocent girls in their charge is a BAD THING is absolutely correct, and quite rightly enshrined in law these days.

That in itself creates entirely different opportunities for perverted thought. Several of my stories revolve around a teacher having to punish his favourite girl (bright, sassy, attractive, a prefect, destined for one of the great universities, requiring private tuition, and so on). The feelings are mutual – the girl respecting, adoring her wise mentor.

But, of course, in a story set in a boarding school of 2006, there could be no corporal punishment. And the relationship would be purely platonic: their deep feelings left unspoken.

Until (if you were having kinky dreams, as I did last night) the final day of the final term of the girl's school career. It's after final assembly. Our young lady heads for her favourite teacher's study to express her heartfelt thanks and say her goodbyes before heading to the railway station.

They stand opposite each other, electricity crackling in the air between them, so many unspoken words leaping through their minds. He tells her to stand up straight: "Just because you're no longer a pupil here doesn't mean you can slouch."

"No, sir."

He walks around her, inspecting her, and then stands close before her. "As you've left the school. you shouldn't be wearing your uniform."

I'll leave the rest to your perverted imaginations...

Etiquette for girls

By Haron on 6 November 2006

I'm in trouble. Not in the sense that I'm about to get a spanking, but in the sense that over the next few weeks I'm going to work very hard not to get a spanking. Because Abel has just invented a very twisted little exercise, called "Torture by Etiquette Guide".

A few weeks ago we heard that Debrett's, the publisher of such useful books as a guide to the British aristocracy, a book of forms of address, and - yes - a guide for etiquette and manners, had brought out a new publication called "Debrett's Etiquette for Girls."* It's thoroughly modern, and includes such complex topics as how to eat sushi politely, the solution to the intricacies of staying the night at your boyfriend's, and how to gracefully stagger home after an evening of boozing.

Usually I find old etiquette manuals very useful for story research: it's important to know what an Edwardian schoolgirl would have been spanked for, you see. I was going to go through the new book if I had a chance, but I wasn't particularly excited about owning it.

Except last weekend we noticed it in a shop, and my perverted husband has decided that it could be put to a better use.

Over the next few weeks - starting this coming Thursday night - he will test me on one chapter of the book. There will be ten questions, with a stroke of an implement of Abel's choice being the punishment for each wrong answer. Each chapter is about twenty pages long, I'll have you know; that's twenty pages more studying for a test than I've had to endure since finishing my first degree.

You might wonder why I'm all worked up, given that I'm supposed to be *into* playing school-related scenes, and being spanked, and things like that.

That I might be, but I'm really not into failing tests. I got a perfect score on every test I've taken since about the age of 14, and I've certainly never had to answer for failing one. This is a matter of honour, or maybe a matter of arrogance: to come away from the tests unscathed. But there are ten chapters in the book - that's a hundred questions, if Abel doesn't get bored earlier. I think I'm justified in panicking here.

I'm sure you'll hear more on this soon.

* By which they mean "young women" rather than "female children".

Corporal punishment for undergraduates

By Abel on 9 November 2006

It's good to hear that the law students at the University of Wales campus in Aberystwyth have been settling down this term to some interesting modules. The one that caught my eye is entitled "A History of Crime and Punishment":

> From corporal punishment to the modern prison, from sanctions administered by neighbours to those handed down by the state, the subject matter of this course concerns societal reaction to wrongdoing. Students have the opportunity to investigate historical evidence and learn of the philosophies and practicalities of responses to crime from the middle ages to the twentieth century.

Actually, the academics seem to have missed out a phrase in the final sentence. I'm sure it's meant to start: "Students have the opportunity to carry out extensive practical research, as well as to investigate...."

I'd like to be a fly on the wall overhearing some of the students' conversations after certain of the discussions. I recall one very mundane maths lecture when I was at college that led to a cute Scottish friend discussing her one school encounter with the tawse. Goodness knows what revelations might have resulted from a whole hour on corporal punishment.

Dreaming of Chalet School

By Haron on 10 November 2006

I had the sweetest spanking dream last night.

Are you familiar with Chalet School books by Elinor Brent-Dyer? It's a classic series of girls' school novels, and there are tons of them. (One of them, "Chalet School and Richenda", even has a mentions of spanking in some of it editions, although on the whole they are very innocent.)

Well, I dreamt I was holding a very rare book, which had practically disappeared from bookshops and libraries, and it was called - yes, really - "Chalet School and Spanking".

Next thing I knew I got sucked into this book, and, because even in the dream I was aware of being *into* spanking, I volunteered to take the punishment the very next time a fellow schoolgirl got into trouble.

My memory of the events is rather blurry in a dreamy sort of way, but I distinctly remember being spanked with a wooden spoon in a legs-up position, and also being taken over an (otherwise) nice female teacher's lap in class.

When I woke up, I was sure that I had actually held that book in my hands, and that if I looked around the bedroom, I would find it. Except, I didn't. Sigh.

Daddy orders a whipping

By Abel on 11 November 2006

My most recent story imagined circumstances in which a University student had to return to her old school to be caned. I named the school St. Christina's and – with due thanks to the Vatican - I ought to explain why:

> St. Christina was the daughter of a rich and powerful magistrate named Urbain. Her father, who was deep in the practices of heathenism, had a number of golden idols, which our saint destroyed, and distributed the pieces among the poor.
>
> Infuriated by this act, Urbain became the persecutor of his daughter. He had her whipped with rods and then thrown into a dungeon.

It gets gruesome from there on in, as most tales of martyrdom do; her relics now lie in Palermo in Sicily, if you ever happen to be in the area.

By the way, St. Christina's feast day is on 24 July – put the date in your diary, in case you feel the need to whip anyone in celebration.

Misbehaving on the school bus

By Haron on 14 November 2006

Yesterday afternoon I had the dubious pleasure of returning home by bus at about the time local schools send their pupils home. In the absence of organised transportation for schoolkids in England, at about 4pm every day the local bus effectively turns into a school bus.

I can't fault the kids' behaviour, really: they were on the whole a pleasant bunch, it's just there were so many of them, in their variously coloured school ties, with huge folders pressed to their chests, chatting over the heads of other bus passengers.

To distract myself, I imagined I was on a different school bus entirely: as a middle-school girl on an organised field trip to a museum, for example. My best friend had a cold and was forced to stay behind, and nobody wants to sit with me or talk with me, and all the snooty six-formers are behaving as though the whole thing is beneath them... I just know that in a few minutes this cauldron will boil over, at which point the supervising prefect will snap: "That's it! I'm reporting the lot of you to Dr. Jenkins the moment we're back!" And we will all get caned - even though I'm doing nothing wrong, I'm telling you, nothing!..

Lost as I was in this fantasy, I didn't fail to notice one of the girls take her tie off her neck and wrap it around her forehead instead, hippy headband-style. In my school, on my bus, one of my fantasy schoolgirls would know better.

He's got the look

By Abel on 15 November 2006

My ears pricked wandering past a gaggle of gossipers in the office first thing this morning, as one of the ladies commented, "He kept giving me that Headmaster look all day. You know?"

No, I don't: care to enlighten me? Is that the "I've seen what you're doing" look? The "I'll deal with you later" look? The "I understand I'll be seeing you in my office at lunchtime", or the "Ah, there you are"?

The "Feigned surprise at the severity of your misdeeds", the "I'm disappointed in you", the "You'd better not argue with me?" Or the "I'm now going to hurt you" or the "I wonder how you're going to take this?" or the "Averting my eyes, up to a point" as the girl adjusts her uniform for punishment?

Perhaps it was the unseen look: from behind, the girl bent over, feeling his eyes on her. The concentration as he measured the cane, the smile of satisfaction at the quality of his ever-so-precise handiwork?

Or the "I wonder if that got through to her", the "I know you're not really a bad girl" - and the genuine, re-assuring "I hope this is our last such encounter" combined with the "Intrigued as to whether you will ever be back for more".

Perhaps I should go over and ask her for clarification?

To spank a student

By Haron on 16 November 2006

We were innocently driving through Norwich city centre when I cried: "Spank Student! Oh my god, there, there, look!"

"Pardon?" Abel, conveniently pausing at the lights, gave me a confused look. Our friend who was with us in the car was similarly puzzled. Of course, we had been talking about spanking just moments before, but for once the conversation had nothing to do with students.

"No, you're not looking!" I stuck a finger at the window. "There, on the left, where I'm pointing!"

Abel looked and cried: "Oh my goodness!"

Our friend looked and cried: "Oh my goodness!"

Here's what we saw. On the wall of the building we were driving past there stretched a great yellow banner, which said (in big, clear letters visible even in winter dusk):

SPANK STUDENT

And underneath, very helpfully: spankstudent.com

There was no hint as to what this was actually advertising - a shop? a newspaper? a bar? a national campaign for the introduction of corporal punishment in universities?

Not that it matters, but it's a chain of clubs (the dancing and booze kind, not the fetish kind), which appears to run discos in several UK towns. The origins of the name are not at all obvious from their home page, though their logo of a cute cartoon character with a very red behind is unequivocal.

Discussing the cane

By Abel on 19 November 2006

The web is littered with discussion boards featuring threads on corporal punishment. Many of the entries are clearly works of fantasy; that said, the entertaining fictional interludes come with the added frisson that they might – just – be genuine.

Take the following, from a poster on The Answer Bank:

> My school had a cane, and it was very rarely used - but the fact that it was there acted as a deterrent.... In fact I only remember it being used once, on a girl (!) who set a fire extinguisher off. Everyone in the school was SO shocked that the cane was finally being used, we didn't dare BREATHE next to a fire extinguisher after that!

I can just imagine Haron breathing on fire extinguishers wherever we go in the next few days, just to show off her bravery...

Chewing gum in the House of God

By Haron on 20 November 2006

We had a friend staying with us for the first time, and, being the good hosts that we are, Abel and I decided it would be nice to take her sight-seeing. After lunch we had planned a cathedral tour, and she and I were approaching it with a spring in our steps and some chewing-gum in our mouths.

I don't think Abel approves of chewing-gum very much, although he doesn't ban it, and even indulgently buys it for me. And now he discovered that he had not one, but two gum chewers on his hands. As we were approaching the grand cathedral doors, he told us that it wasn't appropriate to chew gum in a cathedral, and to spit it out immediately.

I, being a wimp, tossed mine in the bin at once. Our friend, being cheeky, made big eyes and asked:

"What's wrong with gum in a cathedral?"

"The cathedral is the house of God," Abel explained in a slightly dangerous voice. "God doesn't like chewing-gum. Spit it out, now."

For a very frightening moment I thought she was actually going to spit it at Abel, but luckily she's a polite girl, to an extent. She only said:

"Does it matter that I'm an atheist, sir?"

Feeling bad for my own earlier cowardice, I added:

"It's her own gum, sir. She bought it. It's her property. Why should she spit it out?"

Quietly getting to the boil (you can tell by the narrowing of his eyes), Abel took our friend by the shoulder and led her to the nearest wastebasket:

"Somebody you don't believe in disapproves of chewing-gum in his house. Bin, now."

She made a great show of pretending to take it out, but then finally, encouraged by the squeezing of fingers on her shoulder and by the dangerous squinting of eyes in front of her, she got rid of the gum.

So you see, no spanking happened at that time. Because either we're very cowardly, or Abel is very scary.

But we are still unclear on this fundamental issue: does God really disapprove of chewing-gum in church? If so, why? If not, how can we claim our gum back?

Vanilla for a day

By Haron on 22 November 2006

I believe that for at least two hours today I was entirely, completely vanilla. I haven't had any kinky thoughts at all. For a whole two hours, and maybe more.

That was because I was tired. When I'm tired, I can summon up only marginal interest in spanking. I suppose, a particularly juicy startle will cause a mild twitch of my mouth and a disinterested 'Oh...', but I wouldn't expect any more reaction than that.

Luckily, even a short rest is enough to fix me.

The longest I've ever felt completely vanilla was about three months, which was a result of a bad case of flu. Even after the illness was gone, spanking was not a subject I cared to think about, never mind act on. I knew intellectually that something was missing, but I didn't mind that it was gone: it was as though I'd taken a vanilla pill.

The interest returned very gradually, in almost the precise order that my spanking kink had developed in the first place: school and father/daughter fantasies first, then grown-up scenarios, then other, edgier themes.

And one for luck

By Abel on 23 November 2006

So, Irish rockers U2 decide to release a compilation. They call it '18 Singles', since (as you may be able to predict) it comprises their 18 best singles.

However, as the BBC News site comments:

"Brilliantly, the UK version of the CD has a bonus track - which instantly renders the album's title nonsensical."

I'm picturing a young female executive at their record company, spread-eagled over the boardroom table for a whipping this afternoon.

Henceforth, whenever I give a girl "six of the best", I think I should include a bonus stroke.

Traditions, updated

By Abel on 25 November 2006

Awaiting a friend at a railway station. Her text message flashes up: "Think we're a few minutes late."

"One swat for every minute's delay." (I'm fair like that).

So I wait, and the train duly rolls in - four minutes EARLY. I text her, knowing she'll have a long walk along the platform: "No, it doesn't work that *you* give *me* four swats for being early."

Quick as a flash: "4 stroke credit though! To be used at my discretion!"

I look up, just as her beaming face appears before me. "But of course. I shall remember your credit. The next time I give you a traditional ten of the best."

Lots of mini-spankings

By Haron on 26 November 2006

I've spent the last couple of days getting a number of very short, very painful spankings. Each individual one wouldn't really merit writing about, but as a whole they have been kind of building up. Abel is going away on business today, and just as well, because I'm sure that if he didn't, I'd be getting more of these "what are you complaining about, you wimp" spankings.

Firstly, there was my etiquette test. This must have been the most boring chapter ever: clothes and "image management". You might have thought it would be exciting, but it kept going on about the teeniest aspects of a girl's wardrobe. I can't imagine ever needing to consult such a list, never mind having to commit it to memory.

(Question: What are the two things a girl should remember to do if she applies fake tan at home? Answer: Exfoliate and moisturise. Chance of me ever applying fake tan, at home or otherwise: zero.)

Anyway, I got two questions out of ten wrong, mostly because of being unable to stay even relatively awake by the time I got to the last two pages of the chapter. (What are some of the uses for a square piece of cloth? Hair accessory, scarf, SOS banner, sarong. How long may a girl's dress be at a black tie event? At the shortest, it may skim the knee.)

"Take your jeans down and bend over the arm of the sofa," said Abel, trying to sound stern. "I'm going to spank you with my most severe implement."

His hand, you understand.

Oh my goodness, did those two smacks ever hurt! The first one felt more like a punch; he must have swung his arm way back; I could feel it deep in the muscle of my bottom for the rest of the evening. The second one wasn't as extreme, but it was still a damned painful whack.

And then there was yesterday morning, when I got spanked for - I'm not sure what, but it might have been for the crime of having a bottom, and standing around with only some French knickers on while I was brushing my hair in the morning.

So, I'm minding my own business (damp hair), when Abel swoops into the bedroom, sees me and says something along the lines of: "Well, if you show off your bottom like that..." He grabs my Mason Pearson hairbrush, pushes me over the bed, and wallops me with it about two dozen times.

It stings. A lot. Hairbrushes tend to.

So that was that: random, unprovoked acts of violence in the home, and he seemed mighty pleased with himself after all that.

Police chief runs a spanking program

By Haron on 28 November 2006

You know this common spanking fantasy, where an offender - rather than serve a short sentence, pay for a traffic ticket or pay a fine - submits to a spanking instead? ("Please, officer, couldn't you punish me in some other way? Like, spank me, maybe?")

Well, the police chief in Warren, OH decided to run a whole "diversion program" for young offenders, in which "clients were spanked for infractions". Yesterday they were still figuring out his criminal sentence.

I wonder if it'll be a judicial paddling?

Top five arguments for and against the slipper

By Haron on 30 November 2006

A discussion about slippers with friends recently has provoked a variety of opinions, from "slippers are weird" to "slippers are hot", and I feel the need to give my perspective.

The slipper and its relative, the plimsoll, are not my favourite implements because they are so damn painful. "So what?" I hear you ask. "Tawses and belts are painful. Canes are painful. Hairbrushes are painful." That's right, and I like tawses and belts a lot less than I like the slipper, which is why I said it wasn't my favourite, rather than that it was my least favourite.

The slipper has lots of advantages, which make it one of the hottest implements to fantasise about, to imagine other people getting, etc.

Top Five Reasons Haron Likes the Slipper:

1) It's authentic for school scenes. It belongs in a school scene. I know people who'd been slippered at school. And I like school scenes.

2) Unlike the cane and the tawse, it's a hell of a lot easier to aim, due to not being whippy. I've never heard of a slipper landing somewhere it hasn't been aimed.

3) A slipper is all "thud" and little "sting". I like "thud".

4) It looks really hot laid across a round bottom encased in bottle-green school knickers, preparing to strike.

5) You can slipper somebody really fast, which makes them reach the state of "Oh My God" (identified by the culprit hanging limply over your knee) that much quicker. Come to think of it, this may also been seen as a disadvantage.

Top Five Reasons Haron Is Apprehensive About the Slipper:

1) When you get slippered really fast (impossible to do safely with other school-specific implements - a cane or a tawse) holding on to a degree of control is completely impossible. As part of said control is the ability to keep down the noise, the slipper is, therefore, not very neighbour-friendly.

2) It's really bloody painful! (I can't emphasize this enough. It is. Very painful.)

3) It may be hard for a top to judge just how painful the slipper is, because it looks fairly harmless. It's imperative that you let the top know by every verbal and non-verbal communication method in your collection the impact of each individual thwack.

4) Thick rubber creates little raised blisters surprisingly quickly, and knocking heads off them can draw blood. I don't get unduly freaked by bleeding, but it does put a stop to any further play, even if you've only just started, and it hasn't actually started to hurt that much.

5) Man, are those freaking' things *ever* painful!!

However, if you're lucky, you may get cool tread marks. (I did once, before Abel - sorry, sweetie, I don't believe that's possible any more; that train's gone now.)

So there you are. Make your own conclusions, really; as you can see, I haven't quite made up my mind on the issue of slippers, other than they are hot, and also painful.

Breaking point

By Abel on 3 December 2006

Whilst wartime anecdotes usually fall on just the wrong side of the kink/squick line for me, a phrase in a post on a Yahoo group some time ago was sufficiently distant to be of interest. Discussing the Special Operations Executive, she recalled a lesson from her school days:

A schoolgirl friend had stated that she "would not give away her friends" no matter how she was tortured! The old French teacher asked, very dryly:

> "Well - imagine you are in the deepest cellar of a prison, completely bared, and fastened across a table for what you had been told was going to be the soundest of thrashings. Tell me, my dear - How many strokes of the strap or cane do you think it would take before you were willing to tell everything you knew?!" It shut my friend up - and the rest of us too - imagining!

And me!

Punishment, and Natty's inner appalled feminist

By Haron on 4 December 2006

Over on the Punishment Book website, our friend Natty has started a great discussion about the need for real-life punishment, and the inner blocks many women stumble upon when it comes to reconciling this with their feminist ideals.

In my case the reconciliation took about four seconds many years ago. I've been into spanking since I was born, an aware, active spanko for 9 years - and a feminist for only the last 5 years or thereabouts. When I mentally auditioned the feminist ideology to decide whether it was something I identified with, I made a mental check to see whether it was compatible with my fundamental inner needs.

In the case of my punishment kink, it went somewhat like this: "Can I identify as a feminist and still be accountable for my behaviour if I so choose, to any man or woman? Yes, I can. Check." It's a little simplistic, but overall, that's how it happened, and it's never worried me since.

The same reconciliation has not been as easy for many women - particularly, I suspect, for those who were doing it the other way around: those who were feminists first, and became aware of their spanking/punishment kink later.

Office politics

By Abel on 5 December 2006

I've borrowed an office today that has a simply glorious river view. A procession of schoolgirls headed along the towpath this morning en route to their day's studies; happy couples wander past hand-in-hand at regular intervals (making me think of, and miss, Haron).

There's a high wall at one point on the riverbank. As I look down now, a cute young lady can be seen sheltering almost out of sight of the office, puffs of smoke rising heavenwards.

I'm given to break from my work and contemplate a somewhat different style of employer. Smoking is strictly forbidden; the company disciplinary is much more... traditional.

The HR Director looks out from his office window, catching sight of the miscreant. "Amanda," he says to his PA, "would you be so kind as to ask security to bring the young lady who's smoking to my office. And might you fetch the junior cane from the cupboard?"

Abel. Artist.

By Abel on 7 December 2006

The Guardian tells us that Tomma Abts, the artist who won this year's £25,000 Turner Prize, deploys

> "a process that mingles disciplined severity with pure intuition".

I so should have entered.

Hand caning techniques

By Abel on 7 December 2006

A memoir of 1930s in Castlethorpe Village, Milton Keynes, describes a technique that I might use on Haron:

> Discipline was very strict ... at the senior school at Wolverton where we had to attend from the age of eleven to fourteen. If you behaved very badly you received six strokes of the cane on your writing hand from the headmaster before returning to the classroom to write five hundred lines containing a reference to the offence.

I wonder what sentence a Machiavellian master could devise. Perhaps:

> "I must be a good girl and refrain from using abhorrent, objectionable language to pupils from other neighbouring schools whilst travelling on the bus in the morning in my uniform."

Yep, that'd keep freshly-caned hands going for a while.

PS I checked the spelling of Machiavellian, as I initially typed it incorrectly. Bizarrely, Word offered "lying face down" as an alternative. My laptop is starting to recognise my writing style, but this is just spooky

Dangerous phrases

By Abel on 8 December 2006

Haron just wandered into my office straight after taking a shower. Now, I never can resist a cute, naked woman, and an inevitable swatting followed. Literally: with our leather fly-swat.

After a few whacks, my darling wife commented:
"That doesn't hurt"

Whilst she's often given to provocation, that just about wins the prize for "silliest thing to say to a man wielding a spanking implement". The remaining few did, of course, perhaps more than she would have liked. She's now standing next to me rubbing her backside ever-so prettily.

Naval floggings: the girls take their turn

By Abel on 13 December 2006

One could enjoy the thought of a press-gang, roaming a port in search of fit young men for the navy, making the mistake of rounding up a boyish young woman in a new batch of unwilling recruits. Her protests would be ignored, and once at sea, self-preservation would be the order of the day amidst so many sailors far from home comforts.

Condemned, though, to a caning for failing to strip at wash time, the truth would then be discovered. To maintain discipline on board, the captain would decree that her whipping should continue "as if she were one of the men", before taking her to the supposed safety of his private cabin.

An alternative naval scenario presented itself in a report of a Parliamentary Petition from 1659 describing the conditions facing "white slaves" transported to the colonies:

> Elizabeth Dudgeon, had dared to talk back to a guard. She was trussed up to a ship's grating and mercilessly whipped.

One of the ship's officers relished watching her whipped: "The corporal did not play with her, but laid it home, which I was very glad to see...she has long been fishing for it, which she has at last got to her heart's content."

Time for a trip to the seaside. I wonder if any friendly captains would take us to sea for a day, and look the other way politely whilst Haron was stripped and tied to a mast?

Christmas is a'coming

By Abel on 14 December 2006

I've been so busy at work of late that it's hard to believe that the festive season is almost upon us. Until yesterday evening, that is, when I stumbled upon the choir from an eminent girls' school performing a medley of carols in their local railway station.

I happened to have a few minutes before my train, so paused to listen. Suddenly, a phone trilled. Not mine, dear readers, but that of a young lady in the front row of the choir. She stepped out of formation; spoke anxiously into the handset; returned shamefaced to her position. The supervising staff glared at her; she avoided their eyes.

I've never written a choirmaster story. I'm beginning to think that that's an omission from my repertoire

'I'm not on the train'

By Abel on 17 December 2006

One doesn't mean to eavesdrop, but I've just heard the most spankable comment from the seat behind me on the train. Thanks to the joys of wireless on-board internet connections, I can report it directly to you.

A youngish lass, pretty, smartly dressed, joined at the last station; a sixth-former, if I'm guessing her age correctly. She was chatting on the phone to her dad, and sounding unusually keen to finish the conversation. Opposite her, a small boy with his family accidentally knocked a glass of milk over the table. Cue much commotion.

"It's nothing, dad," cute student mutters. "Just the people next to me in the coffee shop."

'Coffee shop'? Right. That would be the 130 miles per hour type of coffee shop that comes with a locomotive at the front and runs along tracks.

So, dear readers, who's she going to see? What furtive liaisons are planned for her afternoon? And what would daddy do on her return home were he to find out where she'd really been for the day?

Shanghai, scandal and spanking

By Abel on 19 December 2006

I posted recently about branches of British public schools popping up in China. I've visited Shanghai a couple of times in the past few years for work, and picked up a racy (and very well-written) book after my last trip that described some of the city's dubious past. The Pearl of the Orient was so decadent that in the late nineteenth century that one missionary commented, "If God lets Shanghai endure, he owes an apology to Sodom and Gomorrah".

A couple of anecdotes might appeal to our pervy readers. The local Madams "always kept their eyes open for new talent", including foreign women:

> "One madam, the mistress of the chief of police, approached a visiting Margaret Sanger in a tearoom to leave her card: the admiral of the British fleet, the madam informed her, was dropping anchor in Shanghai in the next few days and the demure-looking Sanger happened to be 'just his type.'"

And then there was the British Vice-Consul in the 1850s, who:

> "ran afoul of the Church... by taking as his mistress a pupil at a Protestant girls' missionary school in Ningpo. When he was transferred to Foochow he took the girl with him, which so outraged the head of the school, an upright Englishwoman named Miss Aldersay, that she reported him to the Bishop of Victoria in Hong Kong. The outraged bishop denounced the Vice-Consul from his pulpit, forcing the errant diplomat to send the girl back to her home."

One might presume that said young lady would have been especially soundly whipped on her return to school. Unless she ended up stopping over in Shanghai en route, of course.

The home of gentle ladies

By Abel on 21 December 2006

I find myself this evening in the comparative comfort of a Georgian country house in the South-West of England.

They've thoughtfully provided a history of the property in the bedroom. Its early years saw lavish entertainment: Pitt the Younger visited whilst Prime Minister. But (and this is where it gets interesting) it was soon converted into a home for "ladies of gentle birth and their servants", with preference given to the widows and daughters of clergyman and of naval and army officers.

As if that wasn't enough to trigger my mind into kinky overdrive, they also ran:

"a school for orphaned girls, like the ladies 'to be of gentle birth'."

I wonder if any of the ladies here as conference delegates - or indeed of the ever-so-cute uniformed staff - are game for some historical re-enactments? I rather enjoy Regency-era scenes. There's a birch tree handily positioned next to the car park, and I'm sure I noticed its branches twitching with anticipation as my carriage pulled up...

Of Schoolgirls, end-of-term reports and canes

By Haron on 22 December 2006

This afternoon I got an email from Abel: "This is your end-of-term report: print it and put it in an envelope, but don't read it. Tonight you will come to collect it from the Headmaster."

Oooh, I thought. Ooooooh. I sent the attachment to the printer with my eyes shut.

In the evening, after Abel had arrived home, I jogged upstairs to change into my school uniform. This time it was a maroon skirt, white shirt, maroon-and-silver striped tie and white cotton knickers; it's my oldest uniform, and I'm quite fond of it. I pulled my hair into a neat pony-tail, and made sure I got rid of all nail-polish and cosmetics. (You can never be too careful when going to see the Head, unless you want to be in trouble deliberately.)

Abel carefully opened the document: an end-of-term report. And not a good one. I - or rather this girl called Helen Watson - was in a lot of trouble! She got a long lecture about academic integrity, applying oneself to one's studies and so on, after which she - and I - had to bend over and grasp the edge of the desk.

Up went my skirt, down came my knickers. I was to get five strokes, one for each subject in which I had, quote, underperformed, unquote. Abel had picked a cane that isn't my favourite by any means: a short, straight, very stiff reformatory stick. Each stroke felt like an individual cut. I howled my way through the final three, barely aware of the admonishment to control myself. (My usual thought at moments like this is: "If you don't like the volume of my screaming, you don't have to hit this hard". Not that I ever *say* it - not at the time, anyway.)

Even pulling up my knickers afterwards was incredibly painful, as the elastic brushed against each double welt. I smoothed the skirt back down, and shuffled out of the office - only to come back a second later for my cuddles, now as myself. Abel looked terribly pleased with himself for composing the report.

He seemed surprised that I wasn't keen to continue the scene by bringing the report home to my father, but there was no way I could take any more lecturing, never mind spanking. What does he think I am, a masochist?

Daddy, Sir

By Abel on 23 December 2006

A warm, comfortable living room. Mum reads her novel on the armchair. Dad sits studying papers on the sofa; his daughter leans against him as she revises for the following day's test.

The gentleman glances at the clock, and places a hand on the girl's shoulder. "Time to be getting ready for bed, my dear." They both haul themselves to their feet, the girl going over to kiss her mother. The father continues, "I'll come in and say goodnight once you're in bed: I just have to pop over to my office to deal with something first."

"Do you have to?" she pleads, scanning his face for hints that he might stay.

He took his girl by the shoulders, holding her tight. Understanding. "I'm afraid I do."

And so the Housemaster unlocks the door that leads from his family's living quarters to the school proper. And the girl heads to bed, to contemplate her best friend's imminent fate.

Spanking around the Christmas tree

By Haron on 24 December 2006

Can I just check that the following is a genuine Christmas tradition?

Abel claims that before icing the cake, the husband takes his wife's trousers down, makes her bend over with her hands on the wall, and beats out the words "Fa-ther Christ-mas" on her tush with a wooden spoon.

It had better be true, after all I've suffered…

2007

2007: The Year of the Cane?!

By Abel on 1 January 2007

Those of you in the UK may have caught the BBC's fantastic New Year's Day production of "Wind in the Willows". Fortunately we had glasses of wine to hand when the main characters, plotting a raid to reclaim Toad Hall, armed themselves with staffs and raised a toast: "To the proper handling of sticks!"

Needless to say, we joined in enthusiastically. As a motto for the year ahead, it seemed rather appropriate.

Haron had 'enjoyed' her first 2007 experience of the proper handling of rattan shortly after midnight. A wonderful comment from our friend Rob in Australia recently proposed that we might bring the new year in with a dozen strokes, one per second counting down to the chime of Big Ben. We had company as midnight struck, and the TV pictures of the astonishing fireworks display on the Thames then kept us enraptured - but as soon as we were left to ourselves, we conducted our belated kinky celebration.

My young lady was told that she could choose her cane; she disappeared upstairs, returning with the longest, thickest, heaviest rod in the house – our Singapore rattan, bought more with curiosity than intent. Even the lightest stroke resulted in a spectacular response, and a delightful stripe; the twelfth and hardest engendered a yelp that the crowds in London could surely have heard 200+ miles away!

Caned on the first day of term

By Abel on 3 January 2007

Workers and students are heading back to their labours after the holiday season. I pictured a sixth-former, instructed on the final day of last term to report to the Headmaster after assembly on the first day of this. "A few weeks contemplating the consequences of your actions should help to focus your mind," he'd explained.

She'd be trembling as she walked through the school gates this morning, wearing her thickest skirt and praying that he wouldn't want to cane her on the bare. Contemplation had indeed been the order of the day during the festivities - seasonal joy tempered with the recurring thought of what would follow, imagined by now in so much detail.

Saturday detention, office-style

By Abel on 6 January 2007

A rare foray into the office on a Saturday morning. (Sadly, I do often end up working at home for at least some of some weekends, but I have to have obscenely large bags of cash dangled in front of my eyes before I deign to actually go into work!)

All is silent, apart from my team's fingers flying across their keyboards. Apart from two faint voices, one male, one female, barely audible from one of the lower floors. Hard at work as I am, I imagine the distant conversation fading, to be followed by the distinctive sound of strokes landing on bare flesh. After all, it would be entirely appropriate to instruct a young lady in one's team to report to the office on a Saturday morning to discuss recent issues with her performance, sparing her the blushes of being punished whilst too many of her co-workers were in close proximity.

Who knows - there might be a succession of staff approaching the building nervously; a veritable chorus of lonely whackings ringing out across the office during the day; a procession of punished girls, having learnt their lessons, disappearing down the road whilst rubbing their bottoms ruefully.

That strange, strange desire

By Haron on 7 January 2007

> "The desire to have severe pain inflicted on the most intimate, delicate and sensitive bits of your body defies explanation."

What sort of essay on masochism for beginners was this, you may wonder?

Oh, only a restaurant review by A.A. Gill, who discusses why on earth people like eating chilli peppers. He goes on to write:

> "No amount of boffinry explaining that chillis remind us of orgasms really seems to make sense. I've had an orgasm and it's not remotely reminiscent of inadvertently chewing a little red jobbie."

That's right, Mr. Gill, you tell them. Pain doesn't need to translate into sexual pleasure in order for us to enjoy it on some level!

Snape and spanking belong together
By Haron on 9 January 2007

Today's Professor Snape's birthday*, and if this means nothing to you, you might as well move on to the next entry, because I'm about to go on a Harry Potter geek-out.

It so happens, whenever I think about Snape, he somehow ends up spanking his students. Because he would, wouldn't he? How could he not? He'd be very strict, sometimes mean, not always fair, but ultimately the punishment would be for their own good. Right? Hogwarts would be much improved if spanking were introduced.

Happy birthday, Professor.

* What do you mean, how do I know his birthday is on 9 Jan? J.K. Rowling told me on the phone! OK, fine, I'm lying. Characters' birthdays show up on JKR's official website.

And then there was one...
By Abel on 10 January 2007

I often find myself catching a train to work at around 7.30am. At that time, the opposite platform is packed with commuting schoolgirls.

For a young lady to join the Schoolgirl Express each morning, rather than simply heading to one of the many schools nearer by, suggests that her parents are sending her to a very good school indeed. The neat uniforms re-enforce my view, as does the good behaviour - no rowdiness here. They're good girls, you see.

I departed for the office somewhat earlier than usual this morning. In place of a gaggle of girls waiting opposite was just one, forlorn soul. Head downcast, avoiding the eyes of her fellow travellers.

I guessed why immediately: that note in her locker the previous evening, neatly typed: "The Headmaster wishes to see you in his office thirty minutes before the start of school tomorrow."

She'd be there before her friends filled the corridors with chatter this morning. She'd hang up her coat, place her bag in her locker. Take a final look at the letter, lest it had magically reworded itself into a less ominous message overnight. Set off on a long, lonely, nervous walk through the empty corridors.

Acknowledge her wrong-doing; apologise profusely (have pity; be lenient; even though she knew that a caning was inevitable). Take her strokes with as much bravery as she could muster.

Wipe away her tears; wash her face carefully. Pretend when the others arrived that daddy had been en route to a breakfast meeting, so had had to drop her for the earlier train. Hope that no-one saw her wince as she sat down for the first lesson of the day...

The scary, scary piano tutors

By Haron on 11 January 2007

One of my favourite re-occurring fantasies is to suffer through piano lessons held by a strict tutor, who would alternate between slapping my palms with his ruler (because piano teachers all have rulers, of course), taking me over his knee for a bare-bottom spanking, and making me bend over with my hands on the piano stool for six of the best. Not if I played well, obviously.

So, you can imagine, I got quite a jolt out of discovering the existence of the movie "The 5000 Fingers of Dr. T", which features (according to Wikipedia):

> the surreal Terwilliker Institute, where the piano teacher is now a madman dictator who has locked up all non-piano-playing musicians in a dungeon and constructed a piano so large that it requires Bart and 499 other enslaved boys (the aforementioned 5,000 fingers) in order to play it.

...But does he spank them? Does he smack their hands with a ruler? Does he? Does he?

Morning canings at school, re-visited
By Abel on 12 January 2007

By remarkable coincidence a couple of days ago, on the same morning I'd been inspired by fantasies of a girl being caned before school, our friend Pandora posted an incredibly hot account along similar lines.

My *imaginary* girl was merely getting one caning, mind; *hers* was up for 12 of the best from every morning for a week, before classes. Were I the Headmaster in Pandora's account, mind, I'd vary the punishment routine ever so slightly – the girl would report to me immediately on waking, in her dressing gown and pyjamas. The alarm call would be sounded at 7.15 a.m.; woe betide her were she to appear in my study a moment after 7.20.

She'd know the routine after the first morning: she's remove her dressing gown and lay it carefully over the arm of my leather armchair. Her pyjama trousers (silk, striped) would be lowered to her ankles before she bent to touch her toes.

I'd doubtless pause to admire the quality of my handiwork from the previous days, the marks still clearly visible. (Headmasters are smug like that). And then I'd administer her dozen, making her continue the count from where she'd left off the previous morning – including any extra strokes she may have received to date. "Twenty-eight, twenty-nine, thirty,..."

And then she'd would off to join the other girls in the communal showers, where – despite her embarrassment and her best attempts to hide her caned bottom from view - her stripes would doubtless be soothed and admired. Once dressed, she would find the hard benches in the school refectory to be particularly unforgiving, as she ate under my gaze as I dined at the top table.

And only then would the young lady get to go to class...

The amazing one-handed typing bear

By Haron on 17 January 2007

Abel's parents went on a cruise, and among the things they brought back for us was a carved wooden figurine of a bear sitting at a desktop computer.

The bear's forepaws, attached to a system of strings and bolts, are supposed to tap-tap-tap on the wooden keyboard when you move him about in a certain way.

Only, the bear isn't working quite right. He refuses to type with both forepaws. There he sits, grinning into his wooden monitor, his bear bottom planted firmly on his wooden chair... and he types one-handed.

We suspect, we have a fair idea what he's typing, and what kind of sites he visits.

Caned at the crack of dawn

By Abel on 18 January 2007

The milkman, usually fairly quiet as he creeps up to the front door to deliver our daily pint, woke me this morning with a great clinking of bottles. Still half asleep, I began to ponder an alternative early morning round, this time by the local punishment officer.

Legally-appointed, said official's "morning round" would take in each village or district once a week. Parents in the relevant area would leave a note outside their door before retiring the previous night, requesting the officer to stop by: "Six strokes, eldest daughter", for example. The young lady's punishment would presumably be amplified by the thought that late night passers-by might pause, curious, and read the note.

The girl would be expected to be up and waiting from, say, 6am – showered and in her uniform ready for the school day. The precise time of the disciplinarian's arrival would be determined by the number of other calls he'd had to make on the given morning. Punishment would be swift and firm, administered on the bare with a government-issue cane.

Anyone interested in providing such a service in our local area should apply to... No, hold on: sounds far too hot a scene to let anyone else play in my place. "Eight strokes, wife". Haron won't be sitting comfortably after I've left for work tomorrow morning...

Headmasters: I have seen the future

By Abel on 19 January 2007

According to The Times this morning, a new report for the UK government by consultants PricewaterhouseCoopers suggests that "business leaders with no classroom experience" could be recruited to run schools. Reporting to them would be a teacher, looking after academic issues.

I wonder where disciplinary responsibilities would reside? "Report to the Chief Executive, young lady?" perhaps?

The article is helpfully illustrated with a picture of a cane-wielding schoolmaster. I'm starting to dream about the job advert: "Package: £100k plus car, pension and beating rights."

Full training would be required, of course. "The essentials of corporal punishment" would doubtless form part of the induction course. I'm happy to bid to run "Advanced caning techniques" for those requiring additional advice. All I need now is a gaggle of girls to be used for the practical sessions - any volunteers?

Being good at a spanking party

By Haron on 20 January 2007

We've been invited to a play party at our friends' house; it's an extended school role-play affair. (Naturally, I'm a pupil and Abel's a teacher.)

Once upon a time I delighted at being naughty and inviting punishment at such events; I planned elaborate schemes of pranks, rehearsed flippant remarks and generally thought that the whole point of it was to get spanked as much as possible.

I'm not sure what has changed, but the more I play, the more I enjoy just being good. OK, I can't help showing off my, ahem, razor wit at the most inappropriate moments, but I'm not tempted to plan anything in advance, or to sit down with my girlfriends and decide, "Right, this is how we're going to be misbehave."

Maybe having spanking on tap at home has eliminated the need to cram as much play as possible in my rare play-days, or maybe it's that even when I'm relatively good, I still get spanked an awful lot. Or maybe I enjoy being a schoolgirl so much that I don't want to interrupt the lessons with unnecessary whacking. Or maybe there's a degree of fear that if my play character is bad, other people will think ill of me. Or maybe I'm just really boring.

Be that as it may, all I'm bringing is my uniform and school supplies, whereas before I would have had my pockets full of slingshots, water pistols, silly noise-making gadgets etc. I'm not sure what I think about that.

Haron flagellata est

By Abel on 21 January 2007

The Latin master at my school taught us one particular grammatical construction with the memorable phrase, "The boy who had been caned asked for a cushion."

I was reminded of this whilst reading the quirky bestseller 'Amo, Amas, Amat' by Harry Mount, which explores the joys of the Latin language. Mount's wry humour is quite marvellous – and, not surprisingly, the discussion of school Latin lessons throws up a huge number of startles. My favourite?

> An active verb is exactly that – it means acting, doing something to somebody else. A passive verb means exactly that – i.e. doing nothing and having something and having something done to oneself. So if you are "being thwacked", "are about to be flogged" or "have been bullied", then you're in the passive.

The book comes, as you might imagine, highly recommended.

I had a dream

By Abel on 23 January 2007

I dreamt last night about a girls' reformatory, based in an old Georgian building. Six of the girls had been caught committing some heinous offence and were gathered together.

Six officers appeared. Three took the first girl, three the second, and the other girls were left locked in the room.

Each offender was taken to a separate punishment room. Three warders proved quite sufficient to subdue and strip her, tying her over the whipping frame - and leaving her to wait until they'd returned to take all of the others and tie them in turn in the other cells.

Each officer was then allocated a girl to punish. He returned to her cell, leaving the door open so that each girl might hear her neighbours' cries. The sentence of a severe birching was announced. And administered. Hard. Very hard.

Afterwards, the officer untied the girl (no longer struggling) and returned her to the main room, where the governor checked each offender, ensuring that she had been punished thoroughly.

The arsenal
By Abel on 24 January 2007

I've been sorting out our collection of implements, which had started spilling out alarmingly across the floor on my study at home. So off-putting to be disciplining a girl and to say "just pick a cane up from the pile on the floor", rather than being able to turn to a carefully-sorted collection...

So, sort it I did. And whilst sorting it, I decided to count the number of items we've accumulated over the past few years:

12 canes

11 tawses or straps

12 whips and belts

8 paddles

10 crops

14 miscellaneous household items purchased specifically for illicit purposes

That makes 67 implements. And that excludes anything we own that wasn't purchased explicitly as a spanking toy but that gets abused (such as hairbrushes), or anything that we've made (such as locally-cut birches), or (of course) hands.

Now, I wouldn't want any of the implements to feel neglected. Let's say they should each be used at least thrice a year. That works out at about four punishments for Haron per week.

Seems reasonable to me.

TFI Friday
By Abel on 26 January 2007

It's "dress down day" today in the office I'm working in at the moment. Suits shed; the catwalk begins.

As a service to our readers, I've been studying the latest fashions all morning. Carefully. I'm now an expert on the especially tight jeans that seem to be in vogue for the young ladies of the office. I'm copyrighting a term for the style: "Paddleable Chic".

Needless to say, I'd like to extend the dress-down concept to encompass an occasional "undress, young lady" day. Sadly I'm not confident of support for the proposition from Human Resources.

Google translates a spanking

By Haron on 27 January 2007

It's a common feature with the spanko people I know, that as soon as we get our hands on a dictionary, or a translating tool, or any container of knowledge, we look up *spanking* in it straight away. I do it without thinking, sometimes even before I look for whatever it was I picked up the dictionary to look for in the first place.

Unsurprisingly, when Abel showed me Google Translating Tool, I immediately made it talk to me about spanking.

What I did was type in a phrase, translate it from English into French, from French into German, and from German back into English. What I got was the following:

> If I brought house a bad school report, my uncle made the being located in the corner for me and thinks of my behavior. After the fact that he mean took skirt put up, downward my knee trousers, and fessée hard over its knee gave me. My reason was real endolori for the remainder of the daily.

The original phrase? Why, nothing too sophisticated:

> When I brought home a bad school report, my Uncle made me stand in the corner and think about my behaviour. After that he raised my skirt, took down my panties, and gave me a hard spanking over his knee. My bottom was really sore for the rest of the day.

Alright, I thought, maybe a whole paragraph is too much to ask; let me try something simple and to the point. Through the same simple process (English => French => German => English) I got this:

> Do not ask very honoured gentleman the stick; I promise, I it yet will not make!

Five points ~~to Gryffindor~~ to the first person who figures out what this said before little translation elves had their ways with my prose!
(It was *"Please, sir, don't cane me; I'll never do it again!"*)

Slides and spanking

By Abel on 29 January 2007

To Tate Modern, the art gallery on the south bank of the Thames built within the former Bankside power station. The cavernous internal space has been filled with a collection of near-vertical slides, catapulting visitors - who should presumably be concentrating on the Picassos - from the upper floors to ground-level at great speed.

I imagined a group of girls out for the day in London, queuing for their turns - in the highest of spirits, excepting one of their number, for whom the realisation had just dawned that the previous evening's thrashing would make the impending trip down an excruciating experience.

And then I became more practical in my pervy thinking. The Tate issues timed tickets for the steepest descent. There's a budget hotel within a few minutes' walk. Booking both in advance, and timing the exercise carefully, one could therefore despatch a freshly-striped behind down a slide within minutes of the girl's bare-bottomed caning. Best of all, the look on her face would be plainly visible for all to see via the webcams at the foot of the slides...

Spanking on honeymoon
By Abel on 1 February 2007

Excavations in my office; I found a scrap of paper from the hotel Haron and I stayed in on honeymoon, some time back now. Awwwwwwww :-)

I'd scribbled down three story ideas, with which I'd entertained my new bride. Just snippets, no more. There was the school that worked on the principle of demerits for any misdemeanours: ten demerits would get you send to the Head. Girls on eight or nine would clearly be impeccably behaved.

Then there was the school groundsman, responsible for tending the sports pitches. He lived on a cottage in the school grounds, alone with his bright young daughter. The school staff had all known her since she'd been a little girl; she was almost 'one of the family'. When she reached an appropriate age, she was awarded a scholarship to the school – and then fell immediately in with the 'wrong crowd' and had to be caned for misbehaviour in her first week…

And we speculated about a two-part punishment form. The teacher would fill in the top half with details of the offence; the girl would be despatched to the Headmaster, who would complete the remainder, to be handed back to the original teacher by the girl when she returned, caned, to the classroom.

Forty-two of the best
By Haron on 2 February 2007

The saga of morning canings continues, except now it has passed from the realm of Abel's fantasy to the realm of 'Haron's bottom is too sore to sit, because she's just had a week's worth of caning in one morning'.

This morning Abel was going away to Brussels for four days. His taxi was due to pull up at 6am to take him to the airport, but a good hour before he had to get up, we both found we couldn't sleep. We cuddled and talked of perverted things, and at some point he decided it would be a good idea to give me a caning to remember him by.*

"I wonder how many strokes I should give you," he said, warming my bottom with a few initial smacks over his knee. "Six of the best, I think. For every day I'm away."

A bright spark that I am, I blurted: "That seems like a fair number" - because I felt bluesy that he was leaving, and also, I hadn't quite woken up yet. The reality of what he had just suggested didn't hit me until it was quite, quite late to protest.

Abel grabbed a cane and instructed me to bend over the edge of the bed. Which I did with some trepidation.

The first few strokes were fairly light, and I began to think that not running away screaming at the suggestion of this caning might have been a good idea. I held on to the bed covers and quietly hissed as Abel counted six. "This is for today," he said. "Let's move on to Saturday, shall we?" I swallowed and managed: "Yes, sir."

It didn't take long to recognise that tomorrow's strokes were much crisper than the first batch. Each burned like a little individual knife slash, and I had to grit my teeth to keep from yelping. (It would have been impolite to wake the neighbours at 5am, I thought.)

"Time for the hard strokes," said Abel. "This is for Sunday." The next six were proper scorching licks of the sort that would fit into any school scene we might play. I swallowed my screams with a great feat of willpower, and after each one it took me several long seconds to return to the proper caning position.

The Monday half-dozen would be coming next, and Abel confirmed what I knew anyway: these strokes would be the hardest of all. My eyes watering, I dug my fingers into the bed covers, and pressed my mouth into the soft duvet, hoping it would muffle the screams I couldn't hope to contain. The most challenging part of a hard caning is that out of the corner of my eye I can usually see Abel draw his hand right up, as high as the size of the room allows it**, and this can be more terrifying than the pain itself. I held on as well as I could through the great cracks of wood on skin and the branding pain, counting down until all twenty-four were done.

And then it was time for more cuddles in bed.

Except, it would be a mistake to think it was over. I made this mistake too, but a little while - and much bottom-squeezing - later, Abel said with quite a pensive look on his face:

"You know, I don't get back until quite late on Tuesday."

Huh? What? Before I could give him a good kick for even suggesting evil things like this, he was out of bed, and had a cane in his hand again, and I was on my tummy, clutching the pillow and counting the swoosh-cracks, and gritting my teeth in pain. Admittedly, these strokes were not as hard as the Sunday portion, but neither had they lightened up by much.

I let out my breath after the last one and looked at Abel over my shoulder. He had that pensive look again, like an ogre who had just eaten a little girl who wasn't quite agreeing with his digestion.

"That was five lots of six-of-the-best," he said. "You know about that schoolgirl who got caned every morning before her lessons? On our blog? If I gave you another dozen, you would have had her whole punishment in one go. I think that would be quite cool."

I thought that it would be quite a sacrifice for the sake of I wasn't sure exactly what, but I was the one with an upturned bare bottom, and Abel was the one with the dragon cane, and thus he seemed to be at a rhetorical advantage.

I had never had a dozen stripes delivered quite so fast. Not harsh individually, together they grew into a long, continuous stretch of sharp pain. I cursed the day I ever showed Abel how to use WordPress for blogging. When it was over, I decided not to point out that the schoolgirl in the fantasy had received a dozen strokes every morning, but he knew that, and didn't seem to mind.

We had just enough time for our final cuddles before his alarm clock started bleeping. I was sore, but content with what I had taken - and glad it was all over.

And it wasn't even dawn yet.

* Because obviously a girl is capable of forgetting her husband the minute he's out of the door. Obviously.
** The Ralph Lauren polo-player logo always reminds me of Abel's cane at the apex of its rise. This makes department stores quite disturbing.

The captain's belt

By Abel on 3 February 2007

A vote of thanks, please, for the crew from the leading airline who kept me entertained with their wonderfully indiscreet conversation at the table next to mine at dinner last night. I nearly choked on my moules and frites several times, and had to order at least two extra beers lest I finished dinner before their stock of anecdotes had run dry.

I loved hearing from the cabin attendant who had had to put out a fire in a plane's oven mid-Atlantic on a previous trip. A colleague had put her shoes in the oven to dry, and was padding around the cabin barefoot. She forgot all about the shoes, and inevitably they combusted after a few hours.

It appears that young Kimberley, the stewardess concerned, was dismissed. I imagined a different outcome, in which the stern, older captain sat quietly at the end of last night's table had taken matters into his own hands. The crew had arrived safely at their destination in some far-flung land, and checked into their hotel rooms. Kimberley emerged from her post-flight shower, and slipped into casual clothes for a night on the town - before spying a note that had been slipped under her door: "Captain Watson would like to see you immediately in suite 2505."

He'd still have been in his uniform. He'd have been unimpressed to have been kept waiting. An uncompromising of lectures about flight safety would have followed. "Do you realise the possible consequences of your actions today, Kimberley?"

She did. She apologised, swore it would never happen again.

"It certainly won't, young lady." He proceeded to outline his three options for the return journey, having total responsibility for the plane and the crew. "I can dismiss you now, and you can find your own way back to the States. I can take you with us under suspension; you can travel as a passenger and be taken to Human Resources as soon as we touch down. Or I am allowed under airline rules to use my discretion to address any disciplinary matters as I feel fit, so we can deal with matters now."

"Please, sir," she pleaded. "Let's deal with it now. Whatever it takes."

'Whatever it took' involved a conversation about how the captain had punished his two daughters in their wilder teenage years and through into their recent times at college. "They're your age: good girls with good jobs. We're all very close. It worked for them, I think."

It involved a shamefaced Kimberley responding to the query as to whether her father had dealt with her in the same way in the affirmative.

It involved her sitting at the desk in the captain's suite, taking out a sheet of the hotel stationery and writing a letter to him asking him to punish her.

It involved her taking off her tight designer jeans and folding them neatly over the arm of the chair; the captain looking at her sternly until, as agreed, her underwear followed.

He'd have cleared his desk of the usual hotel paraphernalia – the leaflets advertising the spa, warning of the exorbitant phone costs, forms seeking feedback that would inevitably be ignored.

He'd have removed his jacket, braided with so many stripes. Unbuckled his thick, airline-issue belt and doubled it over.

He'd have had her bend over the desk's cold wooden surface, reaching over to grip the far side.

He'd have punished her. Not one of those a-few-gentle-licks-will-be-enough, it's-the-very-act-of-punishment-that-will-correct-a-girl type corrections. Not a daddy-dealing-with-Kimberley-for-a-bad-report type admonishment. A full-blown lesson in airline safety, in the risks she'd caused for the captain's aircraft, an if-this-is-the-alternative-to-dismissal-it'd-better-be-hard type thrashings.

She'd have fought not to cry; he'd have whipped her 'til she did. And then he'd have had her stand, pull on those too-tight jeans with a wince, told her how brave she'd been, confirmed that the incident was now closed. Offered her a hug, gratefully received, holding her tight as she sobbed and her tears dampened his captain's shirt.

Fitting the punishment in

By Haron on 4 February 2007 in The Punishment Book

One of the things I noticed about working for yourself is that you never have enough time. For anything. Even for most of your work. Everything needs to be extensively planned, squeezed into the calendar, finished in too little time, crossed off the to-do list.

This seems to include punishment. Unless it's planned ahead, or cramped into a tiny pocked of the day when neither Abel nor I happen to be running mental circles around our tasks - it's not going to happen. Luckily, we've got pretty good at finding time for things like that, but it also means that I'm losing any ability to worry about a punishment much beforehand. Otherwise I'd spend days and weeks waiting for a snatched moment, fretting.

A few weeks ago Abel woke me up before going off to catch a train, and informed me I was in for it: I had let the credit on the gas meter run out again. (We are old enemies, that gas meter and I.) I sighed, and agreed, and fell back asleep until my alarm clock went, and then there was work, and more work, and over the next few days we remembered that a punishment was supposed to happen, but we failed to find that small shred of time and aloneness that would make it possible.

Days went by, we went on a trip, and played with others, and worked more, and worked and worked.

And then we had half an evening relatively free. I was in a silly mood, and teased Abel about - well, something; I'm sure he deserved to be teased about whatever it was. He told me to stop being cheeky; I didn't feel like letting some quality teasing go to waste just because he was going to smack my bottom for it.

Sure enough, he grasped me by the upper arm and dragged me to the living-room, where he manfully threw me over the arm of the sofa, and manfully whooshed his belt out of the loops, and manfully doubled it over. I was enjoying myself far more than my position dictated.

Three or four smarting licks later Abel paused and asked me if I had anything to say for myself. I decided to quit while this was still fun, and offered him my most humble apology (perhaps, not very humble by other people's standard, but I did my best).

"While I have you here," he said.

I twisted around to look at him: "Yes?"

"There's that issue with the gas meter we haven't dealt with yet."

Oh, great, I thought, just when I was having fun. "Wasn't it kinda long ago?" I said. "Isn't there some sort of statute of limitation for punishments you never get around to giving me?"

"I've got around to it now," he said impatiently, "Let's not waste any more time on it."

I saw him raise the belt and stuck my face into the cushions.

Three strokes - not much longer than two seconds - that was all it took. I didn't even have a chance to get scared, or to cry out in pain. A brief moment of pain, like a lick of fire from a flame-thrower, and Abel was telling me to get up, and pulling his belt back through the loops.

"Is this it?" I asked in surprise, rubbing the sore spot on my bottom.

"Why, do you need more?" Abel laughed at my expression and put his arms around me.

I was really glad I hadn't spent the previous two weeks freaking out over the upcoming punishment: the build-up was going to have been for not very much. Still, the punishment was proportional to the gravity of the offence, so making it worse just to rise up to the two-week wait wouldn't have been an answer, either.

And then I had to wait another two weeks until I had a little time to write this account, but that's another story entirely.

Belgium: spanking snippets

By Abel on 5 February 2007

I like Brussels: I've worked here a fair amount over the past couple of years, and the city's grown on me.

A stroll on Saturday stimulated several silly spanko snippets. There was the jacket shop, named "Leather Victim". (Many tawsed, strapped or belted girls would presumably associate with that!).

Then came the advert in a recruitment agency window, seeking a "Frontdesk collaborateur (M/F)". I can do the M/F bit: I wonder if that'd get me the job?

Next, the immaculately-uniformed group of girl guides, ever-so-well behaved in the Grand Place – possibly Europe's most beautiful civic space. The group of slightly older girl guide leaders, chasing each other around the square, shrieking loudly. My hand was twitching... Oh to be a girl-guide-leader-leader.

And finally, the very distinguished shop in the very distinguished arcade, with the long stick in the window and the notice entitled "Canne Toulouse-Lautrec". Apparently:

> This cane is a replica of the famous Toulouse-Lautrec cane. The original is in Albi's art gallery.

Wow! I must go and check some of his paintings... I didn't know he'd caned his models. And then I read on, realising that absinthe was a more likely explanation: "Inside, you will find two glasses and a bottle with a silver-plated stopper". 445 euros, if anyone's interested.

I do quite like the idea of caning a girl, then pausing to unscrew the implement's "silver-plated knob" and pouring two shots, one for me and one to help calm the thrashed girl!

The joy of sitting uncomfortably

By Haron on 6 February 2007

It takes quite a lot of spanking for me to feel it when I sit down. Even then, most of the time I have to squirm around, so that I feel the elastic of my knickers digging into the area of my bottom that's red and sore.

When it does happen - when I do get spanked hard enough and for long enough to feel the shadow of pain over the next few hours, the pleasure is unique and exquisite.

How unfortunate is it, then, that to get this wonderful aftertaste I have to take a really, really hard spanking, possibly with a strapping or a caning on top? I like the idea of spanking, and the anticipation, and the ritual, and the afterglow, and can I even occasionally get into the right head to surf the pain and turn it into pleasure, but most of the time pain is pain. I don't like being in pain.

But afterwards - oh, afterwards. Hard wood of a pub bench pressing against the pocket seams of my jeans. Tight elastic of my knickers across swollen welts. I think I'll take the pain.

Flogging in Europe, 1900

By Haron on 8 February 2007

Going through old newspaper archives, you discover the most interesting things. For instance, the April 8, 1900 edition of "Washington Post" contained, apparently, an article entitled "Flogging in Europe". (You never know when people in Washington may need to find out all about the whacking habits across the ocean). The table of contents looks ever so enticing:

> Lash for Youthful Offenders Favored by England
>
> Russia's retention of the knout
>
> Corporal Punishment in England
>
> Great Men of England Who Have Been Whipped at School - Lord Salisbury Holds the Record in that Line at Eton — Gladstone Never Flogged.

Shame you have to pay $11 to get the copy of the article itself. I'm not that dedicated, I'm afraid.

But: "Gladstone never flogged"? Where on earth did he go to school, to have managed to escape it?

Uniform fetish

By Abel on 9 February 2007

A recent post mentioned a conversation by an airline crew that I happened to overhear in a restaurant in Brussels. The other anecdote they told one another that amused me concerned a loophole in their employer's process for ordering uniforms.

Anyone, it seems, can order any uniform – so if you stand at the gate checking boarding passes, but feel like parading in a captain's garb, go right ahead.

One of the pilots described boarding a flight the previous week and doing a double-take when seeing one of the stewardesses. Immaculately turned out, from her scarf to her skirt to her stockings.

The captain looked her up and down, and then recognised her from previous trips: "Stuart?" "Good morning, captain," came the gruff reply.

PS the most senior of the group proceeded to tell tale of a young, newly-qualified pilot who'd annoyed him immensely in the cockpit during a recent flight. "I'm 'Captain', or 'Captain, sir', or 'sir'", the senior office explained. "I don't take kindly to 'Captain, dude'."

Valentine's Day and spanked schoolgirls

By Haron on 14 February 2007

This morning we lazily imagined a group of schoolgirls who send their teacher a rude card on Valentine's Day. Something cheeky, perhaps. Something witty, but which none of them would have said to his face.

We imagined the discovery: first, the English teacher would identify the hand of the girl who'd written it out, and then the rest would admit to the deed, because they wouldn't be willing to let their friend answer for all of them.

And then I remembered that in my last year at school, my friends and I did, in fact, send a cheeky valentine to a teacher we didn't like. My school had a tradition of a few younger students walking about with small mail-boxes, where you could drop your cards during the break, addressed to "Schwartz, Max, 5a", or "Maria Ivanovna, physics classroom". During the lessons the messengers would knock on classroom doors to deliver the cards amid the giggles.

My friends and I weren't bad girls, so the note we sent to our maths teacher was actually a rather complicated puzzle, which we'd hoped he would spend much of his spare time solving, just like we had to spend much of our spare time on his ridiculously difficult homework. And of course, he thought it was hilarious, and had the answer by the end of the lessons.

This was exactly 11 years ago, and I haven't thought about it since. But of course, girls who send their teachers cheeky valentines should get punished. Shouldn't they?

Taking one's time

By Abel on 15 February 2007

To a lovely hotel earlier in the week, where I've stayed for work a couple of times before. Unlike the nondescript, albeit comfortable, chain hotels in which I seem to live for half of my life, this is family-run and wonderfully friendly: a real home-from-home. The owner was in the reception area as I walked through the door. "Abel," he said straight away, "how lovely to see you again."*

Dinner is always excellent: very traditional, with excellent ingredients from local farms. The waitress was lovely – petite, friendly, desperate to please, delightful in her old-fashioned black uniform. Despite there being only five diners, she was rushing from table-to-table with alacrity, to the extent that it was hard for guests to relax. The inevitable happened, and in her haste she dropped a tray of vegetables.

Her subsequent (imagined!) punishment would have served perfectly to illustrate the advantages of taking things nice and slowly. Once the final diner had retired to the lounge, she would have been bent over one of the dining room tables.

The owner would have delivered a long, slow caning: plenty of pauses between strokes allowing the impact of each to tell its full story, each whack plainly audible to the guests next door. He'd have talked to her throughout – calmly, sympathetically, explaining that it was better to take one's time; that rushing was rarely the most effective way...

*Actually, she used my real first name, rather than "Abel" – it's not quite *that* much of a home from home!

Workplace flogging

By Haron on 16 February 2007

Occasionally I do some work for Abel's business. Yesterday one of the guys wrote to him wondering why I hadn't sent him a file he had supposedly asked for a week ago. Having never seen the original request, I just shrugged and mailed the file - but in the meantime, Abel and The Guy had the following conversation:

> Abel: Just checked - she hadn't had the note. Good thing: I don't like having to flog the staff...
>
> Guy: Fibbing as well as ignoring requests from colleagues...someone is having a bad influence on her!
>
> Abel: A flogging it is, then...

Can you sue your own husband for sexual harassment in the workplace? Or would this just lead to further ~~corporate~~ corporal punishment?

Caning in assembly

By Haron on 18 February 2007

Flicking through channels on Friday night, we caught a History channel documentary about schools. Mostly it talked about the division between grammar and secondary modern schools, interviewed people who had gone to each, and showed archive materials of exciting things they taught girls in home economy classes.*

But it wouldn't have been a programme about British education if they hadn't mentioned corporal punishment.

And here came a surprise. One of the interviewees, a woman who had gone to a secondary modern school (though we'd missed which - damn) claimed that when somebody was particularly bad, they got called onto the stage in assembly and got given six of the best.

You mean, this isn't just a scenario from a kinky fantasy? This actually happened? I would have found it hard to believe if I read the claim on a spanking message board, but hearing this spoken out-loud, unprompted, in an otherwise vanilla documentary, made me re-assess what I'd thought of the practice before.

I'm feeling an incredible urge to write a story along these lines.

*Serving tea doesn't strike me as something on which I would particularly want to be examined.

Training the secretaries

By Abel on 19 February 2007

The ground floor of the office in which I'm working at the moment has large, expensive TV monitors switched for most of the day to the BBC's News 24 channel.

It's fascinating to pause and watch the real-time subtitling on these rolling news channels. Their high-speed misinterpretations can be quite wonderful to behold: last week, for example, I learned that:

> "Tony Blair has been killed this morning by MPs - correction 'grilled'."

Anyway... A notice has appeared recently, announcing that:

"Only the secretaries that have been trained are allowed to use these screens."

I'm torn in two directions. First, I wonder where they keep the untrained secretaries: wild women, fighting, flinging computers across the room, hurling abuse at their bosses. And then I picture the secretaries in training. Collared, demure, obedient, their trainers instilling the necessary discipline with regular cracks of the whip.

Tax Collectors with Whips

By Haron on 21 February 2007

According to yesterdays Times, in Spanish carnival tradition there exists a mask of *peliqueiro* - a tax-collector from the 18th century. It's described thus: "their painted faces are mute and macabre under the street lamps, their leather whips punishing whoever fails to leap out of their way. The authority they exude bores through the revelry like a hot iron."

They also, apparently, had a habit of chasing people through the streets.

I know what costume Abel is wearing if we ever end up at a Galician carnival.

Exclusive! Caning movie wins Oscar!

By Abel on 25 February 2007

As Hollywood steps centre stage for tonight's awards ceremony, let's pause and contemplate the movie that that captured the Oscar for Best Original Screenplay sixty years ago.

The wonderful Internet Movie Database describes "The Seventh Veil" as a "Pygmalion story about a concert pianist and her cruel guardian" and a review goes on to provide further commentary:

As for Ann Todd, a pretty wooden doll, her performance can be judged by the awful scene at the beginning of the film where she is caned by the headmaster of the school...Francesca retells the story of her life, from when at the age of fourteen, she was caned by her headmistress, to when she was sent to live with her "uncle" Nicholas, an abusive and domineering guardian.

Note to any Hollywood types who want to be walking up the red carpet twelve months' hence: a few good canings seem to find favour with the academicians.

Lock up your daughters

By Abel on 27 February 2007

Vivaldi, to be filmed shortly with Joseph Fiennes in the lead role, tells how the composer is ordained as a priest, before he "realises he is not suited to the profession and is moved to a school for abandoned daughters of Venetian courtesans". Vivaldi gave them a thorough musical education, the girls joining a choir and orchestra:

Gerard Depardieu is to play "a French aristocrat seeking to place the girls in the care of wealthy French families."

Completing the cast is London-born actress Zuleikha Robinson as a 'twenty-something' orphan girl. Heavy hints are dropped that she and Vivaldi have a romantic liaison.

Haron is swooning already at the very thought, and at the plethora of kinky diversions that the movie could inspire. Apparently, the institution concerned, the Pio Ospedale della Pieta, still operates today, taking in eight pupils a year. However, the building is also home to an hotel: I wonder if they offer themed weekend breaks?

Spanking on a dark country road

By Haron on 28 February 2007

There is something about the empty road through the fields at the back of our house that whispers to Abel, "Spank your wife, now."

The emptiness of the road is really open to chance. Plenty of people drive there and back along the unevenly paved track, and it's a great quiet spot for joggers, dog walkers and riders. But not, as we have often found, at eight o'clock on a wintry Saturday night.

We were at a drinks party at our friends' house, and I was flagging.* We were lazily gearing up for the walk home, when Abel leaned close to my ear and said: "You're getting your bottom smacked when we're in the lane." The promise gave me a pleasant chill, and perked me up enough to go looking for my boots and coat. I would normally feel apprehensive about this, but we'd had a few vanilla days before that, and the evening had been mostly vanilla too, so I quite fancied a reminder that I am, in fact, kinky.

There are no streetlights along the road. When we turned into it from the village green, the first few paces were still lit from behind our backs, but all the rest was darkness. The trees were obscuring the lights from our village ahead, and the town that lies across the fields was curtained with mist. We walked and held hands. I was still warm from wine and anticipation, but Abel was shivering.

"I think, I need that spanking now," I said, without adding: to warm you up, mate.

"Ah, yes," he said. "Bare your bottom."

"Huh? What? It's February!" I can't pretend I hadn't counted on this, but foregoing the haggling part is like cheating at spanking.

He heaved a very put-upon sigh and reached under my short coat to unbutton and unzip my jeans. Rolling my eyes,** I wriggled my trousers down together with my panties.

Abel's hand pressed into my back, and I bent down with my hands on my knees while he swept my coat up onto my back. His other hand cracked down onto my cooling behind; the pain was startling: bracing, like the cold of the evening. I couldn't help dancing around as the smacks descended. Slightly out of breath, Abel ordered me back into position, and spanked on. I yelped, but there was a wide grin on my face.***

"Right, this is enough. You may dress," he said, waving his hand in the air. "Ouch, that hurt!"

"No. Really? Poor you." I pulled my jeans up again with a hiss, and gave Abel a hug and a pat on the head: "Aww."

We walked on. He rubbed his hand, and I rubbed my bottom. We weren't cold any more.

P.S. The next morning we had to walk back again to collect our car, and I got a few licks of a switch while watching out for joggers and riders, but that's a different story.

* My switch-off time is 9pm, after which I turn into a pumpkin, or some sort of vegetable, anyway; it was nearing eight.
** Which I'm sure he didn't see: it was dark.
*** Which he also didn't see.

Three-dimensional spankings

By Abel on 1 March 2007

To an IMAX theatre, donning silly coloured spectacles to watch a 3D movie on an immense screen the height of four double-decker buses. We found ourselves on safari deep in the heart of Africa.

The 3D effects really are quite stunning. Objects appearing with vivid clarity and form, as if in touching distance.

Objects such as the extremely pert backside of the exceptionally cute conservationist who was driving the Land Rover.

I lost all concentration on the wildlife for a good few minutes, plunged into reveries about the type of 3D film that I would really like to see. If anyone who makes spanking movies is reading this, I beseech you to invest in the technology, no matter how expensive.

"Explain yourself, young lady."

By Abel on 3 March 2007

I love it when vanilla friends utter hot comments, completely inadvertently. One such acquaintance was recently trying to decide whether a particular young lady's failure to complete some task or other resulted from her being: "stubbornly disinclined or pathetically incapable."

I rather hoped it was the former, and felt smug knowing that I'd be rather ahead of my friend in my ability to correct the situation. And, of course, I memorised the phrase: so perfect for a future scene.

Palms outstretched

By Abel on 5 March 2007

At a recent wine tasting, I listened to a fellow taster describing a trip to the Pyrenees. He'd visited a leading Armagnac producer, whose staff adopted a novel sales technique at the end of the tour. Rather than proffering a small glass to taste, the young lady in the cellar would pour a drop into her hands, rub them together, then offer them so that that client could absorb the aroma of the brandy.

Needless to say, the sales girl in my mind immediately had freshly-punished palms: bright strap marks or vivid cane lines, maybe.

And perhaps her hands would be trembling slightly, eyes pleading with the visitor to make a purchase, knowing that failure to make a sale would lead her imminently to yet more strokes in the back office.

Flogging as healthy exercise

By Haron on 6 March 2007

I discovered a hilarious article: the writer has discovered that "golf" spelled backwards is "flog", and continues to write the article substituting one for the other at every turn.*

Particularly juicy quotes: "And yes, I flog. I have been doing so for a year and a few months. It was a 50th birthday present to myself. Take up flogging..." and "never underestimate athletic ability in flogging! You can't afford to get tired after a few whacks, you know."

I've been flogged by golfers, and they have a perfect aim and an admirable swing. Shame the sport is so dull.

* But not, I notice, where it concerns golfing balls. Because "flogging balls" sounds a little iffy for a respectable newspaper.

Caning on the Edgware Road

By Abel on 7 March 2007

BBC radio played straight into my hands in its morning broadcasts yesterday. I'd already started fantasising when they reported that store managers are outraged at the lenient sentences being doled out to shoplifters: one commented that thieves deserved "the ultimate sanction". Later, a government spokesperson, commenting on the same story, spoke of the need for "swift and effective justice."

It wasn't any old store that I pictured with the young woman bent over the flogging block, wrists tied, for a very public meeting with the rattan. No, it was specifically the branch of Woolworth's in London's Edgware Road, the thrashing taking place just inside the front windows! (I've not even been there for a year or more: strange how the mind works).

A small crowd had gathered: they gasped as her buttocks were bared, and winced collectively as the strokes fell. No gentle spanking, this: full-bodied blows, red stripes clearly visible for all to see…. Swift and effective justice, indeed.

And then the sobbing offender was untied, and was free to go, pushing her way tearfully through the crowds and out onto the street.

P.S. Will the girl who got two very hard smacks from her boyfriend next to the chocolate stand before the Keane gig in Newcastle Arena yesterday please delurk?

The ideal fantasy school

By Haron on 8 March 2007

It will surprise nobody if I say that Abel and I rather like school stories. We don't only ever fantasise about spanking in school settings, but it's very much a favourite fantasy for both of us. It's also the framework within which we role-play a great deal.

Despite this compatibility, Abel's fantasy school and mine are different in certain ways, some of them major, some of them not so crucial.

I should really let Abel speak for himself if he wants to (sorry, sweetie) but when I think about the differences, I can't very well describe them without putting some words into his mouth.

Both of us see ourselves in a British school, and we'll both research the education system and histories of famous public schools with great interest. We both enjoy enriching our fantasies with authentic details. Authenticity is important to both of us.

To an extent. And there has to be this limitation, because, of course, in a real, authentic British school under no circumstances would a male teacher cane a schoolgirl on her bare bottom. Or her clothed bottom. Or at all. And of course, the caning of the (pretend) schoolgirl on her bare bottom by a male teacher is the single act which we love to re-enact and describe in many guises, and so reality must be stretched a little.

Other instances on which we are happy to compromise with reality - and where we resolutely draw the line - can be used well to describe the similarities and differences in Abel's fantasy world and mine.

While Abel accepts that, as I mention, a male teacher can discipline a female pupil, he won't compromise on his conviction that it would be inappropriate for the teacher to spank the girl over his knee, or to use any implement other than a cane, or a tawse, or a plimsoll. (Maybe a big paddle, if he's being adventurous, but we aren't fans of paddles, so this rarely comes up.) Anything else - other than a cane or a tawse used on the girl's hand, or those two plus a plimsoll on her bottom - doesn't feature in Abel's fantasy school.

Girls in his school are very rarely punished in front of the class, and, on the whole, corporal punishment tends to be rare - and thus every instance of it is an extraordinary event. A girl gets the cane once or twice in her school career, and carries the memory of it throughout the rest of her life. For their part, teachers do everything to play up the importance of the occasion - and the significance of the fact that the girl has been caned before. (Every punishment must be more severe than the last. Or, conversely, the first punishment must be extraordinarily severe, so that there isn't the second time.)

So, you could say that his school is on the whole not too strict, but that each separate occasion of corporal punishment is a terrifying, traumatic event.

My school is, perhaps, a less authentic establishment, but I've been carrying its general image in my head since before I knew what authentic corporal punishment regimes could have been like. It is at the same time a stricter and a more lenient establishment than Abel's.

It's stricter, because corporal punishment is used there frequently, and is, if not the first response to any misdeed (for then we would never have lines, demerits, corner time, extra homework and detention), something that everybody expects to experience and witness on a fairly regular basis. Even the best-behaved girl in the school can't avoid getting spanked at least once a term; the bar is set quite low. So, you see, it can be seen as a fairly strict place.

However, each individual instance of corporal punishment in my fantasy school isn't necessarily all that scary. It can be anything from a single, embarrassing smack on the clothed bottom, to a bare-bottom caning in assembly, but more often than not it will be a moderate punishment: painful and undesirable at the time, but not overall too traumatic. The girl will worry about it beforehand, and cry at the time, and squirm on her chair afterwards, but the next day she'll be bright-eyed, bushy tailed and ready to sin again.

Where implements and positions are concerned, I'm also willing to commit some crimes against authenticity. In my fantasies teachers are allowed to take girls over their knee for a hand-spanking, and on occasion they use decidedly domestic implements, like a hairbrush, or implements borrowed from other times, like the birch, or places, like the paddle.

There you have it. Two school fetishists, two different fantasy schools. Isn't it lucky we are pretty good at communicating?

Army discipline

By Abel on 9 March 2007

Her Majesty's Army has issued a "pocket guide to instructional behaviour" to NCOs. It 'lists the maximum penalties that instructors can mete out to recruits who fail to achieve their exacting demands'.

The 'punishments allowed' include:

200 metre run

15 sit-ups

25 press-ups

12 strokes of the cane

(OK, I'll be honest. Guess which one of these I added to the list?).

Post-flight entertainment

By Abel on 11 March 2007

A conversation with colleagues reminded me of a business trip to Hong Kong at the height of the SARS crisis a few years back. They'd installed scanning devices at the airport, testing for anyone with a high temperature (a possible sign of infection).

I suddenly thought of an alternative trigger for the machines: young ladies with glowing backsides. Daughters who'd been spanked mid-flight, misbehaving super-models in first-class who'd been thrashed by the captain, stewardesses who'd been disciplined for leaving their aircraft in an untidy state... punished miscreants one and all causing panic as the heat-sensitive alarms rang out...

Spanking writer on the move

By Abel on 14 March 2007

The well-spoken gentleman was having as little joy as I connecting to the internet on the train. We swapped technical suggestions: none worked.

He wandered through to the next carriage, returning a few moments later: "No luck," he said. Then, with a broad grin, he continued: "There's a chap further down browsing hard-core porn of the most obscene nature, but he swears it's on his hard disk."

I giggled; he returned to his seat; the train continued for another hour.

The gentleman passed me again, laden with luggage, as we approached his station. He glanced from afar at my laptop, watching me type. He shook his head in mock outrage. "Disgusting!" he joked.

Had he been able to see the screen, I wonder if he'd have blushed. There are those who would concur with his opinion, had they realised that two girls had already been flogged in the story I'd been writing, and that a third was about to hear the court's sentence...

Nature versus nurture, spanking-style

By Abel on 15 March 2007

I am becoming ever-more convinced that my interest in spanking is inherited from my father, who's forever alluding subtly to my favourite topic.

Last time we stayed with my parents, we browsed the bookcase in the bedroom that we were using and discovered a battered copy of Juanita Carberry's autobiography. For those of you not in the know, it describes her childhood in the "Happy Valley" area of Kenya, and is littered with descriptions of whippings from her father and her governess (his mistress). My father's well-worn copy fell open conveniently at the appropriate pages, which made for some very nice bedtime reading, whispered into Haron's ear.

The following evening, I happened to mention an autobiography I'd bought, by a poet I know him to like. In return, he generously offered to lend me John Mortimer's biography: "It's very good." Any of you who've read the reviews of the author and barrister's life story will know that it attracted a certain amount of prurient comment as a result of his predilection for spanking and being spanked. One incident reported a visitor asking Mortimer's young secretary why she seemed flushed, for her to respond, "Well, how would you feel if you had just been spanked?"

Interesting, too, that a google search on "mortimer spank" turns up a reference to the movie "Young Adam". In one scene: "(Ewan) McGregor beats co-star Emily Mortimer on the bottom and then has sex...." and apparently "McGregor did actually spank Mortimer, daughter of writer John Mortimer" although "they weren't spanking very hard." Yet more proof of genetic influences over our kink interest?

Strict agony auntie

By Haron on 16 March 2007

A preview of the agony aunt column in the Times on Wednesday: big letters over the top of the front page: "You did wrong. You know it. Now you're being punished."

Oh yes, give those correspondents a good scolding.

(The article itself is about a normal relationship train wreck, but mmm, the quote...)

The canes in the cupboard

By Abel on 18 March 2007

An Observer columnist reminisces: "Many of those who taught me at school had returned to teaching after the war.

They had the habit of command, a love of classics and a handy supply of canes in the cupboard."

But how did the canes get there? I picture an entire procurement department in the Ministry of Education. There'd be the forecasters, making careful calculations of the number of rods required for the whole country, based on estimates of the number of punishments in the coming school year, and the durability of the typical cane.

The most senior buyers would take a more strategic view: calling in samples of new products. Having them tested. Checking the results.

The supply chain experts would co-ordinate the whole process: working with rattan growers, appointing master craftsmen to manufacture the canes, arranging for shipments to each school just in time for the new academic year.

Did the masters in each school then select their own canes, from a large stock in the staff common room? Did the eve of the new term see them taking practice swishes with the new stock, seeking out the ones that offered the perfect weight, balance and length? Did the more senior staff get first choice?

Perhaps the teachers called into the Headmaster's secretary for supplies? ("I'll take an extra senior cane, please, Miss Crowther. I think this year's sixth-form will be an especially tricky bunch.") Or was one of the prefects responsible for distributing fresh stocks to each cupboard, and replenishing supplies at regular intervals?

Maybe the staff procured their own? Picture the late summer call into their gentlemen's outfitter: "A new mortar board and gown for the coming academic year, Dr. Jenkins? But of course. And anything from the rattan department while you're here? Did last year's selection perform as you would have hoped?"

Budgets of days gone by

By Abel on 21 March 2007

So, Chancellor Gordon Brown has announced his spending and taxation plans in the coming year. As he gave his set-piece Budget speech in the House of Commons, I cast my mind back to tales of the famous budget of 1904.

The then-Chancellor Herbert Smithers arrived at the despatch box drunk, waving a bottle of single malt at hecklers on the opposition benches. Removing his clothes during the early stages of his speech, but protected by ancient conventions that forbid members of parliament to interrupt the Budget, Smithers proceeded to berate his own Prime Minister, Alouisious Fotherington-Smythe, for 'overseeing a collapse in moral standards that threatens the very future of our society'.

Most of his controversial measures - such as the trebling of tax for men with beards - were repealed within minutes, as the government invoked ancient rights under the terms of the Treaty of Salisbury of 1763.

Yet his announcement of substantial additional aid for the farmers of South-East Asia went through unchallenged, allowing the emerging rattan industry to expand significantly, and leading directly to the rapid growth of the cane as the preferred instrument of discipline in England's public schools.

Indeed, to this day, misbehaving girls at one leading establishment find themselves on the receiving end of "six on the bare with a senior Smithers", the great man's name still intimately associated with the products of the industry that he spawned.

ROSLA revisited
By Abel on 25 March 2007

Education Secretary Alan Johnson has announced a plan to raise the school leaving age in the UK.

One can't help but think about the last time this happened: some teachers considered that their existing implements would not be sufficiently impactful to deal with older students. Fortunately for them, leading tawse maker John J. Dick came to their rescue by producing a double-thickness strap – known as the ROSLA, for "Raising of the school leaving age".

A nail-biting story
By Haron on 26 March 2007 in The Punishment Book

Last night I caught myself chewing my nails. I haven't done it since I was about - oh, six or so - and decided that coming back to the habit twenty years later wasn't something I wanted.

"Uh-oh," I said to Abel, with my mouth full of nail. "I think, I need a beating."

This is exactly the sort of matter where any initiative from Abel would have been firstly, impossible, secondly unwelcome: if he had seen me nibble on the nail and forbidden me to do it under the threat of a punishment, he would have been invited to take a hike. However, helping me with an issue that I brought to his attention myself is a sort of husbandly duty. (The poor guy is so exploited.)

He sat on the bed, bent me over his lap and tugged down my knickers, and gave me a few experimental swats with his hand.

"Ouch," he said. "This hurts."

Hmm, no bloody kidding. I nearly said "this is supposed to hurt", but I didn't want to convert a sort-of disciplinary spanking by my own request into a solid walloping for untimely cheekiness. In the meantime, he reached out to the night-stand and grabbed a hairbrush.

It was the same brush I had been tearing through my hair five minutes previously. It's a fine, effective brush in both senses. I yelped and owwed for a few strokes, and cursed myself for turning his attention towards my nails. There are so many things with which I can deal without any painful encouragement from him, I thought - why not this? It was too late, though. A dozen swats into the punishment I gave up trying to contain my wailing, and howled in earnest.

"What are you crying for?" asked Abel in a very surprised voice.

"I'm letting you know the spanking is working!" I squealed.

"Oh."

I would that all questions were so easy to answer.

Abel gave me a few more whacks, and put the hairbrush away.

"Up you get," he said. "What do you have to say?"

I scrambled onto my feet and yanked my knickers back up. "Um. I won't bite my nails again? And thank you for punishing me?"

He nodded. "Good girl. Get ready for bed."

On the whole, that was probably the most effective spanking I've ever had. I have no doubt that I really won't bite my nails again. Whatever fluke had urged me to chew on them in the first place seems a thing of the past now. So does the pain of the spanking, for that matter - but the memory of it remains, as does the warmth from the hugs I got afterwards.

I wish spanking worked the first time for every kind of behaviour I've ever wanted to change.

Creating the Headmaster's study

By Abel on 27 March 2007

A dear friend was discussing a possible move into a new home. She was working out how to furnish it, and would love a room devoted to her spanking interests. The problem, I guess, is what you'd do if family or friends inadvertently wandered in. "We were wondering why you need a school desk and a blackboard?" might be a tough question to answer!

My suggestion was to furnish a room in the style of a Headmaster's study. Imagine the fun you could have finding a grand oak desk just wide enough for a girl to hold onto – reaching up on tiptoes, fingertips clutching the far side.

Leather armchairs, slightly careworn, could be angled towards the desk, awaiting parents craving news of their daughter's progress, or over whose arms girls could be positioned. A high-backed wooden chair could rest against the wall to one side.

Think of the old school photographs, and the slightly worn trophies handed out to victors on the sports field. The bookcases: a fair selection of volumes in Latin, I think, together with histories of famous scholarly establishments. Perhaps the Headmaster's degree certificate, framed on the wall?

The gown hanging behind the door. A mortar board? A punishment book on the desk, or in a drawer? Would the canes be out on display, propped against the wall, or locked away?

Oh, the hours of interior design fun one could have on eBay. And all perfectly suitable to be converted back into an ordinary home office before guests arrive!

The bottom of the beholder
By Haron on 28 March 2007

"You spanked me last night," I whined to Abel on the phone as he rode the train to work. "I was falling asleep. I had already fallen asleep! And you spanked me! Really hard! Why?"

"Well," Abel said pensively. "You were *there*."

I had been conveniently resting on my tummy, hands tucked under the pillow. Abel took this as an invitation: he pulled back the covers, and walloped me with his hand at least a dozen times. At the start, I was too sleepy to do more than squeak, but that didn't last.

I fell back asleep, but every time I drifted half-awake in the night, and felt him turn, I wondered if he was going to do it again.

"Anyway, it wasn't that hard," he said. It was pleasant to think of him trying to form his responses tamely enough that the whole train carriage didn't share the conversation.

"Yes, it was."

"It wasn't."

"Was," I took a sip of my coffee. Coffee puts me in a philosophical sort of mood. "You have to understand that whenever I get a spanking, *at the time* it's the hardest spanking I've ever endured."

He had nothing to say to that. Because it's true.

Spanking on American Idol?
By Haron on 1 April 2007

"Reality TV Magazine" quotes a contestant voted off American Idol: "As soon as they gave me the spanking that they did, I kind of knew that I was going home."

I haven't been following the show at all. What on earth have I missed?

Birched behind the gothic facade
By Abel on 2 April 2007

I've long loved St Pancras station, that incredible neo-Gothic London landmark that's soon to become the new Eurostar terminus. During my recent Tate Modern trip, I picked up a slim volume in their bookstore, in which Simon Bradley describes the history of this remarkable railway building.

Built to contain the then-wonderfully posh Midland Grand Hotel, accommodating passengers arriving into town, the comfort of the guest rooms contrasted with the 'bleak' dormitories provided in the attics for the staff... Whilst staff were generally looked after well, it's noted that there was an 'omnipresence of hierarchy, discipline and petty regulation'.

I filled in some of the gaps, the book being sorely short on colourful anecdotes. Young Beatrice, fresh from the country, would have been one of the most promising maids in the hotel. That she'd fallen for Albert, one of the footmen, was regarded with good humour by the management. That a visiting dignitary, staying in one of the top suites, should stumble across them canoodling in the guests' corridors late at night, was a matter for rather less lenient treatment.

Footmen were two-a-penny: Albert was, of course, dismissed in a blink. But bright, polite, conscientious, pretty young maids were hard to find and expensive to train. Whispered discussions the following morning resulted in the wisp of a girl being led by the wrist through the corridors to the General Manager's imposing office.

Lectured about the perils of irresponsibility, Beatrice was given a choice: follow her paramour, penniless, onto the streets, or bend over the gentleman's desk and have nothing more said of the matter after her punishment had been duly administered.

Her choice was easy, if painful: well-paid positions with training were hard to find, and homeless poverty was an unappealing option in Victorian London. Now, some 125 years on, staff working on the hotel's renovation tell tale of those still nights when the swish of the birch and the ghostly yelps of the penitent girl can be heard echoing through the corridors of the near-deserted building.

Beatrice would have gone on to a life of great prosperity, no doubt - whisked off by a famous gentleman who fell for her charm as she delivered fresh flowers to his room. But Albert would never have been forgotten, and nor would the painful consequences of that innocent first love.

A live-in disciplinarian

By Haron on 3 April 2007

The most recent Sunday Times' "Style" magazine had a neat little feature on a new type of a lifestyle consultant: the guy moves in for however long you can afford him,* detoxes your life, whatever that involves, - and moves out.

You can tell what I'm thinking, right? I've written and read lots of stories where a girl in need of discipline is sent to live in a structured, strict environment, but I haven't come across a scenario where the discipline and the person who wields it comes to stay at the girl's house.

I could have tons of fun with this idea. "What's this in your drawer, young lady? Last year's laddered pantyhose? Out it goes." A tick on the clipboard to mark a stroke of the paddle to come at bedtime. "It's October. Why is your wall calendar still on August?" Another tick. And so forth.

Obviously, seeing how an appropriately strict husband is a good lifestyle guru substitute (!), I don't feel an immediate need to experiment. Even if I did, though, I don't think this regime will work for me very well. And here's why:

I couldn't accept discipline from somebody who didn't care about/for me. Having to pay somebody to take an interest in my doings would smash my self-image all to pieces. Acquiring self-discipline is a long, terrible, ongoing process, a battle with no end. Any disciplinarian needs to pay me constant attention, even when I've been doing well for a while. Simply moving out when a semblance of order has been achieved would be no use.

Even if the disciplinarian worked out of charity, the moving out thing would undoubtedly shatter any progress we might have made. Because being cared for/about somehow involves the disciplinarian person not leaving.

I don't think I could even write this as a story: I can't imagine a girl for whom it would work well enough that she hired such a person.

On the other hand, if she were *sentenced* to receive "live-in guidance" (as it would be called by the courts) - as a form of house arrest, I suppose...

* The article quotes £350 - 500 an hour, plus travel. Eep!

In which Haron narrowly escapes a caning

By Abel on 4 April 2007

"Thank you for being so kind and considerate."

Haron's such a polite girl. I was in my suit, about to leave for work, leaning over to give her a kiss. And I'd just shared my pre-waking dream...

A Housemaster, observing two girls sneaking back into the house late at night... Recognising one of them...

Sending a prefect to wake her shortly before the usual reveille, and to bring her to his study...

Coming straight to the point... That he'd seen her return and would cane her. That he'd observed a companion: "Who were you with?"

The six strokes for the offence itself would be repeated, even harder, for her refusal to name her fellow truant. She'd will herself through them, knowing that her suffering was protecting her friend.

I shared my little story with Haron, as I say. Told her that I thought it had been very kind and considerate of me not to drag her, sleepy and naked, from the bed to enact the scene in my office. It was a good thing that she thanked me, really. Playing safe, I call it...

When fantasy and reality coincide

By Abel on 7 April 2007

Often, I hardly have to close my eyes before a feast of spanking fantasies starts to present itself for my consumption.

I'm fascinated by how kink overlays real-life memories in my slumber. Take last night: the girl trudging disconsolately from the hockey pitch, all muddy knees and worried face, sent off by the referee in an inter-school match. She'd know, you see, that a sending-off (a most rare occurrence) was always punished by a caning.

I watched her on the bus back to the school, sitting in silence, lost in thought and fears. I wondered, as she must have done, how soon after her return she'd be called to the see the Headmaster.

And here's the interesting thing. The hockey pitch from which she trudged was clearly one at my old school. The sports pavilion was there in the background; her lonely walk back to the changing rooms took her past the groundsman's cottage. I could hear the studs of her boots click along the badly-paved pathway.

What other interesting dreams await? Whippings in Waitrose? Canings in the cathedral? Tawsings in the town square?

Pining for a governess

By Haron on 8 April 2007

I've written before about the kinky inspiration I get from "Antiques Roadshow".

Well, it strikes again. On tonight's programme, a sweet young girl was showing off her great-grand-grand-(etc)-mother's embroidery sampler. Careful stitches growing faint from the sun: the alphabet, numbers, a short devotional passage.

I could see that 18th-century girl bending her head over the canvas, licking a prickled finger, stifling a bored yawn. Her mind wonders, the progress hopelessly stalled. A governess frowns, picking up a birch rod...

I'd love to role-play this scene. I'm pretty good at embroidery (a Ukrainian girl's necessary accomplishment), but I'd be willing to botch it up for a suitably strict governess. I've been going through the list of my female friends for the last half an hour, trying to imagine which one of them would be willing to take me in hand. Oh, to be a good 18th-century girl...

Pampering one's implements

By Abel on 12 April 2007

An article I read recently about the unbelievably posh Rocco Forte hotel chain commented that:

> "Staff not only unpack your luggage but also pack it again, layering your undies with tissue paper."

Where would they place certain travel accessories, I wonder, whist unpacking? The cane hanging on the door, the hairbrush on the dresser, the tawse in the desk drawer? Everything laid out neatly on the bed?

Would they smile a knowing smile throughout one's stay? And would they inspect how well-used the implements had been before they cosseted them in tissue paper prior to departure?

Writing spanking stories in public

By Haron on 13 April 2007

I've been very bad, and I'm going straight to hell.

I'm typing this from my ancestral home in Kiev.* On the plane on my way here I was surrounded on all sides by smiley American missionaries. They were going to Ukraine to convert the savages. I was the first real-life savage they'd encountered, and they had a go at converting me too.

The nice missionary lady was very enthusiastic about the idea of converting me - but then she tried to sneak a glance into what I had on my laptop screen. There she saw something along the lines of:

> "You've had your warning," said Alli resolutely. She marched into the cubicle, grasped Ruey by her upper arm and with one deft, practiced move, tipped the girl over her lap.
>
> A horrified squeak was all Ruey could manage when she felt her tunic being flipped up and out of the way, and dull, thuddy swats began to land on her knicker-clad bottom.
>
> "There is always one girl," the prefect lectured. "Always one new girl on the first day of term who feels the need to test the rules and push her luck. You think you're so clever, don't you?"

I always try to use long flights to do some writing!

Obviously, the missionary lady thought I was too far gone on the way to depravity, and bothered me no more.

* Poor, poor Abel; all the girls have abandoned him. First our friend Martha, who's been staying, went home. Then I left for Kiev; all the spanking's dried up for Abel. I'm a little worried for the well-being of our cat, alone in the house with a frustrated spanko man.

My roof, my rules

By Haron on 15 April 2007

One of the fantasies to which my mind constantly returns is that of a young woman - a university student or a recent graduate - living in a situation where her actions and choices are controlled with strict rules as though she was a child. The discipline may be enforced by her parents ("As long as you're under my roof, young lady!"), or somebody who she'd asked to provide structure for her. It's a hot idea. I always think about it, and sometimes write about it, and seek out spanking stories that deal with the subject.*

Funnily enough, this is not a fantasy I enjoy returning to very much when I stay with my mother. "No, you're not going out, it rained earlier!" "Wear your coat! No, the winter coat!" "Why didn't you phone you were going to be out until 10?" "You ought to chew your food properly; you eat too fast." If I ever felt like writing another of the girl-returns-to-parental-home stories, I'll have had lots of practical research to fall back on. Minus the spankings, obviously.

* Though I've never found a story that convincingly explained to me why the girl submits to the childish treatment in the first place, unless she's already into spanking.

A spanking writer among vanillas

By Haron on 17 April 2007

I'm spending much time hanging out with my childhood friends. It's the first time in months that I've been around vanilla people for days at a time. I'm not used to this any more.

Obviously, when I'm with kinky friends, spanking isn't the only thing we ever talk about - yet, it's always there, like a comfortable background tune. This has been the only type of communication I've known recently. Coming to the UK to study, I needed to make a whole new set of friends, and I've consciously stuck to the spanking scene.

Thus, returning to Kiev, I find that I've forgotten how to communicate with people who are not only vanilla, but also chaste, fresh and unknowing. Even the saucy japes we throw at each other are of an innocent kind. We blush when we swear; we don't talk of sex, but whisper. Most of the time, conversations are not just vanilla, but sexless: life, memories of school, work.

When you make a living writing erotica, it's kind of hard to discuss work with your childhood friends. They know, but they don't really want to know the details.

I love my friends in all their chastity. They do baffle me, though.

Spanking from the UK to Ukraine

By Abel on 18 April 2007

I do try and keep Haron entertained while she's away - after all, she's as starved of spanking action as I, and my fast will be broken before hers. This was this morning's account of last night's kinky dream, a variation on one of my favourite nocturnal fantasies:

> A schoolmaster has a favourite student (as ever) - a sixth-former, getting personal tuition. They're close - he's almost a surrogate father-figure. An unsympathetic guardian type lurks somewhere in her background. There's the occasional chaste hug to re-assure and support her, in their one-on-one tutorials.
>
> Someone has misbehaved in his class. The master fills in the standard punishment form, expressing his displeasure as he does, and announces that the culprit will be sent straight to the Headmaster for a caning.
>
> And then he asks who was responsible, before finding it was his favourite. As she takes the form from his outstretched hand, she notices that he's ticked the box for 'serious' in the

section that asks about the level of the offence... and knows that will mean six or eight strokes on the bare.

She reappears 20 minutes later, tearful, every eye in the room watching her reaction as she sits down painfully behind her desk, on the hard wooden chair...

That should have kept my darling girl entertained for a little while!

Spank that man
By Haron on 19 April 2007

One of those "Huh?" news stories for you. The Chinese are building what's effectively a FemDommeLand: a town in which women are in charge, and disobedient men are spanked:
Shuangqiao district in China's Chongqing will have a motto proclaiming its philosophy: "A woman never makes a mistake, a man must not refuse a woman's request."

Li Jigang, the town's director of tourism, said:

> "In any tour group entering this town, female members would play the deciding role concerning shopping and other items of the itinerary ... A disobedient man will be punished by kneeling on an uneven board or by washing dishes in a restaurant."

...Tour groups? There are to be tour groups?

Scottish spankings
By Abel on 20 April 2007

To Scotland, a couple of weeks back, to host an event in the Old Library of a once-grand hotel near my spiritual home (Lochgelly, of course, the historic centre of tawse-making!).

The shelves were lined with an undistinguished collection of cast-offs from the local library: "Disasters at

Sea", "A Doctor's Life", "I Heard the Owl Call My Name" (this last incident presumably being shortly before the nice medics in white coats arrived....)

There was a smattering of risqué romances, in which "the dashing captain entered Emma's chamber". And then there were the self-published local autobiographies, quickly skimmed, telling as they did of girls spanked with mother's hairbrush, and fathers who took off their belts to ensure a "disciplined upbringing".

Later, over dinner, a delightful young waitress took orders. One of our party didn't want dessert. "Can I put you down for a chocolate cake, then?" she asked. "I really like that."

Later on, she looked dismayed. I asked why. "Chef caught me with the chocolate cake." I did wonder whether she might have ended the evening receiving a taste of a local product of a somewhat different nature.

Uniforms for college students

By Haron on 21 April 2007

Oh my goodness. While I've been gone, one of Kiev's universities has introduced uniforms for its students. These would be girls and lads from 17 to 22 years old, plus any mature students that care to attend.

The girls wear straight navy skirts, white shirts and navy ties, with a pin in the shape of the college's logo.

I took them for students of one of our military schools at first, but my friend mentioned in a casual conversation: "University A. is thinking of introducing uniforms, now that University B's done it and it's been such a success."

The city is full of grown women in schoolgirl gear.

Writing spanking science fiction and fantasy
By Haron on 23 April 2007

Over the weekend I sat at a lecture by a well-respected Russian writer of fantasy. He said many useful and wonderful things about writing: nothing I didn't know, exactly, but plenty I could do with hearing again. About fantasy and SF he said that if it's good, it needs to be constantly surprising. Bad fantasy is based on recognition (ooh look, another elf!), good fantasy keeps you amazed.

Many people may disagree, but if he's right, I may have just figured out why it's so bloody hard to write good spanking fiction (or any erotica) set in a fantasy world.

I'm convinced that a good spanking story, if it is to appeal to your id, mustn't be surprising. We have our kinky buttons. We like them pushed in a particular way, just so. There's only so much room for manoeuvre before a piece of erotica becomes too surprising, too creative, too vaguely connected with your particular brand of kink.

This isn't to say spanking stories have to be boring: just that there shouldn't be so much extraneous stuff that you get distracted from having a finger jabbed at your buttons.

Where good fantasy fiction must surprise and amaze, erotica must provide enough familiarity to still get you off.

When you try to mix them in together, well... Chances are, one side will suffer: either the fantasy element will be weak and cliché, or you'll get so excited by the magicky gadgets that the spanking side of the story will limp along, as though it was put there as an afterthought.

One or the other will sound jarring. One or the other will seem extraneous. "Why did you put all this spanking into a good space opera, huh?" "Why did you mix in all this complicated geekery and spoil my spanking story?" Well, see, I really tried to make it work, but...

I'm still convinced you can do fantasy erotica well. I am, in fact, convinced that some of my own fantasy erotica is pretty good, you know? But it's *hard work*. I've noticed before how hard it was to keep the balance. I guess, now I know why.

Caught on camera; caned

By Abel on 28 April 2007

Tourist information departments are most inventive these days. Wandering round a city centre before a meeting last week, I spied a high-tech multimedia booth.

Behold, an electronic, touch-screen map of our attractions! Marvel at the email ability: just touch the picture of the establishment you want to visit, and you can send them a note! Look shocked at the two schoolgirls standing next to the machine, typing what (from their giggles) was clearly a rude message...

Had I designed the system, it would have had an additional feature...

Picture said girls standing later in the day before their Headmaster...

See him pass the grainy photograph across the desk: not the highest quality, but recognisably the two girls in front of him...

Hear him comment on how prescient the tourist board had been to fit the booths with in-build cameras...

Watch him walk over to his cupboard to extract a cane...

Wince as the girls take their turn touching their toes for their salutary lesson...

Only, I doubt it quite transpired like that this morning, cameras and canes being absent from the multimedia equation.

Nostalgic about spanking

By Haron on 30 April 2007

A reader of The Chattanoogan has fond memories of her upbringing: "I remember growing up. Everybody was your parent. When you were in church, at school or outdoors, you had to be the best-behaved child. Any adult that saw you doing anything out of the way sure would give you a spanking and, before you got home, your grandma or mother knew."

So, hands up if you think that being grabbed and spanked by random adults in the street would have helped you grow up a better person than you are.

What, *nobody*?

That said, in my virtual folder of fantasies is one where I'm a child growing up in a small community where every adult takes part in bringing up every child. Lots of spanking happens, naturally. However, in my fantasy, none of these adults are evil, morally suspect or even less than very wise, which makes it work this much better for me.

Unearthing old punishment books

By Abel on 8 May 2007

The libraries archive in East Riding contains some gems, according to their online catalogue. There's the "Offences and punishment book" from April 1938 – March 1947 for a workhouse and school in Bridlington, for example:

> "Arranged by date of offence. Includes details of name, date of offence, punishment, approval for number of strokes if corporal punishment, date of punishment, master's initials, observations."

I wonder what 'observations' were made? Detailed accounts of the extent to which the young ladies writhed under the birch, perhaps?

And then there's Hull Newington High School's records, including its "punishment book 1945-1967".

What price Data Protection?! I somehow doubt they asked pupils to sign a disclaimer: "I accept that I am about to be caned for misbehaviour, and agree that it's OK for the authorities to make the details available publicly in the local library in forty years' time."

Playing with punishment books

By Haron on 9 May 2007

I feel compelled to tell you about a role-play I invented for myself when I was about 10 years old.

My aunt, who was a teacher, often brought "spoiled" forms from her school for me to play with; rather than be tossed in the bin, they were my sketchbooks and notepads. Once she brought an empty class register: a thick book with spaces for names, subjects, contact details in the back, teachers' notes, the works. A secretary had made a mistake filling it in before the year started, and it was dismissed as unusable.

Unusable by the school, perhaps. But not me. I tore out the offending pages, and began to run a school of my own.

I came up with 35 names, boys and girls, and listed them in my best hand. I invented the subjects they studied, and their teachers names, and their marks. And in the form where the teacher would normally record homework for the following time, I kept a punishment book. The school was set in the future, after corporal punishment had returned.

Don't ask me where I'd got the idea: at the age of 10, I was inventing the wheel, and adjusting it to my own headspace. As far as I was concerned, this was the most wonderful game in the world: to list names, and offences, and the punishments they suffered.

There were never any particular details; these were in my head, in case anybody found my book and questioned my strict running of the imaginary classroom. I had "Sokol, Anna - tardiness - 10" (strokes of the birch, of course). Detention featured as well, though not much else: I stuck to what I thought would be reasonably used. In my head, though, I had entire stories, with lengthy dialogues (the begging; the scolding), additional punishments (a miscreant kneels in the corner, holding the birch: I'd read that one in a book), colours and sounds. It was a whole world.

Since then, every time I come across a real punishment book, I can't help imagining the world behind it, with its own colours, sounds and stories. A simple list of names can send me on a adventure in an imaginary school, with its imaginary rules. If the book is authentic and detailed, all the better, but it doesn't matter: a world grows around it all on its own, without much help from me.

I think I destroyed my original punishment book in a fit of horror, when I found out that my spanking addiction could be seen as a sexual perversion. When you're sixteen, you don't want to be a pervert. Maybe some other books survived, though; I was never any good at cleaning. I'd love to know for sure what I'd written.

City of the banned

By Abel on 10 May 2007

I saved a magnificent article from Time Out a couple of months ago, which listed little-known legislation that still applies in our capital city. Did you know, for example, that a London taxi driver has a legal duty to ask all passengers whether they are suffering from smallpox or the plague, before letting them climb into the cab? Or that it's illegal for commoners to permit their pet to 'have carnal knowledge of a pet of the Royal House'?

What really caught my eye, though, was the work of the "statute law revision team", which repeals obsolete legislation. According to its team leader: "Most of the London acts we're repealing are about provision for workhouses."

I wonder... Some deep, dark, dusty legal tome... An ancient Act, permitting - nay, requiring - gentlemen to administer sound thrashings for misconduct on workhouse land... A new building, constructed on the site of the old workhouse (so still deemed legally to be covered by the Act)... A girl misbehaving... The subsequent thrashing administered with the full authority of the law, even in these modern times...

Whips not votes

By Abel on 13 May 2007

Far from championing women's rights, Queen Victoria was passionately opposed to the emerging women's emancipation movement. Eminent historian Lytton Strachey quoted a fascinating letter from Her Majesty on the subject, following an 1870 meeting in favour of Women's Suffrage:

> "The Queen is most anxious to enlist everyone who can speak or write to join in checking this mad, wicked folly of 'Woman's Rights,' with all its attendant horrors, on which her poor feeble sex is bent, forgetting every sense of womanly feeling and propriety. Lady —– ought to get a GOOD WHIPPING."

I wondered which "Lady" might have been the one to be whipped. A quick search reveals that the most prominent such was Lady Amberley, whose diary for 1870 does indeed record one of the first meetings of the Women's Suffrage Society. Aged 28 at the time, she was described as "vigorous, lively, witty, serious, original, and fearless". Just the characteristics to make her eminently whippable, in my book!

Heading to her flogging?

By Abel on 14 May 2007

Warren Street station. The young woman next to me peers anxiously at the densely-typed sheet of instructions in her hand, then studies the tube map.

> "You will report to the designated Punishment Centre at Pimlico at 5pm prompt, so that we may administer a birching to you, as ordered by the court." *
>
> It was already 4.30 ; no wonder she looked nervous...

* At least, this is what I assume must have been written on her piece of paper.

Martha's letter home

By Abel on 16 May 2007

Our dear friend Martha really is good at this scene stuff! I was staying at her place the other night. She arrived home that evening with a crisp white envelope, neatly addressed to me. Inside, a letter, from her Headmaster.

> With regret I must write to inform you that I had cause to speak to Martha regarding a disciplinary matter at school today. A routine IT check revealed that she had been accessing my private email...
>
> The school views Martha's actions as an extremely serious matter and proposes dealing with them accordingly. I have spoken to her today and she has admitted the security breach.
>
> I would be grateful if you could complete the attached Disciplinary Form (Serious Offences Category) to indicate how you would prefer this to be dealt with, and return it to me, via Martha, at your earliest convenience, so that we may take the appropriate steps.

Attached was a form... I rejected the option of suspension or a meeting to discuss matters with the Headmaster, instead opting for both of the other two choices:

> "I will deal with this matter myself at home and will inform the school of what action is taken"

and

> "I sanction the use of corporal punishment by the school to resolve this matter".

I don't know... what some girls get up to in the office during the day! And thank goodness no-one else picked the form up from her office printer!)

Dominant Fashion

By Haron on 17 May 2007

I'm not a very fashionable person on the whole. I like to know what's in, but I don't always go out of my way to dress according to current season's demands, even if I like the style. Jeans are good.

However, I quite like the sound of what they've got going on in India, if you believe this article:

> For the moment, it seems to be all about spanking style! If one had to take a cue from international catwalks, the look du jour is chainmail micro-dresses, metallic whips, studded stilettos and leather eye masks. The dominatrix is ruling the catwalks – and don't you dare disagree with her!

Apart from the fact that the described style is more general BDSM than spanking in particular, I could still see myself turning into a good little consumer if the new fashion hits the stores.

If a spanking theme is where it's at, does this mean we can expect a great range of adult-sized little-girl dresses, cute pyjamas, replica uniforms and fashion paddles?

The iced girl cometh
By Abel on 20 May 2007

The hotel we've been staying in this weekend has a well-signposted 'Ice Room' on each floor. How very considerate, I thought, of them to help with their guests' disciplinary needs, picturing naked girls being led through the corridors and locked in said room. There, they'd shiver and contemplate, until they were retrieved and led back to their bedroom for their thrashing.

I was most disappointed to find that, rather than a mini-igloo for miscreant daughters, wives, girlfriends and colleagues, the room merely contained an ice machine. Then again, I thought, even that might be a source of some interesting fun...

Art, human condition and spanking
By Haron on 21 May 2007

Have you heard about the new exhibition in London by sculptor Antony Gormley?

At the centre is an installation called "Blind Light": a glass-walled box the size of a small room, filled with dense white mist, in which you're invited to get lost for as long as you can bear. Once inside, you can only see a few inches in front of your face; the rest is a bright, fluffy cloud, disembodied voices, and a vague outline of a human being when somebody stumbles within an arm's reach.

While unveiling the work, the sculptor wondered about the effect this will have on the visitors:

> "On the one hand, you have lost all sense of location - left/right, front/back. You immediately are lost in space and that makes you anxious," he said. "But at the same time I think there is a sense of euphoria that you are almost free of the body whilst being returned to it in a new way.

It's a climatological experiment but also a sociological one. I don't know how people will react to art of this kind. Light and water are two ingredients, but the third ingredient is the human content of the work and I will be interested to see how that evolves."

Abel and I held hands for much of our trip inside.* Except for the moment when we stopped, peered at each other through the cloud (you have to move really close together; really, really close), and he whispered to me:

"Touch your toes."

One smack, two, three. Not too loud; we don't want to spook any other wanderers. Still, I wonder if I was the first person to have been spanked inside "Blind Light"? It's only been open for a few days, right?

Obviously, we weren't just fooling around in a room of artificial fog. We were experiencing this work of art as a couple: two lovers in a world in which we know nothing but each other, and as the mist threatens to rise between us, we cling to the intimate core of our relationship.

Without the eye of the beholder this piece of art misses its subject, it's not complete - and we completed it with the most sincerity we could offer.

We were also fooling around a little, of course.

* He admits to anxiety from the loss of direction; I was at the euphoric end: I spend most of my time lost anyway, and here I had an excuse to be.

Enslaved, whipped, freed?

By Abel on 23 May 2007

"Be cautious in dealing with slaves, and remember that Romans regard slavery as an unfortunate affliction that might happen to anyone... Some slaves even go on to become the adopted children or heirs of their former owners."

So wrote The Independent recently, in an extract from 'Ancient Rome on Five Denarii a Day', a fascinating new 'travel guide' that is surely destined to be added to the large pile of as-yet-unread books on our living room floor.

Where to start with such a theme? My mind's spinning...

"Will you whip me now, sir, in the same way you did when I was a slave?"

Or "Take off your slave's dress, young lady."

Or even, "We have one remaining matter to deal with before I sign the paperwork confirming your new status. Bend over the table."

Oh for a toga party...

Doctor Who, Edwardian schoolmaster

By Haron on 25 May 2007

From the previews for tomorrow's episode of Doctor Who, it looks like he will be disguised as an 'ordinary schoolteacher in 1912 England'.

We had great fun the other day discussing the adventures you might have if you land the TARDIS in a school. Abel suggested that the Doctor's assistant would need to infiltrate her mother's old school. There she would find out why Mum was always so paranoid about her daughter wandering out of bounds: after a night-time monster chase, the girl is brought to the Headmaster for six-of-the-best.

Or how about this: the Doctor steals a girl straight from the bench in front of the Headmaster's study. After many adventures, he returns her, but his usual sloppy driving makes him miss by a few months, and corporal punishment has been abolished. I quite like this one, actually...

Interrogation

By Abel on 28 May 2007

Tired, jet lagged; waking this morning in Savannah was a slow process. My mind wandered, dazed, to the day ahead. I'm heading out with a colleague; we've agreed to meet at 9 for breakfast, with pen and paper to scribble notes for the conference presentation we're giving later in the week.

I recalled, in my sleepy state, that I've brought with me a small notebook perfect for the purposes. Purchased in Japanese store Muji, it's the same size and colour as a passport. I picked up several the other week – thoughts of girls being caught with 'forged' documents sparking some fascinating scene ideas.

I daydreamed back to a scene we'd played the evening before I left for the US. There were six of us in total: some of the very best spanking role players I know. Three girls, three teachers. Fighting outside the common room; sound spankings, carefully-administered canings - and a superb rapport between the members of the group.

And then the logical leap. I pictured the same group of six; the girls with the forged papers, on the run from the authorities, possessors of some clever code that the State needed to know. We caught them, of course; interrogated them; flogged them, but to no avail – silence prevailed. So each officer took a sobbing girl away into a separate room: used fair means and very foul to extract confessions. (I'd better spare your blushes with details of the precise methods used!).

Two gave up their secrets: the third did not. They were brought back into the main room: the girls tied facing each other. We alternated strokes between them, the one uncooperative girl's resolve tested by her own whipping and that of her friends, until she finally gave in.

I guess I ought to dig out that notebook and head off for breakfast...

The Plimsoll Line
By Haron on 29 May 2007

When I saw a review of a book called "The Plimsoll Sensation", I got terribly excited. Wow, somebody has written a whole book about what it feels like to be whacked with a plimsoll! But wait, why is the review in "The Observer"?

Unfortunately, the book is not about the gym shoe you get smacked with, but about the person, Samuel Plimsoll. Apparently, he invented the "Plimsoll line" on a ship, that is, a line that shows how low a vessel can sit in the water while loaded. Hmm, fascinating.

I wondered if he had also invented proper plimsolls, you know, the shoes. He hadn't. But the connection is not entirely random, either! Apparently, plimsoll shoes are so called because 'the band around the shoes that holds the two parts together reminded people of a ship's *Plimsoll line*'.

More on the Doctor and the cane
By Abel on 30 May 2007

Being away, I missed the Doctor Who episode in which he caned an entire class of Edwardian schoolgirls. (At least, that's what I'm hoping happened). My beloved described a couple of the fantasies that the episode idea stimulated when we heard of it, including one in which the Doctor rescued a girl from the bench outside the Headmaster's study.

In my mind, the scene finished differently. The girl and The Doctor go through all sorts of adventures. As the time for him to return her draws near, she starts to worry about the impending caning. The Doctor comforts her, but apologises – the Tardis rules are such that he must return her to the precise time and place from which she had been taken. The episode ends with the Doctor disappearing, and the girl knocking nervously on the Headmaster's door.

And why stop at one girl? Perhaps there were three, queuing up in pyjamas and dressing gowns for a late-night scolding. The Doctor rescues them; time-travelling escapes follow; he returns them safe and sound. They knock on the door, walk in – and realise his error: no longer is it 2007, but an earlier age. It's a different Headmaster who faces them, armed not with the modern threat of lines and a grounding, but flexing a cane…

The Romans again
By Abel on 31 May 2007

Amazing how my little Roman slave fantasies of the other day keep cropping up again.

Last night's dream, for example. A writer sitting by a window, high up, looking out as a young woman is led into the courtyard of a neighbour's house. She catches his eye, as she struggles: a defiant look.

Her tunic reveals her to be a slave. Her master removes it, roughly, and ties her hands above her head. She's positioned facing the writer. She looks up at him again, realising that her ordeal is being closely observed. She averts her eyes, ashamed.

Her master proceeds to lay on the strokes: hard, fast, purposefully. The writer can no longer see her eyes: they're downcast, the girl absorbed totally in her flogging.

She's untied. She grabs her costume; covers herself; runs inside. And the writer records what he's seen, and reflects on what he doesn't know: the girl's name, her offence. Whether it was her first whipping. Given she was facing him during the flogging, how she'd marked. Who'd comfort her afterwards.

Where the Tudor daughters were birched

By Abel on 1 June 2007

Ever been to Hampton Court Palace? It's one of my favourite places, a palpable sense of history surrounding one's every step. I was there recently, and hope the young lady in authentic Tudor dress realised quite how much inspiration she provided.

The attendant in Henry VIII's great hall explained how the décor was designed to intimidate visitors and inspire fear and loyalty. Each tapestry, it seems, is made with so much gold and silver that it weighs a ton; each cost the equivalent of a warship.

In the kitchens, there's a wonderful model of the palace as a royal banquet takes place. My mind wandered, as it's oft to do. The king was presiding over the feast; he was in a less than festive mood, having been kept waiting as the more tardy guests arrived. Indeed, there were still two seats empty as the meal began.

Two immaculately-dressed young women - beautiful, head-turning - arrived in the hall, curtsying and heading for their seats. "Come forward," His Majesty bellowed. "What do you mean by turning up late and keeping me waiting?"

They apologised, profusely: they'd got lost in the gardens, they'd lost track of time, they were so sorry...

"And what do your excuses matter to me? I do not expect to be kept waiting. By any of my subjects." The King turned to the girls' father. "I hope that you will punish them for such insolence and disrespect, Baron?"

"Of course, Your Majesty."

"And I'm sure that you will wish to demonstrate your loyalty to your King, by dealing with the matter with the severity it deserves, Baron?"

"Yes, Your Majesty."

"Then I shall ask the courtiers to set up the flogging block in my private chambers," glancing across at his own daughters, "where the princesses are punished if they misbehave. I shall come and watch after lunch, to show how seriously you treat such disrespectful behaviour to your monarch."

"Thank you, your Majesty."

"You are a good and noble man." The King turned to the other diners, all listening intently. "A true test of a gentleman's loyalty, passed with honour. Girls: sit down: you've kept us waiting quite long enough. Now, on with our feast...."

Fine art of implement buying

By Haron on 2 June 2007

A couple of months ago Abel, before watching the Grand National, backed the winning horse - just because its name was Silver Birch. He immediately decided that winnings gained thanks to being kinky have to be disposed of in a kinky fashion, and invested the whole lot in new implements.

He didn't tell me what he was buying. He just smirked. And snorted. And cackled. And told me to wait and see.

Well, as my luck would have it, the implements have arrived now that he's away for a couple of weeks, so now I have to wait even longer.

Good job the mysterious elongated package has a customs form stuck on it. This should tell me exactly what it is. It says... Hang on, it says...

"Six wooden sculptures."

Right. That was helpful...

Dr Freud will see you now

By Abel on 3 June 2007

An interesting work-related conversation with a friend in a pub the other night. We were talking about organising various events; I raised the topic of the impact of recent regulations.

Only I didn't call the new law by its correct title - 'The Disability Discrimination Act'.

Oh no.

Completely unintentionally, I commented on 'The Disciplinary Discrimination Act'.

Fortunately, said friend is 'one of us', although the folks on the next table looked a little surprised.

A room with a view
By Abel on 5 June 2007

I'm in the middle of a few days post-conference break in Atlanta. What a lovely city: I've been extremely pleasantly surprised. A kinky friend joined me here for the weekend.

Our hotel room is up on the 63rd floor, with panoramic floor to ceiling windows. One does have to wield the cane with slightly more purpose to make a girl concentrate and avoid her being able to distract herself with the views below. I do hope that passengers in passing planes are not in the habit of surveying the city with binoculars...

PS I must apologise to the cleaning staff for the pair of handprints left on your nice, clean windows. You can rest assured that the culprit was soundly thrashed.

Wrong kind of spanking
By Haron on 10 June 2007

Apparently, a particular internet provider's help forum has become flooded with spam, to the point where you can 'click on an innocent link to learn how to fix your phone and you're more likely to come across "Mel Gibson spanking" or "Katie Holmes touching her boobs"'.

Mel Gibson spanking? Eww! Ewwwwww! That's so wrong!

Makes you realise why spam is bad, doesn't it? It puts images in your mind that you just can't unimagine. (Shudders.)

Yet more Roman whippings

By Abel on 11 June 2007

Now that my mind's started to ponder matters Roman, toga-clad fantasies keep popping up at inopportune moments. Sitting eating breakfast in the hotel Starbuck's in Atlanta last week, for example.

A noble girl had been brought before the court for some heinous offence. The evidence had been heard: her guilt had been proclaimed.

The distinguished judge was a friend of the young lady's equally distinguished father. He understood the impact that the usual punishment – of banishment from Rome – would have on their family.

He decided to be lenient: "I know that you come from a good home. I know that your father has served Rome well. I know that your behaviour, whilst totally unacceptable, has been out of character. I believe that you should be offered a second chance."

"Thank you, sir."

"On this occasion, I will therefore replace the customary sentence of banishment with a flogging. Lest anyone feel that I am favouring the nobility unduly, your whipping will be in the public square, where it is common criminals who are usually punished. Guards: take her away, strip her, tie her in position, and see that every stroke is laid on with all due diligence."

Ethically harvested implements

By Haron on 12 June 2007

Sunday's Observer magazine was on its "ethical issue". I prepared to yawn my way through it, but luckily for those of us with a one-track mind they've included a "green sex" column - which informed me that, apparently, there are people in the world who would "only wish their rump to be 'struck by a paddle' if made from sustainably harvested timber".

I wouldn't mind my rump to be made from sustainably harvested timber, either...

I can just imagine the conversation. "No, no, sir! I shan't bend over! That cane's carbon footprint offends my green sensibilities!"

"A king-sized bed with ropes, sir?"

By Abel on 13 June 2007

Can I really be the only person to have glanced at a poster for 'Real Simple Travel' magazine on a newsstand in the States and marvelled at its feature on "Kink-friendly travel".

Closer inspection revealed that I really should wear my glasses when tired, as the article was actually intended for travellers with *kids*. Shame, really. I was beginning to picture their review of my ideal hotel...

> Maids stand demurely in Victorian uniforms, curtseying in the reception area as one arrives. Large suites each contain a four-poster bed, with an interesting array of other furniture. Staff take particularly care when matching guests to rooms, ensuring that each gentleman is allocated a suite in which the furniture is at just the right height for any lady/ladies who may accompany him to bend over.
>
> In an unusual touch, a selection of rattan canes hangs, ready for use, over the fireplace in each bedroom, with a further collection available in the hotel's library for more public use.

The nearby forest is available to guests should birches be required; one could take a brisk stroll, or ring the concierge to ask for fresh rods to be cut and delivered.

The rooms are, of course, immaculate in every respect. This is entirely to be expected, given the neatly-typed letter handed on arrival to gentleman "requesting and requiring" them to "deal promptly and severely" with any housekeeping errors. Indeed, many guests are known to conduct a full room inspection each morning shortly after breakfast. Beware, though, that many a Sunday morning lie-in has consequentially been interrupted by the sounds of correction being administered in neighbouring rooms, despite more than adequate sound-proofing.

An afternoon of paddling

By Abel on 15 June 2007

We passed a lovely sunny afternoon recently at a local rowing regatta. Teams from schools, universities and rowing clubs from far afield chased each other down the river in the pursuit of glory and trophies.

Not a kinky outing at all, you might think. And so did I, until I watched a women's "eight" in a line alongside their boat, simultaneously bending over its upturned hull.

I believe that they were actually about to manoeuvre it towards the river, but the thought of the coach walking along the line with a paddle (of course) to address the team's poor performance in a race was far more enticing.

Later, I marvelled at how efficiently the whole event was run. Race upon race, starting on time, crews and boats always in the right position at the right time. Yet what if one participant lost track of the hour as she socialised with friends: the cox for a leading men's eight, for example. She'd suddenly see her boat zooming past on the water, a substitute at the helm steering with wild and inexperienced inaccuracy.

The team would lose, of course: the gentlemen in the boat would be most unimpressed with her lack of diligence and dismissive of her apologies. A discussion would take place; consensus would be reached; the young lady would find herself bending tight over the boat as each rower in turn expressed his displeasure in a manner both traditional and forceful.

The message in the mirror
By Abel on 17 June 2007

I've just had a guilty thought. In Atlanta recently, my friend and I noticed that when the bathroom mirror steamed up after a shower, the phrase "19" emerged, having been handwritten by some previous occupant. (A lover aged 19? Their 19th lover? 19 notches on the bedpost during their stay? 19 strokes?)

Of course, we couldn't resist: "SPANK" was scribed neatly onto the glass. Lo and behold, next time the mist appeared, our message revealed itself, as it did for the remainder of the trip.

...and as it still, presumably, does, as I forgot to wipe the word off before checking out. I wonder how many guests we've startled since? And the brat deep within me wonders what else we could have written had we known we were bequeathing a note to future occupants.

Some might say that the hidden text suggested an appropriate remedy for the hotel maid for not cleaning the mirror properly, of course. Mmmmm... The duty manager inspects the rooms, notices the message, calls in the maid...

The tawse in her hands
By Abel on 18 June 2007

The lady opposite me on the train is using her bookmark as she reads, sliding it down the page line-by-line.

It's made of brown leather. About six inches long by two wide. Its end splits into multiple tails. "OMG," I thought, when I first glanced in her direction, "she's reading with a tawse."

It isn't. Quite. But it might be rather effective. And it's got me thinking. I wonder if I could get away with using the small, authentic hand-tawse that I bought for Haron in the same way, on some future journey?

I'm even picturing the conversation with a customs officer at some airport. "It's a bookmark. A *torze*? No, officer, I'm sorry, I don't know what you mean."

A former school for a few million
By Haron on 19 June 2007

The Sunday Times had this big (and otherwise incredibly dull) article about a derelict, completely neglected former stately home that's just been sold for 42 million pounds.

Apparently, right after it was a stately home, it was run as a boarding school. As nobody thought to do it up afterwards:

> "the trappings of boarding-school life are still apparent: the house has a muddled layout, with few bathrooms, while the classrooms, gymnasium and a woodwork studio have been left pretty much untouched".

Well, that sounds good. I wonder if the property developer will rent it out as a venue for spanking parties? It could get him some of his millions back, right?

The good old days?
By Abel on 20 June 2007

Some interesting records unearthed in the archives of past court proceedings here in the north-east of England:

> Durham Assizes, August 3rd 1782
>
> Yesterday se'nnight the Assizes ended at Durham... Margaret Walker, to be whipped. Mary Hunter and Mary Gilhespie, to be privately whipped.
>
> Newcastle Assizes, August 19th 1786
>
> Elizabeth, wife of Thomas Smith; Elizabeth, wife of William Thompson; Mary, wife of John Brown; and Frances, wife of James Atkinson; severally for grand larceny within the benefit of the statute, were sentenced to be privately whipped, and afterwards committed to the house of correction; there to be kept to hard labour for the term of one year.

I'm curious to know where the public whippings took place in the area. I sense the need for a historical reconstruction.

Caned for climbing the school fence
By Abel on 21 June 2007

As I waited in the reception area of a client's office recently for an early meeting, I happened to glance out of the window. Across the street was a school playground, surrounded by a high mesh fence, and full of surprisingly well-behaved students in immaculate blue uniforms.

A supervisor monitored new arrivals. At 8.20 sharp, he reached for his keys and padlocked the only gate. Tardy new arrivals continued to drift up, but the entrance remained firmly locked in their faces.

Doubtless there'd be letters home and detentions to serve. Apart, perhaps, for the one girl who tried to climb the fence, aided and abetted by three of her friends in the playground.

The supervisor would catch them: they'd be hauled up to wait outside the Headmaster's study. He'd call in the three 'insiders' first: young ladies should understand the importance of upholding school rules, not aiding those who would seek to undermine them. Two sharp strokes each would teach them the error of their ways, and they'd be sent on their way to their classroom.

Their fence-climbing friend would, by now, be in no doubt as to her fate, having heard whacks and yelps as she waited outside the office, having seen solemn faces and clutched bottoms as her punished friends passed her by.

There was her late arrival: not for the first time this term, thus incurring a standard two strokes. And there was her attempt to break into school premises: "quite disgraceful behaviour", as the Head would describe it. "Dangerous and dishonest conduct cannot fail to result in the most severe punishment."

Five strokes in total, came the judgment, "as I am minded to err on the side of leniency since this is your first visit to my study." Like her friends, inflicted on the bare as she touched her toes. Unlike her friends, administered with the *senior* cane and a short run-up. And equally unlike her friends, attracting an extra stripe for failing to hold her position after one particularly excruciating whack.

A caning conundrum

By Abel on 23 June 2007

Royal College of Disciplinarians

Examination paper – June 2007

You are administering a caning of twenty strokes. After 12 strokes, the young lady in question asks politely whether she might rub her backside. Equally politely, you decline.

After the fifteenth stroke, she stands up and clutches her backside. What is the correct course of action? You may choose only one answer from the following list.

A. Hug her, and tell her that as it's obviously hurting so much, you will waive the rest of the caning.

B. Make her return to her position and administer the remaining five strokes.

C. Make her return to her position and administer the fifteenth stroke again, followed by the remaining five strokes.

D. Make her return to her position and administer the full twenty strokes again from the start.

I'm fairly sure I got the answer right when faced with this dilemma whilst playing with a friend last week!

Contemptible behaviour

By Abel on 27 June 2007

How many times have I written, fantasised or played scenes in which a girl reports at the appointed hour for some well-earned judicial thrashing?

It's only just occurred to me that a young lady facing such a predicament might be tempted to fortify herself before her appointment.

The court officials would smell the alcohol on her breath, of course. They would wait until the judge who had originally heard her case had a gap in his schedule for the day, and would take her before him.

Her insobriety would cost her dear, for the judge would not be amused. Her birching would be deferred for one week. "In the meantime you need to be taught the consequences of your contempt for this court."

The court officers would be asked to detain her for the remainder of the day, until the judge had finished hearing the afternoon's case. "And then you are to give her a cold shower to make sure she sobers up, before bringing her to my chambers so that I may punish her."

He turned to the culprit. "I shall be giving you twenty strokes of the cane on the bare when we meet again later. I hope that the afternoon will give you sufficient time to reflect on your behaviour and anticipate its consequences."

Hit it for six!

By Haron on 28 June 2007

Abel went out to a see a day of cricket, and came back with the two signs they get handed at the match, the ones you hold up when the batsman scores a 4 or 6. He thought they might be useful in announcing the number of strokes in a scene!

I'll do my best not to giggle. Though, knowing him, I'm now slightly concerned about him combining the scores to award me 46, or even 64.

Hmm, recycling bin, I think.

The vice van

By Abel on 29 June 2007

Peering out of the window of the hotel restaurant earlier in the week, through the Swiss rain, I spied a parked van. It displayed a website address that intrigued me:

vices.group.com

I was ready to change companies; over my croissant and coffee, I started to mentally polish up my resume.

Sadly, when I stood up, I noticed that the rest of the address was obscured, and the vehicle belong to the 'services' division of a large multi-national. Oh, well...

Lonely Planet guide to spanking

By Haron on 30 June 2007

Last night I caught myself having the oddest, perviest thought.

It was quite late, and I was tired, and I was shuffling books around our book-case, making space for more books. I picked up one of Abel's travel books - a guide to Brussels, all glossy and nice - and leafed through it.

And realised that I was thinking, quite dismayed: "But it doesn't have a section about spanking! Where do you go in Brussels to get a spanking? It just doesn't say! Not very good for a travel guide..."

Fancy meeting you here

By Abel on 1 July 2007

Interesting test of kinky etiquette last month. We were in Coffee, Cake and Kink – which regular readers will know to be our favourite London hangout...

...when I spied a familiar face. A very familiar face: a good friend whom I know through work.

Haron's copy of Debrett's Etiquette for Girls sadly lacks counsel on the protocol to follow in such circumstances. But what to do?

Now CCK is a relatively tame place: the emphasis is on the C & C, enjoyed by kinky and open-minded people, rather than on the actual practice of pervery. But, inevitably, some customers may not want to flaunt their real names and work-related identities. (Hey, we're fairly open here, but I don't link to my work website, do I?)

So, "Hello, N—–" was out of the question, and we studiously passed by – before swapping giggly text messages a couple of hours later, starting with my:

> Either you have a doppelganger in London, or you have very good taste in coffee and cake!

By coincidence, she and I had arranged to have dinner two nights later. It turns out that neither of us would have minded a conversation at all, but better no doubt to be safe than sorry. And you can guess where we're going to meet up...

The smoking ban

By Abel on 4 July 2007

So, day four of the (quite wonderful) ban on smoking in public buildings dawns across England...

The court papers for the first offenders will have been filed by police on Monday, the overnight print job generating piles of legal paperwork for despatch on Tuesday. They'll have been landing on doormats across the country today.

"An official letter arrived for you while you were at school, darling. The envelope says it's 'On Her Majesty's Service'. I wonder what it could be?"

Indeed. For they wouldn't even know up to then that their daughter smoked, let alone that she would have been in a pub on Sunday night when she'd gone to her best friend's "so we can revise together for next week's exam.".

Imagining the consequences is all too painful - although, dear readers, I suspect many of you will be doing precisely that.

My spanking motto

By Haron on 7 July 2007

I liked the slogan I saw on the side of a local ice-cream van:

"Often licked but never beaten!"

I'm so stealing it for personal use.

The price of truancy?

By Abel on 8 July 2007

Hold on. It's still term-time. Yet as I sat in Top Shop last week waiting for Haron to try on a small selection of trendy garments (think, enough to clothe a small village), I must have been passed by several dozen young ladies who should instead have been sat in demure uniforms at traditional wooden desks, pencils sharpened, listening intently to the pearls of wisdom being passed down by their teachers.

Sadly, the shop assistants went about their business as if oblivious to the disciplinary crisis unfolding before their very eyes.

I was minded to take a roll call; pass on names to the appropriate Headmasterial authorities. But if the store would like to adopt a more immediate solution, in the interests of restoring its reputation, I'd be happy to wander the floors on their behalf, wielding a cane or tawse.

He's got it all backwards

By Haron on 9 July 2007

Sometimes, the most bizarre stories pop up on my newsreader. Take this item from a gossip column about Prince Harry:

> Last week, it was claimed Harry had spent the night in bed with a blonde barmaid after getting drunk in a sleazy club. Katherine Smith claims the 22-year-old prince took her back to his rented house before dressing in a blue and orange sarong, taking off his underwear and spanking her bottom.

Hang on a minute. *He* was wearing a sarong? *His* underwear came off? But it was *her* bottom that got spanked? Somebody should tell him that when people talk about a bare-bottom spanking, they usually mean the spankee's bottom.

Dreaming of suburban spankings

By Abel on 10 July 2007

Sometimes I marvel at the level of detail in my kinky dreams - and wonder at some of the points that get skipped over. Take last night's reveries.

A 30s style suburban semi. Slightly grubby net curtains, in the big bay window overlooking an overgrown front garden.

Rays of sunlight, filtering through, onto dated furniture that might have been fashionable in the late 1970s.

The vicar, visiting for afternoon tea, perched politely on the sofa.

The startled gentleman (guardian, father, uncle?) admonishing the young lady for swearing (although I had no idea what she'd said). "Just because you're at College doesn't mean you can use foul language when you come home. Go upstairs and fetch the cane."

The girl returning, shame-faced.

"Would you mind moving down a little, vicar?" so that the girl had room to bend over the arm of the settee. (Wearing trousers? Skirt? Bared? No idea!)

The vicar taking the lass's face quite firmly in his hand, lifting it so he could look directly into her eyes as the strokes fell. (Four strokes? Six?)

The girl standing, rubbing her bottom, being handed the cane and disappearing to return it. (To a wardrobe in her bedroom, maybe?)

The vicar being offered another cup of tea...

Adapting the school uniform

By Haron on 11 July 2007

"Time Out" last week previews an exhibition "Old Skool, New Skool", which is going to be on at the V&A Museum of Childhood in November 2007. London College of Fashion students have redesigned school uniforms after discussions with numerous pupils. The new designs explore:

> "the potential of new materials and technologies to produce clothing that might improve the health, education and well-being of children. Ideas explored include jackets with solar panels, bags with homing devices and shoes that enforce physical activity."

Excellent! Now I would like somebody to create a uniform with a Kevlar panel over the seat area. Put it in the skirt pleats or straight in the knickers. Thanks.

Punished by His Lordship?

By Abel on 12 July 2007

Sitting on a train home from London last week, we found ourselves next to an amazingly posh couple. The gentleman's suit had quite clearly cost more than our car, and the lady's silk skirt had evidently been magicked together by the fingers of a hundred naked virgins working solidly for at least four months under the stern eye of a cruel, whip-wielding supervisor.

Of course, the upper classes are past masters at retaining as much of their wealth as possible, and so their first-class tickets came with a senior citizen's discount. Her Ladyship left her railcard out on the table - and I wasn't surprised to see that she *really* was a 'Lady', a genuine member of the nobility.

Google is a wonderful thing, and the train's wireless internet connection was working for once: our curiosity led us to details of Baron B—'s public school education, service in the Guards, grand stately home and elevation to his (hereditary) peerage.

We particularly smiled at the thought that, although he was in his 70s, their daughters were younger than Haron. She sat for the reminder of the journey with "called into daddy's library to be soundly punished for being naughty" fantasies etched quite plainly across her face. I rather fancied the idea of inviting his Lordship to take her home to thrash - for dunking her shortbread in the tea, perhaps - but I wasn't sure that that would really have been the done thing...

'I'm Lee. Holloway.'

By Haron on 15 July 2007

There was an article about Maggie Gyllenhaal in one of last week's Sunday papers. There were a couple of paragraphs there about 'Secretary', including this one about her working relationship with James Spader:

> These days, she is guarded about discussing this, saying only that "despite myself, sometimes the dynamic that you are exploring in your work spills into your life".

I don't think she meant it the way I'm reading it! Even though I don't think 'Secretary' is the spanking enthusiast's ultimate movie, I'm still sort of sentimental about it. This quote works for me in a kinky way.

The missing spanking phrases

By Abel on 16 July 2007

A competition for you... I was idly browsing for inspiration last week, and was surprised at how many spanking-related phrases turned up no results whatsoever on Google. Here's ten that I tried that were sadly absent from existing web pages:

> "the girl was tied to the mast and flogged"
>
> "the headmaster caned the girls soundly"
>
> "he placed her over his knee and spanked her"

"the tawse cracked down on her outstretched hand"

"report to my study to be punished"

"the headmistress will cane you now"

"I will not tolerate lax discipline in this school"

"she bent over his desk for a paddling"

"he tawsed the girl in front of the entire school"

"the punished girl needed comforting"

I wonder what other spanking-related phrases need introducing to the web for the first time?!

Making excuses
By Haron on 19 July 2007

Last night we played a quick scene, both in our pyjamas - I was a schoolgirl caught wandering the corridors at night, Abel was the housemaster who caught her.

He demanded to be told what I was doing out of bed so late. I was tempted to see if he could keep a straight face, "I wanted to see the lunar eclipse, sir."

Not a giggle from him: "Given the last one was in May 2006, you may have had to wait for a long time. Now, the truth."

Obviously, I got it worse for lying. First came four crisp, firm whacks over the pyjamas for wandering about, then four more on my bare bottom - pyjamas pulled down but not right down, just to bare enough flesh to stripe.

Then we admired my stripes together, and cuddled.

"Did you like my excuse?" I asked.

"Did you like my response?" he asked back.

"Yeah, but actually," I said, "there was a full lunar eclipse in March this year; I just thought I wouldn't bring it up."

"Really?" he said. "Well, you would have still got the cane."

Funny how that happens... eclipse or no eclipse!

Newsflash! Girls queue for birching!
By Abel on 19 July 2007

Your correspondent is able to report exclusively that floggings are imminent for a queue of girls in school uniforms in London's Piccadilly.

Staff at the punishment centre were seen moments ago carrying large bundles of freshly-cut birches into the building.

(Haron assures me that the young ladies are awaiting tomorrow's Harry Potter launch party in the big Waterstone's branch, and that the implements were broomsticks, but we all know better...)

Daddy, the book, the bedroom, the belt
By Abel on 21 July 2007

Saturday. 7.03 a.m.

My darling wife's downstairs, curled up in pyjamas on the sofa with a book. *That* book. She joined the hoards at the local Waterstone's at midnight; returned home triumphant; hasn't been to bed. And she's still only half way through (page 356, to be precise).

Naturally, when I woke, I too pondered the plot of the final work of the Harry Potter series. Or, at least, the one major outstanding issue... Hermione must *surely* be caned in this one. Surely? *Please?*

And then my thoughts turned darker. A daddy, walking sleepily downstairs first thing in the morning. Catching his daughter reading; realising that she'd been up all night. Without permission, of course. Indeed, against his specific instructions.

Tearing the book from her hands. Dragging her upstairs, bending her over the end of the bed. Thrashing her soundly on the bare with his thick leather belt - for staying up late, and for disobeying him.

I mentioned my idea to Haron as I flicked on the machine to make a much-needed coffee. "Don't touch my book," was the grumpy refrain. That'd be 'no' to playing a scene, then...

PS No, we don't want anyone posting helpful hints about the ending to save Haron some reading time, thank you very much.

Spanked, on the tube
By Abel on 22 July 2007

Haron's a clever little minx. We'd been staying in a hotel out near Heathrow; as we finished breakfast, I checked that she'd brought her Oyster Card with her. (Those of you not familiar with London might need to know at this stage that Oyster is a pre-paid smartcard for public transport, which roughly halves trip costs).

She hadn't. Again. And the previous time it had happened, she'd been left in no doubt as to the consequences of future forgetfulness.

She fluttered her eyelashes, held my hand. To no avail. So she embarked on a long discussion of alternate ticket types on the tube - the pros and cons of travelcards, single tickets, buying a new Oyster card.

I became quite engrossed in trying to work out the right option as we walked back to our room. So engrossed, in fact, that I quite forgot about the spanking element of the discussion. Perfect diversionary tactics from the young lady, I'm sure you'll agree!

Fortunately I did then remember, and over my knee she went, but it was a close run thing!

The percentage game
By Abel on 26 July 2007

Inspecting my girl after a recent scene, I traced my fingers gently (and then not quite so gently) along the raised weal made by a rather high whack of the cane.

She'd been playing with someone who's an uncannily accurate administrator of severe strokes. "Oh well," I commented, "even the most experienced players have to be allowed the occasional miss."

This provoked debate, as you can imagine. I'm personally horrified when I lay the odd stroke astray - a little high, a little low, wrapping a little too far round. But it does happen, from time to time. And, of course, every girl has her own definition of 'accurate'. Woe betide anyone who stripes Haron's thighs, for example - whereas one dear friend simply loves to receive cane strokes there.

But what's an "acceptable" ratio? What's par for the course? Two inaccurate strokes in six of the best would be well and truly out of order: even one stray strike in a half-dozen would feel a little high.

Here's the thesis, then... The best we could come up with was the ninety per cent rule. That is: unless you're playing a scene in which the caning is deliberately (and by agreement) wild, *at least* nine strokes in ten must be entirely accurate. Any views, from either end of the rod?

Not all canes are scary
By Haron on 27 July 2007

Abel's father has been suffering from back problems recently, but yesterday he was talking about going back to the office, where they've missed him for the last couple of weeks.

"Perhaps you should take a cane," said Abel to him on the phone.

"Oh, yeah, that would scare them!" replied his dad with enthusiasm.

Abel's jaw dropped. He finished the conversation, then turned to me and said: "I actually meant he should get a walking stick, but it's not what *he* meant, is it?"

...Yes, the interest is definitely genetic.

Roald Dahl's spanking poetry
By Haron on 29 July 2007

Abel and I were both influenced in our kinkiness by Roald Dahl's writing. "Galloping Foxley", the short story from "Tales of the Unexpected", was one of my earliest introductions to the world of British boarding schools and their savage rituals. I found this stuff horrifyingly compelling. When Abel and I first met, I was delighted to find out that he was also fond of this story - up until then it had been my secret pleasure; I'd met nobody else who had read it.

When we became aware of the existence of a Roald Dahl museum, we had to go, even if it was unlikely to be entirely dedicated to the part of his writing that interested us the most.

It's a tiny place, and it isn't at all kinky, if you don't count a couple of pictures of larger-than-life canes on the walls. (Not that pictures of canes didn't amuse us. It doesn't take much to amuse us, really).

However, Abel stumbled upon a piece of spanking writing, which (as far as I remember) Dahl sent in a letter to a group of school kid correspondents, starting: "My teacher loved using the cane, He would thrash me again and again..."

I thought this was worth the admission price. Not that the rest of the museum wasn't interesting. I hadn't expected to find a local amateur theatre acting out "Galloping Foxley" for me, but the museum wasn't really geared for grown-ups.

Nice of them to give us a spanking poem, though.

Paddles at the ready

By Abel on 1 August 2007

A story from the Dallas News last week is just too remarkable - and has too much potential for sparking the spanko imagination - to let pass without comment. Apparently:

> Thirty-three high school cheerleaders from Dallas and Midland were involved in a scuffle at a camp in San Marcos this week... as the four-day Universal Cheerleaders Association camp was winding down. Squads from both Dallas Skyline and Midland high schools were staying in Blanco Hall... Eleven Midland girls and 22 Skyline girls were involved...

A school statement explained that "If disciplinary action is warranted, it will be taken according to the guidelines established in the student code of conduct."

Principals? Once the miscreants return to their respective schools, the girls being called in one by one to bend tight over the desk?

Coaches? At the start of the next practice session, working their way down the line of toe-touching cheerleaders, or waiting to dole out punishments in the changing rooms afterwards?

Disappointed fathers? Adding excruciating weight to the chorus of disapproval, in their daughters' bedrooms?

I scarcely know where to start, but Haron will be finding scholastic paddles descending rapidly in her direction, together with parental belts, whilst I try to figure out how this whole sorry state of affairs might have ended for the 33 young ladies concerned.

The Cheerleaders Association itself "did not plan to take action because [the incident] occurred at the end of camp." As for how they might have dealt with matters had the fighting broken out at any point *before* 'the end of camp'...

A traditional sort of school

By Haron on 2 August 2007

A notice in the Guardian talks about a former headmaster of a grammar school, 'a rather traditional establishment where the cathedral, the cane and the class curriculum loomed large'.

I thought it was a charming turn of phrase. "The three Cs of traditional education'. Or would that be the four Cs, seeing how the *class curriculum* is really two C words? I'm also almost as fond of cathedrals as I am of canes, but I'd never thought of uniting the two in one sentence.

Deliberate mischief

By Haron on 4 August 2007

This is an episode from "Life Begins", an autobiography by Jack de Manio.

> Before breakfast we had to draw our bed clothes back so that the beds aired. But on this particular morning I waited behind, carefully concealed. Then the terrible vengeance was enacted. I got jugs and jugs of water and went round two of the other dormitories and made sure that everybody else's bed was absolutely drenched. There was a terrific row, of course, when the headmaster came back, and I got a minor whacking. It was not very severe, as he was a rather humane man.

It isn't often that you hear about people being so deliberately bad, despite knowing the consequences. It's one thing to be caught doing something illicit but pleasant (such as drinking, or skipping lessons), but it's so very different to engage in this sort of mischief.

I very rarely think of any interesting schemes for our school scenes, but reading this has made me wonder what it would be like to have done something so calculated. Unfortunately, I don't think I'd get away with a 'minor whacking'.

The Master librarian's cane

By Abel on 5 August 2007

We took in a particularly beautiful library on our travels recently. A set of old, high-backed wooden chairs lined the room, as if awaiting a group of girls to be lectured - or, perhaps, scolded.

We pictured them there: freshly changed into their new uniforms, on the first day of their year of study. Competition for places in the Library College would be intense: only the very brightest, the most committed, would qualify for the honour.

They would each be seated, marvelling at the antique tomes and the magnificent ceiling. Then the grand wooden doors would swing open, and they would leap to their feet as the librarian came in: a tall, imposing figure in gown and mortar board.

He would welcome them. Outline the syllabus, inform them of their responsibilities. They'd learn the finest calligraphy; to transcribe, to catalogue, to illustrate to the highest standards. Positions in the greatest libraries in the world would be theirs for the asking at the end of their study. If they met his standards.

He'd invite questions; none would be forthcoming, the newcomers too scared of this daunting figure.

"There is one other thing," he would add, and they would all know what he had in mind. "You've probably heard tale of the disciplinary regime here." Girls shuffling nervously. "Yes, I do cane girls. And yes, I do cane them hard. Of that you can be sure. But you need to know. my two golden principles in relation to punishing my students. I presume that most of you were flogged at your previous school?'

Embarrassed nods, murmurs, red faces.

"I can't hear you".

A chorus; "Yes, Sir."

"Much better. So, my principles. The first is very simple:: a girl will never be punished for an honest mistake. But those of you who are repeatedly careless; who choose to be disrespectful or dishonest; *you* should fear the consequences."

Gulps; nervous clenching of fists. Staring at the carpet. Mental vows all round to uphold the highest standards.

"And the second is that I punish girls very infrequently. So much better that you live without the constant threat of the rod, so you can concentrate on your studies. But rest assured: when I do need to punish one of you, I shall do so with all due severity, in front of the rest of the group."

He would pause, speak more quietly. "It is rare that any girl is foolish enough to earn a second punishment during her time under my supervision."

And then he would walk down the line, looking each girl in the eyes. On reaching the end, he would turn - "Any further questions" met with an inevitable silence, before "Might I wish you every success." And he would walk through the still-open doors, closing them firmly behind him.

Running the reformatory

By Abel on 7 August 2007

"Oh, the stresses and strains of running a reformatory these days. The grants from the parish funds never quite cover the costs, you know. We're forever having to seek new ways of raising monies.

The Governors kindly approved my two latest schemes this morning. We'll have to see if they do the trick.

"Reform Your Daughter" is obvious enough. So many gentleman bemoan the challenges of bringing up young ladies in this modern era. At a dance last month, Sir C——, for example, bemoaned young Mary's impudence, even though she has been lately striped with his riding crop. And it struck me that we might just have the perfect solution here in the Reformatory – all the equipment, the location, to administer thrashings that could just resolve their difficulties.

How I can imagine the conversation: a girl led by her governess into her father's study. The gentleman reaching for the cane, administering a sound punishment. Then threatening that any repetition of her misconduct would result in a trip to the Master's office in the Reformatory. That should cure them – or, if not, add a few gold coins to our coffers here.

"Sponsor a Birching", though, is my favourite, a bright idea that came to me as I was watching young Victoria howl her way through her stripes last week. For a modest fee, our benefactor would be sent details in advance of the time of the forthcoming flogging, and the number of strokes to be administered. His (or, maybe her?) name would be read to the offender before the punishment commenced. And I am proud that the reformatory's staff have developed the girls' literary skills to the extent that the offender could be made to sit at a wooden desk to write a lengthy "thank you" letter to her sponsor immediately after her thrashing.

We have some premium services in mind, too: witnessing the birching might raise another guinea or two. And regular customers might even be allowed to wield the rod for a suitable fee. Of course, we'd have to be confident that they were proficient: we couldn't risk the punishment being too light, as we do have to comply with His Majesty's Regulations. One might have to interview – nay, inspect – a few of their servants to check that they knew how to administer discipline in a suitable competent and severe manner."

Abel (Master, Spankville Girls' Reformatory)
August, 1807

Cane stripes in the classroom

By Abel on 9 August 2007

A nice anecdote from a pupil at John Ruskin Grammar School, dating from the late 1960s:

> I was taught physics by Messrs Cook and Preddy - I believe it was Mr. Cook who used to administer the rank of lance-corporal, corporal, or sergeant to wrong-doers using a chalked cane.

That'd be one stripe, two stripes or three, for those of you unfamiliar with British army terminology...

Whipping the waitress?

By Abel on 11 August 2007

A spanking get-together last month was followed, that evening, by dinner in a particularly fine restaurant. (The pheasant, my darlings, was simply divine!)

The staff were immaculate: polite, attentive. Waitresses were neat in austere black skirts and white blouses, with that professionally ever-so-slightly-submissive demeanour that works so well for me for some strange reason.

Strange thing was, the waitress looking after our table was the spitting image of one of the girls who'd been caned at the earlier party. It wasn't actually her, but I wondered whether she knew what her virtually-identical twin sister was into.

There's an interesting angle on this, of course: the team from the Judicial Punishment Centre must *eat*. They'd choose a popular restaurant nearby.

Either, a young lady might find herself waiting on their table at lunchtime, knowing precisely who they were but they oblivious to the fact that she was due to be one of their afternoon visitors.

Or, perhaps better, a girl may have to head painfully to work in the evening, after her judicial flogging, wiping away the tears - only to find that the officers who'd punished her had arrived for their dinner...

The school prefect's cane

By Haron on 12 August 2007

Yesterday we ended up in our favourite second-hand bookshop, and completely cleared it out of anything even vaguely related to any facet of our kink. One of our precious finds was a book by A. Davidson "Blazers, Badges and Boaters: a Pictorial History of School Uniform".

It does have many fine pictures, which will be very helpful in assembling uniforms for my future imaginary schools. It also has the following amusing passage in the chapter on distinctions in uniform:

> The prefect's most terrifying insignia of authority, albeit on the periphery of school uniform, is the cane. Its swishing sound is enough to set many a junior's teeth on edge, even if it is not applied to his back seat. The cane, when it is applied, proves a far harsher instrument of punishment in the hands of an eighteen year old boy than in those of a doddering old schoolmaster.

I think, my own doddering old schoolmaster will be quick to dispute the fact that any eighteen-year-old could give a more painful caning than him. It would make an awfully amusing competition, actually. Trust me, I would not bet on the youngster.

Elvis in trouble

By Haron on 16 August 2007

My desk calendar claims that today is 30 years since the death of Elvis. (It obviously doesn't subscribe to the theory that he was an alien and left Earth for home on this day). A clipping I've kept from one of the pile of papers I've read recently is of a letter from a teacher who started work in a large London comprehensive school in 1956, the year in which Elvis rose to prominence:

> I shall never forget the elderly senior mistress coming into the staff room one morning and saying sternly: 'I must speak to a boy called Elvis Presley because he has carved his name on every desk in the school.'

I'm guessing that when the angry schoolmistress went out looking for blood, no Elvis impersonators would have been around to take his place...

A-Level Results Morning

By Haron on 16 August 2007

Abel is away; he has clearly been watching nubile young ladies opening their exam results on hotel television. Here's what he emailed me this morning:

> From: abel@spankingwriters.com
>
> To: haron@spankingwriters.com
>
> Sent: 16 August 2007 07:53
>
> Subject: A-Level results
>
> ----
>
> Your father would like to see you in his study now."
>
> The butler escorts her, knocking politely on the door.
>
> She enters. The heavy door is closed behind her.
>
> He sits at the far end of the room, behind his desk.
>
> There, in front of him, the crisp unopened envelope containing her results.
>
> Next to the envelope, a cane. And a bottle of champagne.
>
> "I do so hope that we will be able to *celebrate*, my dear."

He takes the antique silver letter-opener, carefully slices open the envelope. He reads the results, raising an eyebrow, then looks up at her...

Watching my girl's caning

By Abel on 17 August 2007

Haron took a pretty hard thrashing from a friend recently.

Actually, strike that. Haron took quite the hardest caning I've ever seen her get. Stripped, tied in position, an improbable number of strokes laid on in rapid succession at full strength from a hard, experienced, unforgiving player.

Whilst I stood silently to the side, and watched.

Interest experience, that, observing one's beloved taking such a severe, relentless whacking. The flogging had been long-anticipated: her sentence pronounced by email, the date fixed, the event anticipated with dread curiosity.

My natural instincts, of course, were to rush to protect my girl - especially once she started to struggle. To *really* struggle.

Yet I didn't. I just watched. Saw her writhe, heard her cry out. Observed as he took her into a deep, dark, beaten place.

And then - soon, yet an eternity after starting - he finished: the binds came off, and I could comfort her. Tell her how beautiful she'd looked, how brave she'd been. Held her especially tight. Re-assured; soothed; admired her stripes. And before very long she was bouncing around as usual, a quite spectacular set of marks and a wincing reluctance to sit down the only visible evidence of her recent ordeal.

A school notice

By Haron on 18 August 2007

The email I got from Abel a few days ago (copied also to our friend Martha, who is coming up for the weekend):

<u>School notice - [Name of our village] Academy</u>

Girls are notified that there will be a full uniform inspection by their housemaster at 4.30pm this coming Saturday.

Any recent misconduct reported by other masters at the school will also be discussed at this time.

Hmm, my bottom is twitching just a bit...

A whipping for the servant girl?

By Abel on 20 August 2007

Diarist Samuel Pepys was not a happy man on this day in 1663. His brother had helped to find him a new servant girl:

> "she told my wife her name was Jinny, by which name we shall call her. I think a good likely girl, and a parish child of St. Bride's, of honest parentage, and recommended by the churchwarden."

Unfortunately, within the day, his judgement had been shown to be incorrect:

> "This evening the girle that was brought to me to-day for so good a one, being cleansed of lice this day by my wife, and good, new clothes put on her back, she run away from Goody Taylour that was shewing her the way to the bakehouse, and we heard no more of her."

The following day, Pepys dined at his brother's house and "told him how my girl has served us which he sent me, and directed him to get my clothes again, and get the girl whipped."

First, catch your girl. The local parish constable obliged, but the diarist had obviously decided to be lenient however and merely "stripped her and sent her away."

I suppose this classes as a happy ending.

The cane as a memory aid

By Haron on 21 August 2007

"What were you supposed to remind me?" Abel said to Martha. She looked completely blank and slightly flustered. I couldn't help her: I hadn't been around when he'd told her to remember whatever it was.

"Well?" he demanded.

"I don't know!" Martha squeaked.

"Fine," he walked over to the arm-chair, where a couple of canes were hanging by their crooks, left over from our scene the day before. "Bend over the couch, I'm going to cane you until you remember what it was."

I suppose, I could have been more sympathetic at my friend's predicament, but I couldn't help giggling, in a horrified sort of way. Martha, growing more and more flustered, bent over the arm of the sofa. "Hold her hands," Abel told me - and I did. More to offer her comfort than to hold her down, because she's a brave girl, and doesn't leap about during a caning anything as much as I do.

"Can you remember what it was yet?" asked Abel, tapping the cane across the seat of her jeans.

"No!" she moaned. "Was it about... er... No, I can't remember!"

"Let's see if I can remind you."

He aimed, drew the cane back and delivered a single, solid whack.

"Oww!" Martha squeezed my hands tight. "Ouch! Binoculars! You wanted to remember to take binoculars when we go out tomorrow!"

"Good girl." Abel sounded delighted. "See? See how the cane focuses your mind?"

We all laughed, and he departed into the kitchen, while Martha and I shared a commiserating cuddle. "From now on you could use 'binoculars' as the answer to anything," she said. "Anything you ever forget. 'Do you have anything to say, young lady?' 'Binoculars'!"

I think it's as good an answer to the main question of life, the universe and everything, as any. Unfortunately, I have a feeling that Abel has now received practical proof that to get the answer to life, the universe and everything is to give somebody a good old whack with the cane.

Quick, quick, slow

By Abel on 23 August 2007

How we must shock people sometimes. Take dinner last night, in a local hostelry, with kinky friends.

Quite shameless, we started to discuss Haron's recent hard caning from a friend. I was surprised when she piped up that, severe as it had seemed from my vantage point, it had been a less daunting thrashing than many I'd given her.

Why, I'd wondered? Were a stranger's blows less intense than a lover's?

Pace, it seemed, was part of the answer. Our friend had laid on his improbable number of strokes metronomically, in very quick succession. My canings are typically much slower - more calculated, perhaps: allowing a girl to savour each stroke to its peak, mentally and physically, before she takes her next stripe.

And there was another dimension. With our friend, the silence had been broken only by the swish of the strokes, and by Haron's shrieks and sobs. He himself had remained silent. Whereas I, of course, talk incessantly: commenting, counting, scolding. The voice, it seems, is the harshest implement.

The librarian and his cane(s)

By Abel on 25 August 2007

I love writing blog entries with Haron around. We spark ideas, toy with phrases - and sometimes moderate each other's ideas.

Take my recent musings on the strict Master Librarian. I ended up writing a line in which he, rather menacingly, explained how rarely a caned girl returned for a second punishment. I'd originally toyed with a slightly different phrase:

"I always present a girl with her cane at the end of her punishment. It acts as a reminder and a deterrent. It is rare that she has to bring it back to me to be applied a second time."

I rather liked this - especially combined with the idea of a nail above each dormitory bed, on which the canes were to hang: an ever-visible mark for the girls who had been thrashed.

So did Haron, but counselled that a librarian with a seemingly endless supply of new canes might just possibly be seen as a tad pervy. And, as that wasn't at all the impression I was trying to create, the lines came out. I think she was right, but it was a close-run thing.

His cane, his gown, his mortarboard

By Haron on 26 August 2007

As I mentioned last week, our friend Martha and I were summoned in front of the Housemaster for a uniform inspection, and to discuss the various sins that had been reported by other teachers.

We admitted to having been seen drunk and disorderly at a ball the previous term. Martha was sentenced to four strokes for this; I was a prefect, and thus got six.

Added to these were the strokes for our uniform infractions: I had an incorrect hair grip (a genuine mistake: I'm not yet used to having my hair at a length that requires grips, so I didn't think twice about picking up a rather ornate, inappropriate clasp), and got one stroke for that. Martha had complicated issues with her shirt - lack of button, messed up collar, things like that - and her socks were not pulled up properly. She got two additional strokes.

While Martha bent over for her caning, bravely taking the first turn, I caught myself on a completely inappropriate thought. You would imagine that I would be full of compassion for my friend. Right?

Or at least that, with seven strokes to come, I would focus on the painful caning I was about to get.

...Right?

Well, no. In fact, all I could do was look at Abel - dressed splendidly in a suit, an academic gown and a brand new, never-before-worn mortarboard - and think: "Oooh boy, that Housemaster is so hot. He's hot, hot, hot. Will you look at that. Mrrr-eow."

I might have day-dreamed through Martha's entire caning like that.

Obviously, my own punishment, which followed in due course, woke me right up: there's nothing that makes you remember your priorities like seven slashes of the cane over your white cotton knickers.* Still, I was quite surprised to have become so distracted.

Oh, well. If spanking play no longer brought any surprises any more, what would be the point of following the same familiar tracks?

* Except maybe those same strokes delivered on the bare, but the knickers were hitched right up anyway, so I don't know about that.

Prefectorial punishments

By Abel on 27 August 2007

Having been a prefect at a British public school in the mid-80s, I was intrigued to spot so many the similarities with the Prefects' Charter online from a similar establishment, some thirty years before.

It pointed out that prefects "will normally continue in office as long as they are in the School but the Headmaster will remove a Prefect from the Board where this seems desirable or necessary". I can imagine that such removal would have been a rather painful procedure.

Saturday detention, overlooked

By Abel on 29 August 2007

Waking up with Haron in a rented apartment not long ago, I glanced out of the window to check the weather. (Europe, summertime: yep, it was raining).

Opposite was a large, imposing, austere–looking building - which, it being a Saturday, was completely deserted. I imagined it as some educational institution - soon to be filled with students called in for a weekend detention. Inevitably, the morning would culminate with a queue of girls outside the Headmaster's office, awaiting their five minutes of shame.

That room up there - top floor, far end of the corridor. That'd be the one. He'd draw the blinds, of course, but on a clear day the retort of the cane and the punished pupils' squeals might well echo around the courtyard...

Paddling both sides

By Haron on 30 August 2007

An article in a Guardian magazine last weekend recommended that "to avoid paddling one side, try paddling over a short distance with your eyes closed."

Oh, yeah. It was an article on kayaking.

Please, Abel, do not try to paddle with your eyes closed. You won't travel very far, anyway - though I might. Vertically.

Stiffening the School Tawse

By Abel on 31 August 2007

It seems as though obscure folks of a certain age feel impelled to include spanking references in their autobiographies, perhaps to boost sales to the likes of us. A quick bookshop browse can invariably turn up a startle.

Take the following description of the tawses in use at the school attended by David Findlay Clark, taken from "Remember Who You Are":

> "Some were so hardened by soaking in brine that they could be used as pointers in class"

Now, I'm familiar with said technique for making birches more flexible; it's fascinating to see that it has the opposite results for the tawse. I may have to experiment with one of ours to see if I can replicate the results.

The same book contained an interesting reference to the daughter of the rather fierce Headmaster being withdrawn from her father's establishment. One wonders to what extent his strict approach at school was replicated at home.

Grounds for a girl to be caned

By Abel on 4 September 2007

The Ross family were posted from the UK to Kuala Lumpur, despatching Rosemary "to a boarding school in the Scottish border region until she was nearly 16". Thereafter, she was completed her education in Malaysia, where as a sixth former at the Victoria Institute in 1960-61 she "was the school's first and only British girl".

Rosemary describes how she slapped a prefect who had taken her...

> "to task for loitering in the Sixth Form Block at recess. I claimed I hadn't known the rule which had come out the day previously (in my absence) and he called me a liar! I asked

him to repeat it and he had the cheek to do so and I saw red! I was summoned by Dr. Lewis [the Headmaster] who was sympathetic to the aspersion cast on my honesty and integrity, but was obliged to hand me over to the prefects...The School Captain... gave me Detention and 1000 lines - each one an apology for my sins. I squeezed all of them on one side of A4 paper in the tiniest writing possible!"

I have a rather different outcome in mind: "Miss Ross, how would a girl have been dealt with for such behaviour at your former school in Scotland?"

"With the tawse, Headmaster."

"Indeed. And you will doubtless realise that we use corporal punishment here, too, for the most serious incidents of misconduct."

"Yes, sir."

And then she would have been told to bend over the desk, for four strokes across her skirt with Dr Lewis's whippiest rattan. By far the most effective form of lines, methinks. Mr Ross might well have been rather displeased when she returned home from school, too.

Haron and I are due to visit Malaysia on holiday before very long. I think a browse round a bookstore or two, Educational History Section, may be in order.

Sneaking a spanking at the in-laws'

By Haron on 5 September 2007

Abel and I live in the sort of conditions that any spanking enthusiast would call privileged: we have the house to ourselves, its walls are thick, the neighbours are quite deaf, and there is space enough to swing a cane in pretty much every room.

From time to time, however, we go to visit our respective parents. This is where we get a glimpse of what other, less fortunate spankos with big families have to deal with. Zero privacy, other than in our bedroom; the walls are made out of paper,* and it's easier to forget about real spanking altogether for a few days than to attempt a little bit of play.

Except we can't forget about spanking, or limit ourselves with whispering stories to each other. I mean, I guess we could, but we refuse to be limited by the circumstances.

Our recent parental home adventure was a couple of weeks ago in Abel's parents' house. It was all rather spontaneous. One morning, before everybody else woke up, I was lying on the bed reading. Bottom-up, as one does; still dressed for bed in my knickers and his shirt.

Abel was dealing with his email. He must have read something exciting,** because he walked over to me and landed a big ol' swat on my behind.

"Take those knickers down," he said.

"Oh?" I said. "We're, um, not alone?"

"Don't care," he said. Boy, that email must have been really good.

I wriggled my knickers down, and waited to find out what he would use. A hand-spanking was out of question: the naked-skin-slapping-naked-skin noise is quite loud, even if you don't know what exactly it is. We hadn't packed any canes. The nearest birch tree was way out of reach. As far as I was concerned, he was stuck.

Not so, it appeared. He picked up the electric cord from our camera, doubled it up, and told me to brace myself.

Now, headspace-wise, electric cords don't do anything for me; they don't feature on my fantasy horizons. However, when we're talking about pure physical side of spanking, I don't mind what an implement is, as long as it produces the right sensation.

Or, should I say, the *wrong* sensation: the infernal burning, the branding pain, the flaming cuts... It was quite horrid. And, of course, I had to stay absolutely quiet throughout the ordeal: we didn't want people to come running to my rescue, did we?

Although Abel normally insists that I stay as still as possible for my whipping, we had to get rid of the rule here: I can be either still or quiet, but not both. If I couldn't yell, I had to wriggle, a lot. I enjoyed the freedom, though it took me a lot not to howl at a couple of particularly evil cuts.

The stripes afterwards were quite pretty, and I squirmed all the way through breakfast, but there was nothing to show for it only a couple of hours later. Other than our big grins, I suppose.

* In my parents' place you can hear the neighbour three floors up practising her piano. Every note.
** Which one of you correspondents has been getting me smacked? Hmm?

Horsing around

By Abel on 6 September 2007

I really don't understand young people today. There we were, at a perfectly respectable event over the recent Bank Holiday weekend, when the group of teenage girls next to us in the crowd of 50,000 started misbehaving in the most disgraceful way.

Their game involved one girl being hoisted onto the bent-over back of another, then held tight whilst the remaining young ladies in the group spanked her backside. Hard. They then swapped, ensuring each of their jean-clad bottoms ended up being soundly swatted in turn. Their shrieks filled the air.

Shameful conduct. I was so taken aback that I had to watch carefully, to take in the horrifying scene in full so that I could report back to you. What *is* the world coming to?

The parental rotan

By Abel on 8 September 2007

A mixing blessing with my job is that I end up travelling fairly extensively. That's good, in that I have a deep-seated wanderlust and love exploring. It's bad, very bad, in terms of the amount of time it keeps me away from home.

My current trip sees me in Singapore thanks to a customer who booked flights and hotels for me, then cancelled the event I was supposed to be running. As the travel was non-refundable, it seemed rather a shame to waste it!

I've already had one of the biggest startles ever, on the way in from the airport yesterday morning. The breakfast presenters were discussing a news item about some teenagers who'd misbehaved. "Last time they were naughty, they were locked in their bedrooms", commented the female half of the presenting duo - somewhat to my horror. She continued:

> "Do you think it's now time for the rotan? It's still the school holidays, so call us. How do your parents punish you?"

Then, she turned to her co-presenter, asking, "Did you get the rotan when you were growing up?"

He didn't, and quickly played the next song rather than asking her the same question. Drat! And the cab arrived at my hotel before the phone-in began.

The rotan - the local name for the cane - still appears to be in surprisingly wide use here for parental discipline. According to one report from the Singapore Sunday Times, hardware stores are the place I need to head while I'm here for my souvenir hunting:

Cane facts

COST: 50 cents, made in China and guaranteed to last a lifetime.

WHERE TO BUY: At neighbourhood shops selling household items. Usually found stacked with the brooms and mops on sale or hanging, tied together, from the ceiling of the shop.

NEW LOOK: Rotans today have a plastic hook at the end, which comes in a variety of colours.

At that price, pennies per cane in UK currency (even if the report is a few years old), I may have to purchase a bundle. (And if there's anyone reading in Singapore, do please recommend a suitable shop)!

Bottom-warming after a bottom-warming
By Haron on 9 September 2007

In a recent review of a new car, the journalist expresses his bafflement with the position of the button for the seat-heater: "...the idea of placing seat-heater controls where little fingers can turn them on over and over again as a hilarious joke to see Mummy getting a hot bottom smacks of sadism. Or is that the point..."

Yes, I wonder. Though actually, I've always found heated seats really nice for a freshly smacked bottom. I know you're *supposed* to want to sit on ice, but having my bottom and thighs warmed gently and gradually takes the edge off the sharper sort of pain.

Leaning against the radiator accomplishes the same thing, but I get spanked for that.

What I did on my holiday
By Abel on 10 September 2007

Singapore's a fascinating city, with plenty to keep visitors from indolence. Like, for example, the Chinatown area – a fascinating mix of old and new, local and touristy, temples mixing with mosques interspersed with restaurants and souvenir stalls.

And then there are the local shopping malls, where few western visitors seem to tread. Yet when hunting for hardware shops yesterday, my spanko intuition suggested that – other options having failed – these might be fertile grounds. And so it was, a display of washing up utensils giving way to a far more interesting basket of products.

Do you want the good news or the bad news? OK, dear readers, let's start by being positive. Urged on by numerous comments on my previous post, I had located the famous local rotan, beloved of Singaporean parents. Even better, they're far meaner little implements than I'd expected – a little over two feet (60cm) long, very whippy but with sufficient bite to cut home their message.

But bad news, too: they only had three canes on offer, and one of those was cracked (provoking most inappropriate thoughts about daddy breaking the rotan in mid-use, and sending his daughter to the neighbouring store to buy a replacement, before continuing her punishment).

Not to be deterred, I continued to the next mall, the mammoth People's Place Complex. After much frustrated wandering, I spied the metro station, and was about to give up. And then, there in the distance, glimmering in Xanadu-like splendour, I saw it: the outdoor hardware stall.

Twelve canes, my friends, with their kaleidoscopic plastic handles: reds, yellows, greens, blues! (I imagined a schoolgirl, squirming uncomfortably at her desk after her caning, as her teacher read the freshly-delivered note to the class: "You are to return to the Headmaster's office. Apparently he used the wrong-coloured rotan, and needs to correct his error."). The poor girl on the cash desk positively trembled, putting on her very best behaviour as she wrapped my purchases.

And even more good news! Praise be to the Singaporean finance ministry, for prices have remained at the levels quoted in 1999: the equivalent of two pounds sterling capturing my entire hoard. (More inappropriate thoughts at this point, of a local girl given her weekly pocket money by her father, minus the "50 cents deducted for the cost of the rotan I had to buy"). I wonder how much I'd get on eBay for an "Authentic Singaporean rotan punishment canes, as used for parental discipline"?!

I view it as a matter of public service, really. Think of all the local cuties who'll be spared the rods that I'm exporting... And think of the painful pleasures awaiting those of you who put in requests...

Coffee, cake and a smack

By Haron on 11 September 2007

This conversation happened between Abel and a very cute barrista at a Starbucks last week, before he set off on his trip to Asia.

> Abel: Please, can I have a fork for my cake?
>
> Barrista (nodding at her helper, a sweet-looking girl): Why, hasn't she given you one?
>
> Abel: No. (To cute helper) Sorry, I didn't mean to get you into trouble.
>
> Barrista: That's OK, I'll give her a smack later.

Do you get a feeling Abel is a spanking conversation magnet?

To the German couple in room 766

By Abel on 12 September 2007

Just because the adjoining door separating our rooms is locked, it doesn't mean that your room is soundproof.

Yes, I have heard the slapping noises at regular intervals over the past 48 hours. Very clearly.

No, I don't think you're clapping something on the TV: it's too regular, too drawn-out, and the plaintive little feminine yelps after each smack leave little to my experienced imagination.

Yes, young lady: when we emerged from our rooms at the same time and found ourselves waiting for the elevator together, I did think you'd look good in school uniform.

And yes, he is a *lot* older than you, isn't he?

No, please don't stop. I'm sure she deserves it.

And no, I'm sure she didn't sit at all comfortably at dinner last night. And the restaurant had hard wooden chairs, you say? What a shame...

No, I'm sure you're not enjoying being spanked. You doesn't look like one of those *perverts*...

You know, I can recommend just the place in Chinatown if you want to find a nice authentic local implement with which to stripe her - or I have a plentiful supply if you'd care to send her next door to ask politely for a caning.

And don't worry: I won't tell a soul.

The threat of a ruler

By Haron on 13 September 2007

I read a short piece recently that discussed the fashion for women to go clubbing wearing T-shirts with extremely rude slogans: things like "Your Bloke's Had Me", and other charming messages.

Among others, the writer says: "There are warnings to males, such as 'You Better Not Lie - I Carry a Ruler'".

I did a double take, I admit. Is threatening men with spanking really that popular? It only occurred to me after a minute that they probably meant it completely differently. As in, um, measuring things.

I like my interpretation more.

Welcome to my other world
By Abel on 13 September 2007

Apologies to the client with whom I was working the other week, for any embarrassment I may inadvertently have caused. My lack of knowledge of Microsoft Word means that when I clicked on "File", ready to "Save" the document we'd been working on together, the menu displayed my four most recent files.

I don't think she blushed because of "C:\...\Actions".

"C:\...\The Girl from the Choir" doubtless hinted at my deep-seated interest in Gregorian chant.

But I doubt "C:\..\Whippings in the eighteenth century" left much to the imagination.

And why, oh why, had I chosen to plug my laptop into the lovely projector in their Board Room whilst we were editing the document, thus making sure the titles were displayed on the big screen in the largest letters imaginable?

The repeat offender
By Haron on 17 September 2007 in The Punishment Book

Certain misdeeds chase me like demons of doom: most of the time I get punished, it's for things I've already done wrong before, and suffered the consequences for, possibly several times.

It would be tempting to say: "Well, obviously, spanking doesn't work if you re-offend," but it's not so simple.

I don't react well to being expected to reform once and for all after only one occasion. Whether there's a spanking involved or not, the "go forth and sin no more, EVER" approach only makes me resentful: if I *could* avoid certain undesirable behaviour for the rest of my life, then I would, punishment or no punishment. I expect to live for a long time, though, and I don't anticipate spending any part of my life as a saint - which would certainly be the implication if all my usual quirks and flaws were corrected forever within the next few years.*

One of my pet hates is hearing the phrase "Obviously, last time I didn't punish you hard enough." I don't hate it in a love/hate way: it just irritates the hell out of me. I'm not receptive to punishment when I'm irritated.

On the other hand, the phrase "I let you off last time", said in a hurt, regretful tone shreds me into tiny little pieces.

This is what Abel said to me upon discovering that the space-shuttle-taking-off noise emanating from our coffee machine was caused by an overflowing dead coffee drawer. That drawer and I have a painful history. Our most recent clash happened about two months ago, when the mould creatures that had evolved there had started to take over the inner workings of the machine, no doubt with designs upon the rest of the kitchen.

I was horrified, but Abel must have decided that my terror was a punishment in itself. He pondered dealing with me after all, but in the end he let it go. This time I neither expected such mercy, nor was I given it.

Despite the early hour - the machine had choked on our morning coffee - and the tantalising smell of cooking toast, Abel gripped me by the wrist and took me upstairs. I went as meekly as a Gorean slavegirl. It was then that he uttered the shattering, injured reproach: I let you off last time. I could have cried if I wasn't so pissed off with myself for the unnecessary pain I had brought upon myself.

The retribution was swift and to the point: no delay, no lecture; he simply made me assume the position - over the edge of the bed, - announced the sentence - ten strokes of the cane - and delivered the cuts slowly enough for each one to sink in, but quickly enough that the waiting didn't border on cruelty. One of the advantages of having already been punished for a particular offence is that you've already heard the lecture.

Do I intend to avoid allowing the coffee monsters to breed again for as long as possible? Yes, absolutely. It's not as though I revel in growing penicillin; I'm going to do my best at keeping an eye on it.

Do I expect that it was the last time I'll ever slip up? Not for an instant: there are so many things in life that need keeping an eye on that my attention is bound to slip at one point or another. I'm not applying for sainthood yet.

Do I expect to be punished when the unlucky day comes? Oh, yes. All I can do is make sure it's not any time soon.

* You don't expect I have enough flaws to last me for more than a decade at a push, right?

Floggings on the Royal Mile

By Abel on 18 September 2007

A quite remarkable location for a startle while I was in Edinburgh for the Festival the other week... I wandered past the "Police Information Centre" on the Royal Mile - a police station, but with an added museum to make it seem friendlier to the passing masses strolling from the Castle to Holyrood.

I peered through the window, knowing from past experience that judicial museums often feature *interesting* exhibits. And there it was! In full view of the thousands of festival-goers: the original 19th century whipping bench!

Offenders lay along the low bench - around six feet long, two feet wide, only two feet or so high. Two leather straps were tied across their bodies to hold them down during their flogging. Further stout leather ties on the legs at one end would hold their feet firmly in position as the blows fell.

I nearly pointed out that their birch rod looked rather inauthentically stiff, although I'd guess it was made to the original design. I was minded to suggest that they soaked it overnight, but decided I didn't want the friendly police officer questioning me too closely as to how I knew such things...

Proper training

By Haron on 19 September 2007

On Sunday I got well and truly startled in a cab home from the train station.

In the usual chatty manner the driver wanted to know where I'd been, where I was going, and whether I had any time for chasing boys.

I didn't tell him that I'd just spent a whole day in London dressing up as a schoolgirl and being spanked. I only said that I was away, but now I was looking forward to seeing my husband, who had also returned from a long trip a few hours earlier.

We pulled up in front of the house. "Has he got a kettle on for you inside, then?" asked the cabbie. "Are you training him proper?"

I grinned: "Oh, aye, working on it."

"If you need help like, I've got a whip in the boot."

I don't think my jaw dropped too far. I thanked him politely, and said I had plenty of whips of my own. And then I went into the house, to have Abel's purchases from Singapore tested on me.

If only the cabbie knew...

SSS in Singapore

By Abel on 22 September 2007

To the surprise of passers-by, I burst out laughing in the middle of Singapore's Orchard Road shopping area last week. The reason? A sign outside Swensen's, a family restaurant, that read:

> Student Happy Hour! Check out our special SSS treat and be happily indulged.

I'm used to the concept of frequent flyer points, hotel loyalty schemes and the like. But this has to be the first time

I've seen promotions specifically targeted at members of the soc.sexuality.spanking newsgroup.

"Would you care to choose your waitress for the evening, sir? Here's a little notepad and pen to keep a tally of any mistakes she might make. The canes are kept behind the front desk - just ask when you need one."

It seems it actually stands for "Soup, Side, Sundae". Like I want to believe that?

Talking of Singaporean restaurants, how come it was only as I sat reading a magazine at the airport waiting to leave that I discovered 'Barracks'? This posh new dining spot is set in (yes, you guessed it) a converted army barracks, where "the over-attentive wait staff were all dressed in school uniforms". I'm feeling quite faint at the thought of discipline being meted out to the serving girls back in the days of the colonial officers' mess...

Meanwhile, the recently-refurbished National Museum had one particularly evocative display: an old desk and chair from the Singapore Chinese Girls' School, together with two school reports from consecutive terms in 1936. The second stated that there was "considerable improvement shown this term" by the young lady concerned; my rotan explorations made me wonder what had led her to become more focused, and left me concerned about her "rather untidy" report for Arithmetic.

The delights of short-sightedness

By Abel on 24 September 2007

My eyesight's definitely going. (No comments about age, please. OR ELSE!). I didn't take my glasses with me to Singapore, as I don't really use them other than for driving and to look authoritative in scenes. That led to me discovering an unexpected benefit of being increasingly short-sighted, via a couple of interesting startles as my brain inserted the phrase it instinctively thought should be there into the words I was actually reading.

First up, a shocking discovery in the hotel's club lounge, when I spied an astonishing magazine:

"Spanking and Finance".

('Banking', obviously, as my eyes adjusted).

And then – admittedly not spanking-related, but what the heck... One of the subways on Orchard Road, the main shopping street, is plastered with adverts showing an attractive naked woman. The slogan? "Brazilian waxing." Only yours truly quite genuinely read it the first time as "Brazilian wanking".

At this rate, I could even begin to enjoy golf…
By Abel on 26 September 2007

Haron and I spent a lovely week in Scotland on holiday last month. Neither of us plays golf, but we holed up in a resort that's next to a very famous course. Needless to say, we were tempted out onto the putting green in front of the hotel.

I won. The margin of victory? Yep, you guessed it: six strokes. I'm not sure the hotel management are that used, however, to the victor collecting his winnings by bending his wife over next to the eighteenth hole for the necessary number of whacks with a golf club.

(Me? With my reputation? In a hotel whose female staff all wear kilts? Scarcely a moment passed without reveries of their predecessors being tawsed, in presumably stricter times when the hotel opened 100 or so years ago).

The punishment parade and other London startles

By Abel on 28 September 2007

Startles – those moments when vanilla life generates a comment that excites one's kinky interest - don't have to involve spanking per se. Take two vignettes from a day out in London last weekend.

The first was in the new Household Cavalry Museum, on the caption describing a clock:

> The time is set to 4pm commemorating the moment in 1894 when Queen Victoria, having found the Guard gambling and drinking, ordered a daily inspection at 4pm for the next 100 years. Known as the 'Punishment Parade', it has become a tradition that continues today.

Later, lunching in Imli (our second favourite Indian restaurant), the next table was occupied by a gentleman with his much younger lady friend. She was just 'my type', with a lovely Northern accent. The dialogue as I overhead it went something like this:

Him: So how old is your mother?

Her: 42. She was only 17 when she had me.

Him: Wow, she's only two years older than me.

(Pause)

Him.   And how old's your sister?

Her: 17.

He didn't say much for a minute or two, but I could see his mind on overdrive with all sorts of most inappropriate thoughts. As, indeed, was mine.

Shopping tips for tops
By Abel on 1 October 2007

I discovered a wonderful money-saving technique today, which I feel I must share with other gentlemen whose young ladies are prone to drift into clothes shops.

Haron and I were out strolling. We chanced upon a selection of stylish garments in a sale. She picked out two pairs of trousers to try on... then realised: "But I can't go into a communal changing room like *this*."

'*This*', in case you were wondering, was with a freshly striped backside. Very freshly. *Very* striped.

So now you know. Whip your girl soundly before heading towards the stores, and your wallet will be as safe as can be.

Being a Head Girl
By Haron on 2 October 2007

While we had Martha staying over the weekend, I wasn't feeling great, preferred to abstain from being spanked. Luckily, this didn't mean that I had to be excluded from any scenes.

At one point I found myself being appointed a Head Girl, and was summoned to witness the punishment of a schoolgirl called Rebecca. She had, apparently, returned from holiday late, having been let off with a warning after a similar offence the previous term.

After the girl had been duly lectured, and made to bend over the bed in her dorm, the Headmaster turned to me.

"Head girl," he said. "Remind me what the usual punishment is for this offence."

I had no idea, and didn't particularly want to land Rebecca in more trouble than was fair - at the same time, I didn't want Martha to be disappointed with not getting enough. I gave Abel an elaborate shrug. He helpfully stuck four fingers up.

"Four strokes, sir," I said, wondering why he was going so low.

"Very well," he said. "Since this is the second offence, and my lenience last term was obviously abused, I will double the punishment. Eight strokes."

Ah. This explained the low number.

The poor girl was very brave. It was a hard caning: it started out simply firm, but the second half of it was truly impressive. The cane was going high up, and biting into Rebecca's bottom with solid cracking sounds. I could see each pink welt form. It made quite a difference not to be worried about my own caning, recently administered or yet to come. Instead, I got the full voyeuristic pleasure from seeing a pretty girl's bottom neatly striped.

When the caning was over, I was dismissed, while the Headmaster stayed to lecture the poor girl. When Abel reappeared in the corridor, we exchanged a grin and a high-five. I'm sure that isn't something Headmasters and Head Girls do, but it was pretty satisfying nonetheless.

Tender in the restaurant

By Abel on 4 October 2007

I can't even go to a restaurant without kinky thoughts leaping to mind. That was certainly true recently in Browns in Edinburgh, a branch of one of my favourite chains, who describe their Minute Steak with the wonderfully-descriptive phrase:

'Thin tender rump'.

For some reason, that made me snigger. I can't possibly imagine why. I'm presuming that the dish must be cooked by the same chef who batters the haddock and crushes the new potatoes...

Anyway, it's a good thing I'm not a waiter. Picture me arriving at a table, laden with meals, asking "Whose is the thin tender rump?" or, worse, "Who'll be having the thin tender rump this evening?"

Hey, hard limit!

By Haron on 5 October 2007

This morning in bed Abel and I were lazily planning a possible scene later.

"You can be a schoolgirl who has done something really atrocious," he said dreamily.

"Mmm-hmm. Like what?"

"Let's say you threw stones at the Headmaster's..."

I thought he would suggest the Head's car, and was ready to agree. Instead, he finished the sentence:

"...the Headmaster's *cat.*"

Yeah, right. I'm more likely to chuck a stone at the Headmaster himself. Or better yet, Abel, for suggesting something like that!

No imaginary animals were hurt in the writing of this post.

Shades of spanking

By Abel on 6 October 2007

How strange. My spanking imaginings are usually full of light: girls are whipped in rooms into which rays of sun shine through large picture windows, or in dingy cellars illuminated by bright fluorescent strips.

I've obviously been looking at too many trendy black and white photos lately, for last night's dream took on different hues.

The girl was tied down: bent right over, shaking, vulnerable. But the room itself was pitch black, save for three sharp white lights. The first was directed straight at her backside, marking out the target area. A pool of brightness illuminated the officer with his cane. And the final beam shone right into in her eyes, lest she be tempted to close them in a vain attempt to block out the experience.

Long haul, maximum discomfort

By Abel on 8 October 2007

Anyone here ever taken one of those interminable long-haul flights to some distant land, which stop over for a couple of hours at some randomly-chosen midpoint for a change of crew? Take London to Sydney, via Bangkok, or something similar?

A conversation with a colleague who's about to head off on some such journey inspired a naughty little fantasy. The girls of a distinguished Scottish* Academy would be heading around the world for an exchange trip to their sister school. School uniforms themselves being too impractical, the young ladies would dress identically in white polo shirts with the school crest, and navy blue tracksuits.

It would be a large group – perhaps the entire Lower Sixth would be travelling, say sixty or eighty girls. The Headmistress would travel with them, accompanied by a small number of staff trusted for their ability to maintain good order.

The young ladies would be in high spirits on the internal flight from Edinburgh to London. It would be on the first intercontinental leg of the journey that their conduct would get out of hand. Colonising an entire block of seating at the rear of the plane, they'd sneak alcoholic drinks from the trolley, clamber over chairs, the noise levels becoming intolerable to fellow passengers. The Captain would ask to "have a quiet word" with the Headmistress, as a result of the barrage of complaints.

Yet after the stopover, the young ladies' behaviour would be immaculate for the final stretch of the trip. Silence would prevail amongst the cuddling girls, save for an occasional sniffle. Passengers would be astonished: what might have brought about the change? They'd look at the Headmistress in awe: the power of words, they'd think, amazed at the effectiveness of the scolding she must have given after leading her girls into a side room at the airport.

Few would have imagined the truth: the XH Lochgelly brought forth from her hand luggage; those tracksuit bottoms pulled down, the searing strokes across each girl's backside ("eight, given the degree of misconduct I have just had to witness, and the shame you have brought on the school") guaranteeing perfect conduct once they had returned, uncomfortably, to their plane seats.

* It'd have to be Scottish. A tawse fits neatly into hand luggage; canes do not.

The McSpanking

By Abel on 10 October 2007

A rare, as-ever-unpleasant foray into a McDonald's the other night. (Hey, faced with a ludicrously overpriced hotel restaurant serving rubbish I wouldn't feed to our cat, or a ludicrously unpleasant chain restaurant serving... Oh well, needs must, sometimes).

At the table in the window were two young ladies: sixth-formers, I'd guess. Happy, talking animatedly. Well spoken, nicely dressed. Not really in keeping with the majority of their fellow diners, shall we say.

One of them, I speculated, would be rather less cheerful before the evening was out. The front door would click shut on their return home. Her heavy bag of books abandoned on the floor, she'd wander into the living room. She'd smile at her father and give him a hug, as usual.

"How did you get on at Alison's?"

"Really well. We revised a pile of vocab for French. Got through loads."

His subsequent lecture would talk as much about the need for diligence in her studies as it would about her lies. She wasn't to know he'd have driven past the burger joint – he never went that way, did he? But he had, and he'd seen her, and she'd not been at Ali's, had she?

And no amount of pleading and apologising could prevent her jeans from coming down. He'd make her bend over his knee, and he'd hold her tightly in place whilst spanking her so unbelievably hard - for her "own good" - before sending her to bed in utter disgrace.

OTK at the airport?

By Abel on 12 October 2007

A foreign airport told us that we could carry on one piece of hand luggage, plus reading matter and a:

"Lap-top"

Since Haron had been across my lap for a spanking shortly before the taxi arrived, we giggled rather more than the sign perhaps merited.

Of course, we're now resigned to the fact that we'll forever associate any mention of a "laptop" with a mental image of a girl being placed over her top's knees. And we thought we should share that thought with you, so that you too will end up sniggering at inopportune moments.

Daddy's footsteps

By Abel on 16 October 2007

What had he said? "I want you to go to your room, so that you have some time to contemplate the magnitude of your misjudgement, before I come up to punish you." Oh, she was contemplating, all right.

He hadn't whipped her in three years now. Not since that summer afternoon in Devon, in the caravan, after she and Alice had been hauled back from the forbidden pub. "After you'd both specifically promised not to go back."

But Alice was away at Uni now. Not that she'd wish a share of this on her elder sister.

Her father's footsteps on the stairs, undeniably. Surely she was too old? Surely he wouldn't... But when he entered the room, his hands were already reaching to his buckle.

I love it when ideas pop into my head with such clarity, to be polished and further perverted - even if it does then become a battle to transcribe the phrases before they float away.

I wonder what she'd done?

Whipping, submitting

By Abel on 18 October 2007

A pupil from Rhode Island shows promise and a keen imagination with his homework. In uploading his assignment to a public file-sharing site, he (one presumes inadvertently) provoked some very nice scene ideas. His topic was European History; his theme the treatment of the poor; his fascinating anecdote as follows:

> Regulations for the poorhouse in Suffolk County, England in 1588 demonstrate this corporal punishment. The regulations mandate that each "rogue" should be whipped twelve or 6 times, depending on age and health, merely upon entering the house. These floggings and the subsequent punishments were performed in order to bring the rogues into "reasonable obedience and submission to the master of the poorhouse".

I'm picturing a stray young girl, fleeing from her troublesome home, being apprehended by the locals and handed in to the poorhouse. She'd be stripped and washed; the master would appear to inspect her, before taking her into his private quarters to flog her before expecting her reasonable 'submission'.

Ruling with a firm hand

By Haron on 19 October 2007

Yesterday I watched the first episode of the good old BBC saga "I, Claudius". Among other things that were hot in a very Roman way, there was a monologue from Tiberius, about how he used to be strict with his soldiers:

> He said: "Oh yes, I drilled and flogged them - but I drilled and flogged their officers too."

Apart from my ears perking up on the word "flog" (it doesn't take much to get my attention!), I also had this image of two young teachers sharing rumours about the Head of a school at which they have just started work.

"Of course, he's strict with the girls," one of them would whisper to the other, "but they say he's even stricter with the staff. They say the girls respect them all the more for it."

The other teacher, an old girl of the same school, would surreptitiously touch her bottom, and give her friend a rueful smile.

A family of noble sadists

By Haron on 21 October 2007

This is from one of the weekend's magazines... a family history that has proved pretty entertaining:

> The scandalous family has included Augustus, 3rd Earl of Bristol, who was an avid connoisseur of 'tribaldism, sapphism and flagellation' according to one historian, and his sexual

conquests included an entire convent of Portuguese nuns, a doge's wife, duchesses and a whole cheerleading troupe of maids and courtesans...

Another ancestor, Lord William Hervey, was a bisexual sadist who was so savage and cruel that he succeeded in getting himself removed from the navy at a time when floggings before breakfast rarely upset an officer's appetite.
...Portuguese nuns???

The girl from the choir
By Abel on 22 October 2007

I really shouldn't eavesdrop on conversations. But there were five* things I particularly liked about the young lady in her mid-20s from the touring choir, who was perched at the next table in the Executive Lounge of the hotel the other night:

1) She was quiet, shy, intelligent, with a gentle humour.

2) She was my 'type'. (Any of you who know me in real-life will understand that there's a certain type of girl who makes me go weak at the knees. And she seemed quite oblivious to how attractive she was).

3) She and her two female friends had chosen not to go out with the rest of the group: the others were too rowdy and the three of them felt like a quieter evening exploring. (Show *me* a room full of strangers, and I'll head straight for the fringes!).

4) She was East Coast American. (I have a very soft spot that part of the world, having a number of dear friends from there - my first play partner included).

5) She'd taken her punishment bravely when the choirmaster had paddled her for her wrong note in that afternoon's rehearsal. He'd given her ten whacks across her jeans, right after the others had left. Hard, since the following night's concert was so important.

* OK, only four of these are definitely true. One might have been the product of my over-fertile imagination!

Spanking within: do not disturb

By Haron on 23 October 2007

Abel found a hotel website that's doing a do-not-disturb sign competition. They give you elements of the design, and you can put together your own sign with your own text.

Obviously, Abel couldn't resist. His sign read: "Yes, she is being spanked. But she enjoys it. So do not disturb."

After he emailed this to me, with some of his other suggestions, I couldn't resist having a go with my own creative design efforts: "Girl in disgrace – do not enter". "Yes, it's a spanking you can hear." "Spanked girl within: please provide chocolate."

"Fetch me the cane, girl!"

By Abel on 24 October 2007

A school helpfully publishes a historical perspective on education on its website:

> Teachers handed out regular canings... Boys were caned across their bottoms, and girls across their hands or bare legs. Some teachers broke canes with their fury, and kept birch rods in jars of water to make them more supple. Victims had to chose which cane they wished to be beaten with!

Now, and this is where I could be accused of having a mean streak, I'm imagining a good girl facing her first-ever punishment. Other, less-well-behaved young ladies would have been thrashed regularly before; they'd offer some 'friendly' advice during the break before her caning was due.

"Choose the thick, dark brown one," they'd say. "It may look bad, but it doesn't hurt half as much as the lighter canes."

Only this particular rod would flex and whip just like the thinnest of the rattans – but would be much denser and heavier. The worst of all to choose, in fact. But girls can be cruel sometimes.

Fantasy spanking from a writer?

By Haron on 27 October 2007

We often talk about fantasy celebrity spankers, and somehow, more often than not, they turn out to be actors. That's quite understandable: we see them a lot.

Yesterday I chilled out with an audiobook on my iPod – "The Waste Lands" by Stephen King, read by the author. And I found myself thinking: ooh boy, wouldn't it be nice to get a spanking from him... He has some incredibly hot spanking and near-spanking episodes in his books, and I bet he could create a real feeling of *dread* were we to play a scene.

This made me think. I spend much more time in the company of my favourite writers (or anyway, their books) than I do watching any actor, and yet I had never before pictured one of them as a fantasy spanker.

So, Stephen King is the spanker for me. Who else? I'd have to say, Neil Gaiman. He's not one of my favourite writers, but on a shallow physical level... well, he's hot.

I have considered and discounted Kazuo Ishiguro (he pretends that he doesn't write science fiction, and therefore we have irrevocable ideological differences; damn shame, because he's also hot), Terry Pratchett (hot, yes, but you could never be sure whether he's taking a mickey out of you) and Ian McEwan (although he has a suitably sick mind, I just don't know what he looks or sounds like).

I'm sure I'll come up with more candidates upon reflection. How about you? Which writers would you like to spank or be spanked by?

As you were...
By Haron on 29 October 2007

The Evening Standard last week gave Abel a piece of good news, with a headline reading "Outright ban on smacking is rejected".
    Damn... It was close this time! (Covers bottom with both hands and runs away).

A spanking with a view
By Abel on 30 October 2007

I think I've found the coolest place in the world to administer a spanking. Our friend Martha and I went for a day out to Alton Towers recently (American readers: think Disneyland with the fast rides, but without the folks in the irritating costumes).
    Linking the various sectors of the site is a cable car. And at 11 in the morning, the gondolas are relatively quiet. Like, we had a 10-person car to ourselves.
    Of course, I gave in to temptation, and the young lady was duly spanked several hundred feet above the ground, the gondola gently swaying from side to side with each swing of my arm. And yes, there were gondolas going the other way at the time: I hope they appreciated our attempt to make their journey more scenic.

Worthy of her lines
By Abel on 1 November 2007

Authorities at Newcastle Airport are relieved to report that a medical emergency was narrowly averted on a recent flight, when a passenger by the name of Abel nearly choked on his coffee. Interviewed later, he explained that he'd been entranced by the young lady opposite, learning her lines for a forthcoming play.

The near-accident occurred when he overheard her explaining to her neighbour that the play was "fine, but contains too much lap dancing."

Fortunately, crisis was averted when he realised that she'd actually said 'tap' dancing.

He later explained that she had caught his eye on boarding. "I noticed that she was wearing one of these trendy body-hugging short dresses, so often worn by cuties over jeans. Only she seemed to have forgotten the jeans."

He went on to confess that he had been wondering whether she was learning lines for a forthcoming spanking movie. He had also been speculating as to her likely reception once her father, doubtless meeting her at the airport and likely to be outraged at her indecent costume, got her home.

Five tips for spanking on the London Eye

By Haron on 2 November 2007

The description of a recent spanking at Alton Towers leads me to describe my own experience of getting spanked on the London Eye, a couple of years ago.

Spanking isn't an equivalent of extreme ironing for me, or anything: I don't seek out impossible places in which to get spanked. Our house will do, though historic cottages with no neighbours around also appeal. It's more that whenever we're sightseeing, and suddenly end up on our own, something clicks: "Hey, there's nobody here! Time for an intimate moment!" So over his knee I go.

Having specified this, let me give you some tips for spanking in a London Eye capsule.

1) The queues are insane: pre-book your ticket. In fact, pre-book it even if you aren't planning to do any spanking.

2) Go insanely early, on a weekday. Only then will there be a chance that you'll get the capsule to yourselves. (We

went after picking up an American spanko friend off her overnight Transatlantic flight. The sight-seeing was meant to keep her awake. I suppose, it did.)

3) Check out whether you can see into the capsule below you. This will give you an idea of how much folks above you can see into yours.

4) At some point on the way down the cameras on the ground will be taking your picture, so that they can try to sell it to you as you come out. Decide for yourself whether you want the spanking on the picture. Bear in mind that it will be displayed on the monitor above the sales assistant's head. If you keep your trousers up, you probably won't be arrested, but who knows...

5) Don't go on the London Eye just to spank or get a spanking. There's no guarantee you'll definitely get your private capsule, and the disappointment may spoil what is otherwise a really cool ride.

Obviously, if you happen to get your piece of spanking action on the Eye, come and tell us all about it!

Whippings in the eighteenth century

By Abel on 3 November 2007

I regularly find myself buying books less for their literary merit than for their likely potential to inspire pervy thoughts. They don't necessarily have to be kinky per se – a mere glimmer of a governess, a schoolroom, a reformatory, a country house is more than enough.

One such recent acquisition was "The Scandal of the Season" by Sophie Gee. It's a fun read, and well-researched. And it's set amidst the partying upper classes of early eighteenth century England; a couple of snippets have duly obliged on the kink-inspiring front. Take the following:

> Jervas turned back to his paper. "Another slave run away in London", he announced as her turned to the public notices.

The young lady's description was printed in full; a reward offered. I drifted in familiar directions as it occurred to me that her punishment once found might make for a rather interesting scene. Maids, too, must have absconded on a regular basis, to be soundly thrashed on their return.

And then there was the chapter set in a masked ball, during which the characters flirted outrageously with one another. The following email exchange with Haron, over the course of about half an hour, shows how much fun we have bouncing ideas around between the two of us...

> Abel: Two girls at the ball misbehave, perhaps giggly on wine at their first ball. The master of the house takes them aside, to his library, lectures them and informs them that he is to thrash them with his riding crop. Without, of course, knowing who they are... And then they take off their masks ready for their punishment....

> Haron: I like! They don't need to take off the masks, either. And I love the idea of them meeting him at social events later in the year, and knowing what he'd done, while he has no idea!

> Abel: I prefer the idea of him having their masks taken off... And finding that one was some incredibly important daughter of some grand Duke. The seeing-him-but-him-not-knowing would come when he asked one of them to dance at a future ball, not recognising her because she was in a different outfit and mask...

> Abel: And I'm now rather thinking that one of them might be the youthful daughter of one of the gentleman's former lovers... Or that one of the misbehaving guests might be dressed for the Ball as a boy: the host would have no idea that she was a girl until the mask came off...

Remember, remember...
By Abel on 5 November 2007

"A particularly fine bonfire the girls have made for Guy Fawkes' night this year, Headmaster." The two gentlemen peer from the window onto the merriment below in the school's courtyard. "Indeed, Deputy Headmaster. I do wonder what they've done to make it burn with quite such unusual intensity."

Suddenly, the Headmaster utters a disbelieving cry, pointing into the crowd of revellers: "Those girls are drinking vodka from the bottle!" He rushes to his cupboard: "I must go down and sort this out. I'll cane the lot of them."

But, dear readers, he finds the armoury quite bare, its usual fearsome collection of canes gone missing. The Headmaster turns back to his Deputy. And their eyes turn simultaneously back out of the window, to the blazing bonfire below...

No, Haron, don't get any ideas...

The moment you realise you're going to get caned
By Abel on 7 November 2007

The Education Code Regulations (1973) for Guyana are, apparently, still in effect. They contain provisions that would be deemed outdated elsewhere, outside the scenes that many of us play. "Regulation 94 [Reg. 37/1943]" is the section of interest. Paragraph 3 explains that

> Corporal punishment for girls shall be administered by a female teacher or by the head teacher in the presence of a female teacher.

Presumably a girl knocking on the Headmaster's door would dread opening it to find not just the Head, but a female teacher too – for that could mean only one thing...

Do-it-yourself spanking art

By Haron on 8 November 2007

A few weeks ago Martha and I were making our way through a generously-sized cafetiere at Coffee, Cake and Kink, and admiring erotic art on the wall opposite.

Among other things, there was a black-and-white print of a beautifully corseted girl, her pristine, perfect bottom bare and turned towards the audience.

"Do you know," I said to Martha, "I could see myself buying that picture. The only thing is, Abel would probably get out his red marker pen and draw cane stripes across her bottom."

"Mmmm," she replied. "Imagine a spanking picture covered with wipeable glass… so that you could draw marks on it."

Thus we have developed the spanking drawing set: you would get a picture of an unblemished bottom coated with whatever they use to make whiteboards, a set of marker pens in different shades of red, and a punishment slip template. Every time you get to decide what the girl has done, fill in her offence and sentence in the punishment slip, and administer the punishment with the help of the markers.

You could also imagine this whiteboard being useful in domestic circumstances. When a naughty girl enters the room, she can be informed of her impending punishment by means of a drawing. "Oh no! The girl on the wall had six stripes today!"

My own whiteboard, decorated with nothing more exciting than a calendar and a picture of a coffee cup, is suddenly looking quite dull.

The cause of pain
By Abel on 10 November 2007

Interesting strapline on the ads for the forthcoming movie 'Beowulf', in the foyer of a cinema I just passed in London:

> Evil breeds pain

Indeed. If a girl misbehaves, then she should expect the uncomfortable consequences. Comments suggesting that the phrase may be taken as implying that tops are evil would be entirely misguided.

The odd one out
By Abel on 11 November 2007

US school handbooks are an ever-fascinating source of information on the ritual of academic corporal punishment. One recent find includes defined its terminology carefully:

> CORPORAL PUNISHMENT: Student is given a number of "licks" or paddling with a board of education approved paddle.

Ah, that explains it, then. I'd always wondered... What particularly caught my eye, though, were the punishments for 'Cutting Class'. For the first 'offense', a student received one day's In-School Suspension; for a second, 'two days or a paddling'.

So, picture the scene. A group of truant girls is sent to the Principal's office. He admonishes them, glancing from one to another as he passes sentence:

"You all understand that the punishment for cutting class is designed to emphasise the severity of the offence. You will each serve an In-School Suspension tomorrow. Now, please return to your classroom...

...Other than Jennifer, for whom this is a second offence: you may wait behind to be paddled."

I am to be birched

By Haron on 14 November 2007

I've been sentenced to a birching on Sunday, and this has been in my thoughts a lot this week. I'm going to be a juvenile delinquent who has already had a court-ordered birching, and has now been caught for a second offence and sent to a reformatory. A 36-stroke birching is bundled into the sentence - twice what the girl got last time.

It is also, incidentally, twice the biggest number of strokes of the birch I've ever had. Abel mentioned something about fifty when we were first discussing the Sunday girl's fate, but I chickened out of getting that many. Considering that 12 with the birch normally leaves me in tears, I think 36 will be plenty.

I would be more likely to want to step to the edge if I could count on screaming my head off to ease the pain, but even though our walls are thick and the neighbour is deaf(ish), there are limits to how loudly I can yell. Nothing like practical matters to limit your scene-playing...

The reason I'm fretting about this is that until the time of the punishment, Abel is actually away. It's going to be up for me to choose and soak the birch, clear the space in the spare room, set up the school desk that serves as a whipping bench. It seems like a particularly cruel part of the ritual. I mentally walked through it about three times today while I was on the bus into town.

I'm kinda concerned about that number of strokes... Not concerned enough to not do it, but just enough to worry and fidget days in advance.

Do you suppose this was Abel's idea in sentencing me in the first place?

Arnica and alternatives

By Abel on 15 November 2007

Applying arnica to a well-marked bottom earlier, I wondered how and when this particular lotion was first identified as a source of healing for punished girls.

More to the point, cruel as I am, I wondered what other alternatives had been tried whilst early spankos experimented.

"Come here, my darling, and let me rub in this nettle essence to see if it helps." Maybe not.

"I wonder if this garlic paste might help". Owwwww.

"Bring over the Deep Heat." Now there's an interesting idea...

Little thrills

By Haron on 16 November 2007

It's well known that the smallest things can throw me into fantasy mode, particularly when I start work when it's still dark outside.

This morning, it was the sight of ink on my fingers. I have been writing long-hand (a fetish of mine), with a fountain pen I haven't used for a while (also a fetish object, the sort my mother's generation used at school).

When I took a break and saw the peacock-blue ink stains, I was a girl held back after school, to write an essay I hadn't handed in on time. When I finish, I will have my hands strapped: two strokes on each. There will also be a note to take home.

I will carry it carefully in my inky fingers, praying that the first person to read it will be my older brother, who takes care of me if my parents work late. He may spank me with a hairbrush, but at least he never makes me go outside to cut a switch: that's my mother's prerogative.

Cheerleaders should be paddled. (Surely?)
By Abel on 17 November 2007

I've just stumbled on a phrase that's plain wrong:

"Cheerleader caned."

There, I've made you wince too. Oh, the incongruity of those two words. Cheerleaders are, have to be, American. As American as... as... (the thought that came to mind was 'George Bush', but that might upset some of you). As Thanksgiving, perhaps, as the Empire State Building...

And the cane as a punishment implement? As English as Buckingham Palace, Yorkshire pudding, as "long shadows on cricket grounds and warm beer".

The two just don't belong together. But, with an evil grin, I imagine a public schoolmaster taking up his appointment as head of a distinguished girls' academy in the States. When questioned by the school governors about his radical new disciplinary plans, he'd explain, "If you'd like to show me where the School Regulations specify that one should use the paddle, I will happily convert, but in the meantime the cane has served me to great effect over the years."

My reformatory birching
By Haron on 19 November 2007

I was prepared to start this account with a pitiful description of how much I suffered during the birching Abel gave me yesterday, and how sore I was, and how I wasn't sure how I'd survived this. I thought I would write this, because that had been my experience in all of my previous encounters with the birch.

Not this time. Well, I did suffer at first, and I'm still quite sore, but by the end I found myself riding the pain, and actually quite enjoying it, in a way I have rarely done before.

Yet, as I set up the punishment room in the afternoon, home alone, I was wobbly with apprehension. We have no whipping horse, so I dragged in the school desk. We are not big on rope, so we only own one length, but I laid it out nonetheless. I thought for a minute, and added some handcuffs.

As Abel gave me regular phone updates on how his drive home was going, I tried hard not to let him hear the trembling in my voice. He came up with the truly devious way of playing with my head: when he arrived, Alice Pierce (the delinquent, the girl I would become) would be sitting alone in the waiting area (the living room), waiting to be fetched by the punishment officer. I wouldn't as much as say hello to my husband, before that other man arrived to take the convict to her doom.

I was supposed to have come straight from court, so I kicked off my usual jeans, and dug out a modest skirt, a nice shirt, some heels. When Abel phoned to say he was 15 minutes away, I was still drying my hair after a hasty shower. I grabbed a hairbrush, a bundle of my clothes and a pair of handcuffs, and scooted to the living room. My heart was in my mouth. I laddered a pair of stockings trying to get them on. Still, by the time he arrived, I had morphed into Alice, and even managed to handcuff myself (as she would have been, while the grim guard transported her from court to the reformatory).

True to his promise (or was it a threat?) Abel didn't come to say hello before heading upstairs to transform into the guard. I had a book stuffed under the cushions of the sofa, to entertain myself while he was getting ready, but my hands were jumping, and my breath was catching, and the whole heady dread was too lovely to dilute.

Eventually, or too soon for Alice, he appeared. A surly, sports kit-clad guard, clearly also a gym instructor. He checked the identity of his new charge, undid one of her cuffs and fastened it on his own wrist. Thus, cuffed to this new scary man, I stumbled upstairs after him.

He made me strip, the only comment on my carefully thought out court outfit being that if I was slutty enough to wear stockings and suspenders, perhaps it was a good thing I would spend a few weeks in the reformatory uniform. Then, to my abject horror, he ordered me to get under the shower, and informed me, with a rather bored face, that the hot water boiler hadn't worked for some weeks.

I suppose, the water was actually lukewarm rather than ice-cold, but for poor Alice this was enough to make her teeth chatter and her nipples do the embarrassing perking-up thing. The cold slightly took her mind off the thorough soaping, which she wasn't allowed to do herself, and which included her mouth. The guard was cool and professional as he did this, explaining that all manner of girls entered the reformatory, and not all of them were clean and nicely turned-out, therefore, the washing procedure was the same for everybody.

"Dry yourself well, Miss Pierce", he said, throwing a towel at me. The abject horror of being birched on a bottom that was not just icy, but also damp, made me work the towel with particular vigour.

Finally, there were no more ritual humiliations, no more delays. I was led into the punishment room, bent over the desk, and had my feet tied to the legs with our single piece of rope. The guard was pretty business-like. He didn't bother lecturing, but he did mention that because this was a second offence, and a second birching (Alice had received 18 strokes for drunk and disorderly behaviour several months before, but now she was back for the same offence), he saw it as his particular goal to make sure that this punishment, these 36 strokes, would be the last she would ever earn.

The birch whistled through the air, spraying me with droplets of water it had been soaking in all afternoon. I tried to peek at him, to guess when the first stroke was going to fall. "Face the front," said the guard coolly. "Stretch out and hold on to the legs of the horse. Don't let go or reach back."

The first stroke was so painful it took my breath away. I counted it at once, as ordered, but I could barely get out the words. The second was just as bad; I was choking on the count. The guard placed a steadying hand on the small of my back: "Breathe. Deep breaths. We have a long way to go."

That we did, and I concentrated on breathing through the pain, settling in for the long haul. Although I could feel the tears burn in my eyes, I didn't feel like crying: I felt like getting through this. I tried keeping a backwards count in my head, but somehow "only thirty-one to go" didn't feel like a terribly comforting thought.

When we passed nine, the guard did something incredibly kind, though at the time it seemed a bit evil: he delivered the next nine in a quick succession, too fast for me to count, or to concentrate on them much. They were all of them hard strokes, but they were over with quickly, and with my tears still unspilled, I knew I was half-way, and winning through.

This is where it got really good for me. The first strokes, aimed evenly all over my bottom, had really warmed me up, and I was slowly beginning to float in that peculiar zone were the hard strokes don't hurt you as much, but instead warm you and send you further and further into the endorphin heaven. Although I was fully aware that my bottom was taking some damage, and I could see Abel's shadow whip the birch down with serious strength, it felt exhilarating. Not a trial, but a treat.

I was buzzing when he untied me, but poor Alice was disconsolate. She stuttered out her apologies, and with shaking hands she pulled on the uniform that was handed to her.* She wordlessly followed the guard to the dormitory, where she was to wait on her own, until the next girl had taken her birching.

The guard made her climbed into bed, turn off the lights and left the room.

Seconds later, the door opened again, and Abel came in - all smiles, and hugs, and offers of lotion, and a mirror for me to admire a mass of stripes that were blending over one another. "Oh, hello," I said. "You're home."

*Abel's polo shirt and boxer shorts.

Birched girl, revisited

By Abel on 20 November 2007

Ever get those nights where your mind works away feverishly solving some problem or other, stopping you from sleeping? Last night was one such for me: I've been working on a presentation for a high-profile conference in the new year, and nothing has quite clicked. Give my subconscious time to work on it whilst asleep, though, and suddenly a wonderful concept and structure for the session fell into place.

Thus, still before five in the morning, I had to get up to scribble down my ideas, lest they be forgotten by morning. And after that, as you can guess, my mind was buzzing.

I climbed back into bed, tired but wide awake. Haron was still sleeping: naked, warm, soft, pretty. I curled myself around her, and squeezed her backside, still sore from Sunday night's scene. She protested, in a sleepy "ow - that hurts – do it again" kind of way.

An evil idea came into my mind as I cuddled my birched girl. The Reformatory officers would have held their early-morning meeting with the Governor. As ever, they would discuss any incidents of misconduct the previous day. Young Alice would be deemed to have been insolent to one of the staff: this would clearly need to be addressed. An officer would be despatched to her room: at 5 a.m. she would be woken roughly, the sheets pulled from her bed, the girl dragged to her feet.

She would be led through the corridors to the punishment room: she would be made to touch her toes, and thrashed with the heavy leather prison strap. And then, sobbing, she would be led back through to corridor to her bed, and left until the bell sounded some hours later to wake the other girls.

You might be pleased to know that I held Haron until she fell back asleep, then headed to my office to work on the presentation. Only I was distracted and started writing this instead...

Justice is done

By Haron on 22 November 2007

I heard a shriek from upstairs this morning, and rushed to investigate.

Abel was in the shower. I have never seen him scared of water before, so I worriedly asked what was wrong.

It appeared that the cold weather of the last few days tempted both of us to have hot baths rather than showers, and so the temperature settings on the shower remained the same as during my recent reformatory birching scene.

That is, not quite freezing, but still pretty damn cold. Did he notice this before turning on the water? No, he didn't. Awww.

Paddling encouraged

By Haron on 24 November 2007

Abel, Martha and I saw a sign near a fountain in the courtyard of Victoria and Albert Museum last month with various instructions for visitors. "Please don't sit or swim in the water", "supervise children at all times", "don't stand on the water jets".

Oh, and: "Paddling is permitted, but please keep clothes on."

I'm glad they approve of traditional discipline, and I'm even more glad don't they think the only way to smack people is on the bare.

Hold out your hand

By Abel on 25 November 2007

I do sometimes allow my kinky sense of humour to creep into my work. There's the slide in my presentation on communication skills that discourages the use of abbreviations, with "S&M" included in the list of examples. And there was that keynote conference speech earlier in the year, which offered witty observations on tactics for leading teams, including the advice to "spare not the rod when necessary".

At the start of December, I'm running a session with a newly-formed group, and we'll be doing some team-building work. I've just written an exercise that will have them producing neatly-measured documents against the clock – think a manic production line of scissors, paper, staplers and rulers.

Ah, yes. Rulers. You see, part of the game will be that each team member will be given a card describing a secret quirk. And one of said quirks reads:

> You have an allergy to wooden rulers.

I wonder if any of them will wince knowingly?

And here's a really strange thing. Haron and I went shopping yesterday to buy the materials for the event. And could we find wooden rulers anywhere? Not a chance. Have the Health & Safety mob conducted a risk analysis, and decided to protect potential victims? Have crowds of mischievous girls stormed the stationers and cleared the shelves of the threat? (No, can't be: our Woolworth's still sells wonderfully-effective plimsolls).

I'm heading off on the long drive south for work later today. Haron's been set a task in my absence: to locate and purchase six wooden rulers. That'd be the five I need for the event, and one extra...

The updated anthem
By Haron on 26 November 2007

With barely disguised pleasure, the Times on Saturday reports the hilarity caused by the performance of the teams' national anthems before England's match against Croatia:

> The singer [Tony Henry] ... should have sung *Mila kuda si planina*, which translated roughly as "You know my dear how we love your mountains". Instead he appears to have sung *Mila kura si planina*, which can be interpreted as, "My dear, my penis is a mountain".
>
> Film of the build-up to the game shows Croatian players and mascots giggling as Henry performs.

For some reason, I keep getting images of schoolgirls, mangled school songs and canings in assembly the following day.

The parental exemption
By Abel on 27 November 2007

One school corporal punishment policy helpfully published on the web includes a not uncommon exemption clause:

> Corporal punishment may be administered as a form of discipline unless the parent/guardian files a written, dated objection with the school principal. It is the responsibility of the parent/guardian to see that the written, dated objection is submitted each school year to the principal's office.

I'm picturing her, standing before her father, pleading with him to write an exemption letter for her to take in on the first day of the school year. He looks at her solemnly: "You understand the consequences? That if you merit a punishment at school, but I have submitted this letter, we will deal with the matter still more severely at home?"

This particular school district, by the way, requires a witness every time a paddling is administered:

It must be done with the approval of the principal and administered by the principal or his/her designee, privately, in the presence of another certified school employee but not in the presence of other students.

When watching a girl take a punishment in a scene, it's always a debate as to whether to watch her backside as the strokes land, or to focus on the expressions crossing her face. I wonder which option is preferred in the real-life Principal's office?

Helping your neighbours

By Haron on 29 November 2007 in The Punishment Book

I'm not usually big on practical jokes, because I like people around me to feel good. I'm empathic like that. However, I'm not completely above occasional naughtiness when events call for it.

This time, it felt like the events were *begging* for it. Abel and I were showing our friend Sarah around town when we encountered one of these charity fund-raisers with a bucket: you throw some coins in there, and the guy gives you a sticker to say what a big damn hero you are for giving money away.

So. Abel tosses some coins into the bucket and receives the sticker. Now, if you happen to have a child with you, stickers are great. Otherwise? Not so great. Grown-up clothes don't look so good accessorised with stickers, plus there's icky glue on them. Plus, it's uncool to advertise your charitable donations - particularly, with a big piece of paper stuck to your boob. Therefore, I felt I was justified in rolling my eyes a little when Abel slapped the sticker onto the outside of my coat. "Keep it there," he said sternly.

It felt like he was putting me through a character-building exercise.

Now, if it were just the two of us, I would have discreetly unpeeled the thing as soon as his back was tuned, and tossed it into a wastebasket. But, as I said, we had a friend with us. Who doesn't want to look cool in front of friends?

I unpeeled the thing as soon as Abel's back was turned, and carefully attached it to the back of his fleece. Sarah and I exchanged winks and giggles, and wandered on, as though nothing had happened.

A considerable amount of time later we were walking through a lovely historic square, pointing out old buildings and such, when a tall, distinguished-looking guy walking past us with his wife suddenly addressed Abel: "Excuse me, you have something stuck to your back." (I'm not sure how he even saw Abel's back, considering he had been walking towards us, unless he turned around to stare at Sarah and mine bottoms.)

Anyway, he noticed the sticker, and helpfully unpeeled it for Abel, as we girls stood there looking Extremely Innocent. It took both guys a few seconds to figure out this was a charity sticker, after which Abel made a very sharp deduction, and turned to glare at me.

The helpful guy also turned to me, looking delighted: "It was you, wasn't it? Well, sorry."

I didn't believe he was sorry. He and his wife were almost indecently gleeful as they started walking away. They were still within earshot when Abel said: "You are in so much trouble, young lady."

"Thanks!" I called after the helpful guy. He giggled. He didn't look so distinguished any more.

After we eventually got home and warmed ourselves up with tea, Abel informed me he hadn't forgotten the episode. "Go upstairs and pick a cane," he said.

"But," I said. "We have a guest. You wouldn't want to traumatise her, right? She won't come back again if you traumatise her?"

Sarah looked traumatised.

"Go upstairs and pick a cane," said Abel.

I hadn't really thought it would come to this, as sticking things to somebody's back merits a few smacks over jeans in my mental punishment quota, but hey, maybe there was a taxi-style meter ticking for the amount of time he'd been wearing the thing. I trudged upstairs and fetched a very fearsome-looking, but actually fairly humane thick kooboo cane.

When I came back, Abel directed me to take down my jeans and knickers, and to bend over the arm of the sofa, so that Sarah could hold my hands. I didn't think he was doing that well in the not traumatising guests department.

I got six of the best. They hurt. I made a moderate amount of fuss, because I don't believe in being too stoic - I mean, I wouldn't want him to think he wasn't making an effect, right? That said, I do have some pride, so I didn't scream the house down, like I was tempted to do. Anyway, the advantage of a caning over a hand-spanking I had been thinking I would get is that, even with the strokes delivered in a measured and unhurried manner, the punishment is over so much sooner.

Sarah's holding my hands also helped. I didn't think she was too traumatised in the end; she even promised to come back again when we put her on the train the following day.

But anyway. Dear helpful man in town; if you're reading this - thank you ever so much; I hope you're proud of your snitching self.

Painting a girl's backside

By Abel on 3 December 2007

A debate in the Guardian about the prevalence slipperings in Beano cartoons led to an interesting anecdote from a lady in Yorkshire:

> I was slippered some 25 years ago very infrequently by my mother and was once caned on the hands at school. We had a painting competition ... and threw paint on one of our competitors creations. The 2 boys I was with got six of the best across their bottoms and I as the only girl got the cane

across my hands. It taught me a lesson and I never misbehaved again at school.

The endless variety of offences committed at school never ceases to amaze me. The pupils in my scene version of this would comprise three girls, of course. But one would have to cane them on their hands, for authenticity's sake. All I need now is someone who can offer a room that can get covered in paint. And two girls to join Haron in the competition.

Stripped and Crying

By Haron on 9 December 2007

I swear, when I saw this quote in the "Private Eye", I thought they had picked up a column by Abel.

> Q. In your new series, do you strip women down to their underwear and make them cry?

Nah, it wasn't Abel after all. He doesn't allow you the comfort and privacy of a cosy little room. (The answer was actually from Susanna Constantine, the TV fashion presenter!)

Hanging up his cane

By Abel on 10 December 2007

Every summer, schools would see distinguished old schoolmasters hanging up their canes for the last time as they headed for retirement.

I picture one such boarding school Housemaster, much beloved by his pupils, returning to his study after dinner on the night before the end of term. There, in the dark corridor, waited a girl. "Lisa?" One of his favourites: he'd miss girls like this. The bright ones, the ones keen to learn, the ones whose smiles had made teaching so worthwhile.

"Mr. Rose sent me to see you, sir." Hands trembling, she proffered a folded sheet of paper.

As she bent over a few moments later, he reflected on how easy it would be to lay it on gently. But that wasn't his way; wasn't how he would want to be remembered, wasn't what smokers deserved. Her first caning, his last, would be no different to the others. Although each caning, he reflected, was indeed different: the offences the same, over the years - the strokes, the stripes, the tears alike. But each girl unique, each punishment a sharp, distinctive moment in time for her to fear and then remember.

Afterwards he'd write Lisa's name in the punishment book, with her tally of six hard strokes, bravely taken. Even though, this time, he would take out a ruler and draw a neat line underneath her entry.

Even though, this time, as she wiped away the tears, she would tell him that he would be missed: not just by her, but by all of his girls. And he would permit himself the luxury of giving her a gentle hug as he wished her every joy and every success, and showed her out of the door.

"Flog the girls until they confess"

By Abel on 11 December 2007

As part of my on-going research into matters of interest to our readers, I was delighted to come across a review of "Jeremiah Joyce: Radical, Dissenter and Writer" by John Issitt across at the Thomas Paine Society's site.

One section describes Joyce's support for some Scottish Radicals who had been transported to Australia. Three of them were accused of plotting to murder the captain of their transport ship, 'The Surprize'. Joyce organised, edited and introduced a pamphlet which included "an extract from Skirving's log recording the flogging of two girls to force them to confess taking part in the conspiracy".

Sadly, I can't find a copy of said document anywhere online: the only available copies seem to be squirreled away in the vaults of various Australian University libraries. We'll therefore have to make do with imagining the captain interrogating the two nervous lasses, before instructing that they be soundly whipped until they acknowledged their culpability.

The tutor

By Abel on 12 December 2007

Whiling away the time as Haron and I drove across the Pennines yesterday, I was inspired with a new scene idea.

The young lady – let's call her Amanda – was highly intelligent. The sort of high-flying, destined for a top University girl that I like. Daddy was particularly keen that she should do well in her A Levels, and so had hired a renowned private tutor – a retired Headmaster, no less.

He was excellent, of course: encouraging the young lady to think more creatively, more originally. Their twice-weekly meetings seemed destined to propel her to great things.

But, you see, he didn't seem that strict about time. Amanda found that she could arrive a few minutes late, with scarcely a raised eyebrow. Even the occasional quarter-hour barely seemed to register. And when the other girls were gathering in the park opposite school for a quick post-lesson cigarette? Well, it would be rude – and most un-cool – not to join them.

This time, she arrived over twenty minutes after her appointed hour. "And, pray, what precisely would you like me to say in my note to your father when I discuss your repeated tardiness?" he wondered, pen poised over the crested notepaper on his desk.

She concurred with his view that daddy would be most unlikely to approve of her continued failure to appear on time, and even less of the implicit attitude towards the costs of her lessons. Blushing deeply, she acknowledged that she would be sent to her room... that her father would follow her... that anything would be preferable to letting daddy know that she was letting him down. Or, particularly – as her tutor sniffed the air – that she was indulging in the forbidden Marlboros.

Blushing still deeper, she agreed with his suggestion that they should deal with the matter more immediately, and consented to his suggestion that she should touch her toes "to be dealt with in the way that I've always found so effective in prompting girls to improve her performance." She watched in dread anticipation as he took the rattan from behind the bookcase, trembled as he lowered her knickers, and sobbed as he taught her most firmly that "ungrateful girls need to learn the error of their ways."

And then he would have her sit on the hard chair, for the remainder of their time together and the discussion of the assignment that Amanda had completed oh-so-well.

Father's switch, mother's spoon

By Abel on 14 December 2007

You know, my wooden ruler exercise last week seemed to have just the right effect. Later that morning, a conversation between the two cutest participants in the event drifted across the room to my ears:

> T: "My father used to make my sister and me go out to the yard and cut a switch from the poplar tree in the yard if we misbehaved."
>
> E: "My mother used to use the wooden spoon."
>
> T: "We quickly found out not to cut the thinner branches: they hurt far more. Although the worst thing of all wasn't the whipping – it was the anticipation and that walk across the yard."

E: "Oh, the wooden spoon *hurt*. I can still hear the sound of that kitchen drawer opening..."

As you might imagine, I found it quite tough to keep my concentration during the next part of the session!

Holiday resort spanking club

By Haron on 15 December 2007

We'd been looking forward to our holiday in Malaysia for a long, long time. The last few days before departure seemed particularly long. You know how you wait for Friday night to come? It was like that, only more tortuous.

To quench our longing for warmth and sandy beaches, Abel and I kept paging through the sites of the hotels we would be staying in. Planning wistfully what we could do when we're there. Resort hotels try their best at putting on all sorts of entertainment: jungle walks, diving, visits to crocodile farms and barbeque nights follow each other in a never-ending succession.

"And Tuesday nights," said Abel in a bright infomercial voice, "is when the hotel's spanking club meets."

Yes, yes! That's one thing they website and brochures are missing. "Come along to the blue lounge for our Spanking Extravaganza, where hands clap and bottom cheeks jiggle. Bring your own rattan or borrow ours."

Maybe not. Oh, well. We'll just have to organise the meeting of the hotel's spanking club with what resources we have. In our bedroom.

Guess what we bought?

By Abel on 20 December 2007

We don't allow advertising here on The Spanking Writers, but we thought we'd make an exception today by promoting the wonderful Asli Crafts, at unit G.23 in Kuala Lumpur's Central Market.

We discovered our new favourite store whilst coming downstairs from the school uniform shop (sadly, too complicated and scary to be a source of useful accessories). There in front of us was what looked like a standard touristy stall – but with a large bucket full of lengths of rattan, of varying thickness, in the doorway. Inside, moreover, were further such containers, in which the rods – a hundred or more - had been cut neatly, one end folded to make an elegant handle.

We worked our way through the selection, picking out the prime pieces, and took them across to the counter. The young lady totted up our purchase – 21 Malaysian Ringgit, or about £3 / $6, for four beautifully made canes. (That's comparable value to the implements I bought in Singapore's hardware stores earlier in the year).

We'd noticed her looking strangely at us as we'd been browsing her stock, and she did look extremely surprised: "What are you going to use them for?"

I thought quickly, understanding that sometimes honesty isn't always quite the best policy: "We have a shop at home, and the hooks on the end will be great for lifting down bags from the highest shelves."

"Oh," she replied, looking astonished. "Here they're used to punish naughty pupils at school." With a rueful look, she added: "Our schools are very strict."

I thought I'd press home the advantage of my obvious innocence in all matters relating to corporal punishment. "Only at school, or do parents use them too?"

"Mainly at school." She continued: "These days they only punish them when they are very, very bad. They used to punish you for anything, like making too much noise."

With a friendly smile: "You must have been glad to leave school, then."

"*Very* glad."

We thanked her for her assistance – she'd wrapped the canes extremely neatly for us – and set off on our way, walking around the corner with entirely straight faces until we were out of eye- and ear-shot, and could collapse in a fit of laughter.

Combined with the serving spoon made from sea coconut wood (very, very dense) that we'd purchased earlier in the day, it seems to have been a most successful shopping trip all round. And I'm told by Haron that sleeping on one's front isn't that uncomfortable, really...

Advantages of a mirrored ceiling

By Haron on 21 December 2007

The other week we ate in a cafe that had this grand gold-and-crimson décor: plenty of candles, mirrors all around.

The ceiling was also mirrored. I had the pleasure of observing the top of Abel's head (not something I see often, due to a substantial difference in height), or, if I threw my head right back, I could see – hang on. I could see down my cleavage.

Nearly falling off the chair, I threw a furtive glance around. Nobody else was gazing at the skies. I subtly pulled the neck of my shirt up a bit, and checked the ceiling mirror again to check the effect.

The was when I noticed that a girl at the next table, who was currently leaning over to chat to her friend, was showing a great view down the back of her jeans. I could see a lick of colour of her thong, and pale, smooth skin of her cheeks all the way down to the crest of her bottom.

I'm sad to report that she showed no traces of having been spanked. Because if she had, the marks would have been plainly visible in the ceiling mirror.

Maybe that's why it had been installed. Perhaps, a regular customer had sponsored the lavish décor on two conditions: that the room had a mirrored ceiling, and that a convenient seat be reserved for him, for whenever he felt like checking the behaviour of the local girls who came for their coffee and cake.

Next time we go, I'm wearing a long, high-neck top.

Dealing with your irresponsible daughter

By Abel on 22 December 2007

A thought-provoking advertisement at Schiphol Airport, where we changed planes last week en route to our holiday...

> You leave a fortune and an irresponsible daughter.
>
> Let's talk about your future.

So, I'll pose a quiz question. Was this:

a) an advertisement for a bank, hoping to get its greedy paws on your money, or

b) an advertisement for a disciplinarian, hoping to get his greedy paws on your daughter?

Sadly, the correct answer was (a) – Dutch bank ING – but the latter option seems so much more appealing. And, after all, if you could instil some responsibility into your daughter, you might not need to employ a team of bankers to cream off their commissions from your hard-earned wealth.

(The option of hanging around for a while, so that you don't have to 'leave' your fortune to anyone but can continue to enjoy it yourself, was presumably – and rather morbidly – not on the bankers' agenda).

The room service paddle

By Abel on 26 December 2007

The "guest directory" for our ever-so-nice Malaysian resort lists essential items that the traveller might have forgotten, which can be provided simply by calling the service desk. Contact lens solution, highlighter pens, phone chargers, nail polish remover, paddles, paper clips, staplers and strollers are amongst the items listed.

OK... maybe I've extemporised slightly. But they should have a paddle (or cane, or tawse, or a selection) available, right?

I'm picturing the scene: the young lady who's persisted in fooling around next to the pool, eventually soaking her father and assorted other guests with a particularly ferocious splash. He'd apologise profusely, promising that the matter would be dealt with, and would lead her straight to her bedroom. The phone call would be made; the daughter – still in her swimming costume – made to stand, disgraced, in the corner until the hotel staff knocked some minutes later.

Daddy would make her answer. The hotel employee would proffer the paddle: "I assume that this is for you?" She'd nod.

"Please could you call to for us to collect it once it's been applied?"

From deep inside the room, her father's voice. "Please don't put yourselves to any further trouble. I'll have her return it shortly to the reception desk."

Meanwhile, elsewhere in the resort, another father would have placed a similar call. "Unfortunately, sir, the paddle is currently being used by another gentleman. We expect to have it back soon, though. Perhaps if someone could wait in the lobby?"

And so it would come to pass that the first girl, tearful and freshly punished, would duly pass on the paddle to the second, tearful and about to be punished, giving her a hug as she did and wishing her well. The transaction would take place under the watchful eyes of the hotel employees.

But I wonder? Would the two lasses avert their eyes from one another when they found themselves at adjacent loungers next to the pool the following day? Or would their common bond unite them, acting as a spark to future friendship?

The pair of paddled girls

By Abel on 28 December 2007

I wondered in my previous post whether the two consecutively-paddled girls in the hotel would avoid one another thereafter, or be united in adversity to become firm friends. A comment from our friend Sarah proposed the latter, suggesting that "they would end up getting into mischief together and consequently getting punished together too".

I immediately thought of the excursion programme that our resort offers every morning – dull-sounding trips to dull-sounding places. (Other than feeding the eagles, that is: but that apparently requires spending most of the day at sea, and neither Haron nor I can face the idea).

Fathers, though, would think of the idea of excursions as a 'good thing': their young ladies should 'take in some culture'. It would be 'educational'. By pure coincidence, our two heroines would find themselves, reluctantly, dragged by their respective fathers to the hotel reception at some ungodly hour, for the "Towns and Temples Tour".

The girls would recognise one another, of course, and as they clambered into the minibus together, they would sit beside one another and shyly start to chat. "You two look as if you know one another already," one father would comment. One of the girls would blushingly whisper an embarrassed explanation.

Later, the group would stop to explore a ruined temple. The girls would set off on their own, stern fatherly warnings not to be late for the 4pm departure ringing in their ears. Only neither of them would have a watch; the temple would turn out to be fascinating; they would lose track of time. It would be nearer five by the time they return to the had-been-worried, now-furious waiting party.

Their fathers would step forward; their explanations, their excuses would be brushed aside. "It seems that neither of you has learned from your punishment earlier in the week," one would say.

I can't decide whether the fathers would cut switches from some nearby tree, using the tour guide's pocket knife, and bend their girls over by the dusty roadside, next to one another, to punish them there and then...

...or whether they would be taken back to the hotel, where one father would suggest that it would save the hotel staff some work if the duo were to be paddled together this time. The other would offer the use of their room, and the girls would find themselves bent over the crisp white sheets.

And even in the hotel, decisions remain: would they be bent over facing one another, or side by side? Would they be allowed to hold hands? Would both fathers be used to administering discipline on the bare – or only one? And if so, would the latter require his daughter to lower her shorts and knickers too this time, "as it's only fair that you be treated equally"?

Would one girl be punished, then the other, or would the strokes alternate? And if the strokes alternated, would the paddle be passed from one father to the next after each whack, so each punished his own daughter – or would the first father administer (say) the first ten whacks, five to each girl, before allowing the other a turn?

Paying off her debt

By Haron on 29 December 2007

We were chilling out by the pool in our hotel in KL, when Abel let out an enraged roar, and jumped like somebody had poured a bucket of water over him. Looking around, I realised that my impression hadn't been far off: the gardener who was watering the bushes behind us had missed the plants with her hose, and showered Abel instead.

This would have been funny rather than annoying, if he wasn't holding his iPod, which had come inches from being dowsed in water. I'm reliably informed that this is not good for an iPod.

While Abel glowered at the gardener and muttered unflattering comments in her direction, I imagined a different girl, in a different society to ours. She was not lucky enough to miss a piece of expensive gadgetry when her hose accidentally slipped in her hands. The hotel's important guest's laptop was irrevocably ruined.

There was no point in suing the girl for the damage: the laptop had cost far beyond the sum of the price of all of her possessions. It was clear to everybody that the only way she could compensate the businessman would be to enter into indentured servitude to him.

After a short negotiation in the hotel manager's office, the girl signed on the dotted line, beneath the agreement that made her the man's maid. He would feed and house her (the price of this would be added to the cost of her debt, of course), and in return she would serve his family until she had paid off with her work everything she owes him.

When she put down the pen, her new master gave her a cool look. 'And now, young lady, we have something to discuss. Did I, or did I not hear you laugh after your sprayed me with that hose?..'

I shall leave the outcome of this scene to your rich imaginations...

A startle to end the year

By Abel on 31 December 2007

We finally emerged from the cocoon of our lovely resort this morning, for the first time since we got here 11 days ago. It being New Year's Eve, and that being officially a big day for Ukrainians, Haron wanted to be taken shopping. We hiked for miles in the blistering midday heat (OK, strolled for ten minutes along the lovely shady path), and found ourselves in a duty free shopping mall, where a girl was indulged to her heart's content.

More importantly, though, it meant that we were able to finish 2007 with one of best startles of the year, for next to the shopping centre was a most wonderfully-named complex. Its name, helpfully translated on the sign outside?

Correctional Academy of Malaysia

Our imaginations went into overdrive, as you can no doubt image. The lack of fences suggested that this was not some high-security institution. No, we decided: this would be a school for girls being given their 'last chance' - good girls, from good families, whose behaviour was giving cause for concern.

The regime would be strict, of course. Each morning, at dawn – before the temperature rose too high – the Governor would inspect a parade of all of the students. That day's newcomers would be brought to the front, to be given their introductory caning: six hard strokes, to deter them from incurring future punishments during their stay.

Miscreants from the previous day would then take their turn, being strapped down over the trestle to receive an appropriate number of strokes for their offences. And woe betide any girl who arrived late for the parade: she'd be directed to join not the girls lined up in their ranks, but the back of the queue of girls to be caned.

Now, why do I have a feeling that Haron might be caught later, having escaped from the Academy...

PS a quick search on the internet on our return revealed the Academy to be a training school for prison officers, but who are we to allow reality to get in the way of fantasy?

PPS in the words of one of our favourite songs, by The Divine Comedy, we'd like to extend our very best wishes to "the friends that we've known, and those that we now know, and those who we've yet to meet"

THE MARTHA PAPERS

At Easter 2007, our dear friend Martha came to stay. Over the course of a few fun-filled days, she recorded her perspectives on the scenes that we played...

A Kinky Friend says...

By Martha on 5 April 2007

Day one of my stay in a spanking household and, as you'd expect, it didn't take long for the action to commence! My arrival allowed Abel to test a hypothesis which had been exercising his mind recently, and which now allowed him to exercise his arm too: is it possible to cane two girls simultaneously?

Determined to investigate, he had Haron and I lie side by side, bare bottoms snuggled close together, and tapped experimentally with a particularly long cane, selected specially for the purpose... then let fly. Two girls simultaneously yelped! More strokes followed as Abel warmed to his task and persisted in the name of thorough research.

I had ended up furthest away so my near cheek was bearing the brunt for me, whilst Haron's far cheek bore the force of the cuts for her. We squirmed and squawked our way through eight or so strokes and then he swapped sides, just for a couple to finish.

At which point I concluded that I may've had a rough deal, since being the near girl didn't seem so bad. Or maybe that was just cos I was already well-striped – prettily-striped – by then!

Content with his efforts, Abel allowed us to redress and we walked over to some local friends' for dinner. Abel wore his new jacket which has a particularly pleasing feature: a tawse pocket! Or at least that's what we've concluded it must be for anyway – why else would a jacket have a pocket which runs horizontally all round the bottom hem? A leather tawse indisputably fits it nicely anyhow, and was duly put to good use on our return journey!

I managed to get it snapped briskly across my hands several times for trying to run off when the pocket was unzipped, and was then treated to my – I think – first open air bare bottom spanking, to help me behave for the rest of the walk back. Fortunately the weather was clement for the time of year so this warming effect was not instantly cancelled out by chill surrounds! Also fortunately, it was very dark and in the middle of nowhere!

All in all, a lively start to my visit! I wonder what the rest of the week will have in store?

In an English Country Garden

By Martha on 6 April 2007

Glorious, perfect weather greeted day two of my holiday, so we set off to visit one of the big attractions in the area: the Alnwick Gardens. Think beautiful English country garden, reeking with tradition – and yet this has been purpose-built in only the last few years, the dream of Alnwick Castle's owner, the Duchess of Northumberland. It's an amazing place and, as you might imagine, ripe with potential atmosphere for the spanko tourist!

So many memories to share with you... First the huge, carved wooden chairs in the treehouse restaurant, their towering backs studded with holes at varying heights to suit all subs and positions! We enjoyed enough peace to experiment with a few, Abel obliging Haron and I with some trial swats to ensure authenticity. This obviously laid the foundations for our wanderings up to the walled flower garden subsequently, when he directed us to another secluded corner containing wooden garden furniture. "Take a chair each, girls: kneel up and wait for me." Obediently we did so and I have to say that, despite some good hearty spanks, he was kinder to our jean-clad bottoms than the wooden slats were to our knees!

In high spirits, we continued our explorations and discovered a great addition to any kinky playground: a bamboo shoot maze! Too tender and green to be raided – not that a good girl would do such a thing anyway of course – but still a wonderful idea – privet is so last century darling! And what an open invitation for two girls, scampering along after Abel, to suddenly dive off down a different path and "lose" him! Much schoolgirl giggling and running around ensued as we retraced our steps and tried to find him.

He was eventually spotted, having exited the maze, standing on the main lawn and sending some delightfully explicit "Come here now, you naughty children" body language our way! How delicious to be sternly rebuked for our antics, warned what a repeat of such behaviour would render us liable to, feel the thrill of it chase down my spine!

We then had to be left unsupervised whilst Abel investigated the award-winning public conveniences and were most effectively tethered for the duration. He made us stand either side of a flower urn, Haron's right foot touching one edge and my left foot the other, with strict orders that they were to remain in contact until his return! How can such a simple instruction, and the adherence to it, be so intoxicating?

These are just a few of my happy memories of our English country garden idyll. One last addition though, to complete day two of my stay, and whet your appetites for future Spanking Writers' posts. On our way home, we stopped off at a wonderful second hand bookshop to browse for anything with a corporal punishment slant – for, as you know, Abel and Haron take their research on your behalf *very* seriously! You'll be pleased to hear that the visit was successful, with a number of new volumes purchased and delighted over that evening. One of which was unearthed by yours truly who, having been compelled to pull forth a nondescript-looking hardback entitled "The History of Tommie Brown" (perhaps thinking fondly of Tom Brown and his schooldays?), found it to have the subtitle "Let pain be pleasure and pleasure be pain"! A quick browse bore out this promise, so look out some day for any fantastical anecdotes about King Tawse and his magical powers for making young ladies' palms smart!

Rods for their own backsides

By Martha on 8 April 2007

The next day of my stay with Abel and Haron: a scene we've planned for weeks comes to fruition...

Good Friday dawned and that could mean only one thing: the day the birchings are administered at the reformatory.

Alice and Martha had both nearly completed their sentences; just this final act remained before their release papers could be signed. The Punishment Officer, one Abel, summoned the pair of them to his office and laid out the procedure.

Girls facing a birching were escorted to the local woods and made to select their own rods, under close supervision. Their behaviour during this expedition should be of the highest standard, for this, along with their conduct whilst serving their sentences, would be taken into consideration when the final number of strokes was tallied. Once back at the reformatory, they would then fashion their own birches to the required standard before having their punishments calculated and administered.

Without further ado, the girls were escorted to the woods to source the rods for their own backsides... At times they lagged behind and were reprimanded for tardiness. The Officer even found it necessary to cut a switch and administer further encouragement to Martha at one stage – which just happened to coincide with the one passer-by we encountered cycling past! (Well they do say that if you go down to the woods today then you'll be in for a big surprise!)

As they progressed through the trees to the birch grove, the Officer spoke to the girls about their time in the reformatory; how they had found it, what they had learnt, whether their attitudes had been suitably adjusted. Alice was contrite and well-behaved: her sentence for trespass and stealing fruit had clearly made a big impact upon her. Martha seemed inclined to be sulky and recalcitrant, claiming a wrong conviction for vandalism which the Punishment Officer was dismissive of, trusting fully in the courts' judgement. Kicking a pine cone along the path under his feet earned her third extra stroke and a very stern warning that she was not making life easy for herself...

New spring growth clung to the silver birch trunks and, an hour or so after setting out, each girl was carrying a thick handful of likely-looking twigs. The return journey to the reformatory was increasingly solemn, each step bringing them closer to a painful fate.

They were permitted a glass of water before being set to work in silence, fashioning their rods. Rough edges were removed and twigs bundled and trimmed under strict instruction to form the traditional implement, before being tied and bound at one end to create a handle. On completion of their labours, two solid, unforgiving birches lay ready.

The Officer inspected them closely, swished them hard, and passed them fit for purpose. He asked the girls which they thought was the more severe. There seemed little to choose although Martha felt one had the edge. The Officer then produced a coin to toss: heads and it would be used on Alice, tails and it would be Martha's. It was heads. Both girls still winced.

Now all was prepared and they were sent upstairs to the Punishment Room. A wooden desk was set out in the middle, rope coiled beneath it. Paperwork was laid out ominously on the desk. The Officer explained what would happen next to the girls. They were told to remove their clothes and fold them neatly. Slowly, reluctantly, they did so, passing their neat piles across, left vulnerable and increasingly frightened.

Alice was told to wait, then Martha propelled by one ear to the shower block to be ritually cleansed. No cheek or bravado now, as she trembled obediently in the stream of water, long hair held up on her head, turning and submitting to the no-nonsense hands which scrubbed her. Then rubbing herself dry in the corner as Alice was collected and shooed under the jets for the same treatment.

Soon, all too soon, they were washed, dried and returned to the dreaded room with the desk… Hands that attempted to shield modesty were ordered back to sides and it was time for sentence to be carried out. How many lashes? And who would face them first?

Alice.

Confirmation filled both their faces with fear. Martha, who had been sure that she would be first, was instead taken from the room and made to stand just outside, facing the wall. Ordered to remain there, stock still, and await her turn. Then the Officer left her, went back in, deliberately left the door open. She would hear everything her friend went through, but would not be able to see…

The first thing she heard was the court's ruling declaration:

"Alice Pears, as Punishment Officer for this reformatory, I am commanded by Her Majesty's Courts under the Judicial Punishments Act of 1928 to administer the sentence of a birching to punish you for the crime of which you have been convicted and to serve as a deterrent to others in the community. You have been sentenced by the Court to 20 strokes, to be administered in accordance with the procedure laid out in the Act."

He then addressed her further, personally, saying that he was duty-bound to be both firm and fair in his delivery but would do everything he could to help her get through it, exhorting her to be brave. Finally, he bade her position herself over the desk and secured her there.

Martha longed to crane around the doorframe, to witness the scene within, but did not dare. Instead she heard the command, "You will count the strokes and thank me for them." And then she heard the swish of the birch, the blow landed across vulnerable flesh, and the howl with which Alice greeted it. Heard her breathe hard, count obediently, be lashed again and shriek afresh. Flinched for her friend's immediate pain and also for her own, still to come but which every stroke brought closer.

After around half a dozen strokes, the Punishment Officer renewed his encouragement and support to Alice and afforded her a moment's respite by checking that Martha remained in position. Then the birch resumed its vicious work and Alice's cries became increasingly anguished. The eleventh fell particularly hard and, on checking her again, the Officer found Martha's face averted from the wall, as she twisted subconsciously away from the source of the agony. Face the wall, she was reminded sternly; no moving.

Alice was struggling badly now, the counting of each stroke sounding more like a sob. The Officer knew that he had succeeded, that the punishment had worked. He didn't lay the final five strokes any less harshly but he did deliver them in rapid-fire style. Poor Alice could barely keep up with her count, which merged into one numeric howl. But it was over, done, she had survived.

As she lay gasping over the desk, Martha was summoned back into the room. Her poor friend's sorry rear was the sight which greeted her, scored across with a myriad red criss-crossing lines, back heaving as she fought to regain her composure.

"Untie her," came the command, and Martha quickly knelt to do so, unable to help seeing the evidence of Alice's beating close up from her crouched position as she loosened the knots, knowing that shortly these same ropes would bind her own ankles fast.

Alice was drawn up from the desk, some scant comfort offered as she was led from the room. She in turn was positioned outside, also facing the wall but on the other side, so that a brief turn of the head would grant her an unhindered view of the desk. No need to hold the already-birched girl in suspense of the spectacle...

The Officer returned, fixed Martha with all his attention, took up the paperwork relating to her sentence and read afresh the declaration. She held her breath as the number of strokes was read: also 20. But the Officer had not yet finished his spiel this time.

"Furthermore, under the powers of the Reformatory Act 1948, you have been sentenced to an additional eight strokes in relation to your conduct whilst serving your sentence of detention."

Gooseflesh swept over her naked body. Twenty-eight strokes in total! Oh how she regretted her previous behaviour now! The defiance which had led to two days on bread and water soon after arrival at the reformatory came back to haunt her afresh; her rudeness and lagging behind in the woods earlier seemed deeply foolhardy now. Alice had struggled to take 20, how would she ever cope with another eight?

She would know soon enough. Bent forward over the desk, she felt the Officer secure her ankles, one to each leg of the desk, pulling them apart, increasing her sense of vulnerability. She settled into position, head buried in her arms, hidden beneath a mass of hair as he took up the birch. Her birch. Laid it passively against her buttocks for a moment, then lifted it away and flicked his wrist to bring it back with meaning.

It seemed to fall gently but its effect was disproportionate. Martha yelped; was reminded to count her strokes; counted the first one. Tried not to think about the remaining 27... Gasped again as the second landed, and was writhing by the fourth.

The Officer paused and placed his mouth close to her ear. "Had you behaved yourself today, you would be four strokes into your flogging now." He then dealt her the fifth savagely, as if to reinforce his point. Similarly her eighth, when he again took the trouble to remind her that good conduct would have seen her nearly halfway through by now, instead of which she was actually just about to begin her sentence.

Martha didn't cry. Her howls became more heartfelt, her shifting and rocking within the constraints of her bonds more pronounced, her counting higher-pitched and her breathing more jerky. Nonetheless the birch struck her relentlessly. She thought fleetingly back to the Officer's description of his duties: to deliver her punishment firmly, fairly and fully. He did all three. At the point where, like Alice, he deemed his actions to have taken due effect, he let his arm rise and fall in quick succession, so the eighteenth to twenty-sixth lashes became an almost-continuous wave of pain. She panted, trying to get a grip, knowing that this pause must be to prepare her for two searing strokes to finish, wondering how she would bear them landing on her blazing flesh.

The Officer touched her right cheek, rubbed it carefully then realigned the birch at an angle. My skin's broken, she registered. The kindness with which he avoided the area whilst completing her allocation was offset by the wicked low angle at which the final two landed, the twigs licking around her right thigh, hungry for the unmarked canvass, bringing her shrieking to the birching's climax.

Alice was called back into the room to untie her friend. Martha unpeeled herself from the desk and stood. Girls no longer bothered by the humiliation of their nudity, by fear or apprehension; now simply consumed by a fiery remorse for their actions.

The Officer confirmed that, their birchings completed, this brought their sentences at the reformatory to an end. They were escorted back to the dorm for an hour to rest and recover whilst their release papers were drawn up, then they would be free to go. The Officer hoped sincerely that he would never have to see them again to repeat the actions of that afternoon.

Lying on our tummies on the bed, Haron (Alice, that is!) and I were reunited, hugging and laughing, on a massive high. When Abel returned to add his hugs and congratulate the brave detainees, we knew that the scene was over. We had played solidly for three hours, maintained our roles and carried off one of the hottest scenes of my life!

Upsetting the natural order

By Martha on 9 April 2007

What's the worst thing that could happen in a spanking household to upset the natural order of things?

Illness can interrupt the best-laid of anyone's plans I guess. Similarly, work and travel often seriously get in the way of the important things in life. But these are universals.

It would be hard to say which of the three of us was most distressed when domestic god Abel had a glass shatter on him whilst washing up this evening, resulting in a nasty deep cut to his hand. His right hand! Whilst he struggled to bear his terrible injury in a manner matched only by women who have lost limbs, surely it is Haron and I for whom you should feel truly sorry?

Here we were, primed by our reformatory scene for a holiday weekend of fun, and suddenly faced with the prospect of no spanking, no play – even no discipline: it was that serious! Mournfully I traced the criss-crossed map of my birching with my fingertips, wondering if this was to be an end to my visit's cumulative total of whipping? I cursed Fate's cruel roll of the dice in so protecting my bottom, and considered how many would feel this a lucky escape! There are others, however, who would understand such a disappointment entirely.

And at least I can report a happier ending here than might have been the case. Brave Abel summoned up his healing powers and that sense of toppish duty soon rose back to the surface. Even before I was put to bed that evening, he had managed to grasp a hairbrush with more than adequate dexterity, so his recovery seems to be well underway.

Haron and I are mightily relieved.

A Spanking for Easter

By Martha on 10 April 2007

Earlier in my stay with Abel and Haron, the three of us played an amazingly hot and prolonged scene where the girls at the reformatory were birched for their crimes. Sunday's roleplay was much shorter, perhaps no longer than ten minutes or so, but was equally wonderfully intense, and with a seasonal theme.

Alice and Martha again, but this time sisters who had agreed that they would give up their computer game habit for Lent. Had, in general, succeeded. Except for one lapse, which their daddy had witnessed when coming home from work unexpectedly early one evening. They spotted him approaching through the window and a mad scramble ensued: screen flipped over to TV, consoles hurled into the cabinet beneath, girls scurrying round plumping cushions and straightening magazines. We were tidying up, daddy. Ah. I see. He nodded, said no more and the matter was forgotten. By the sisters at least.

Easter Day dawned. A family day. Eggs exchanged, relatives coming and going, roast lamb sending delicious aromas throughout the house. And the end of Lent. The end of the PlayStation's banishment. Girls gleefully settling down to a Quidditch World Cup battle to celebrate!

"Alice. Martha. Come upstairs please."

Daddy's tone strangely solemn for such an enjoyable day. The girls looked at one another, puzzled, but did as they were told. Followed him to the room they shared; shut the door when instructed. Looked at their father anxiously, but without really understanding why they should feel so uneasy.

He spoke to them about Lent. Asked them to reiterate to him what they had given up, what this meant and if they had done so. A quick glance was exchanged between them, but confirmation was readily given. Two sisters who believed their deceit, their cover-up, to be safely concealed. How foolhardy would it be to admit it now? Pointless, surely?

But no. Instead they dug themselves a far deeper hole and soon found themselves trapped within it. Their jaws went too slack, their eyes too wide, to be able to deny it when confronted by what daddy had seen. Not only caught cheating, breaking their vows, but also compounding it by lying. Their daddy was deeply disappointed in them and they squirmed miserably.

Whose idea had it been? Who got the consoles out? It was me: Martha immediately taking responsibility, the big sister instinctively trying to protect her sibling. Is that true, Alice? Was it really your sister? No daddy, it was me. Several attempts to pinpoint the ringleader were unavailing, with each maintaining she was the guilty one. So their fate was sealed: they would both have to be punished. Severely.

Daddy's thick black belt lay coiled like a snake on the bed. He bade Martha come to him, told her she knew what would happen now. No daddy, please! Please don't! I'm too old for this now, please! Yes, he agreed, you *are* too old, you should know better than this by now. And you know how I deal with it when your behaviour falls short of the standards you should expect of yourself. When you let yourself down, set a bad example to your younger sister. Martha is almost crying as he turns her towards her bed, unbuttoning her jeans. Orders her to place her hands on the coverlet as he pushes them down, along with her knickers. He has always punished his girls on their bare bottoms to bring his message home; this time will be no different. Alice, go round to the other side and hold your sister's hands. You will both learn how very disappointed I am in you.

He means it. The strapping is hard, thick leather striking vulnerable skin relentlessly, the blows raining down. Nowhere is spared, from the very crest of her bottom to her tender thighs. For all her howls, for all the writhing against Alice's hold, for even the choking sobs to which she succumbs, are useless when she knows she has done wrong. Knows that she deserves to be punished, feels so awful for letting daddy down too, not just herself as he'd told her. Feels her emotions wrenched to the surface by the pain of his belt biting her flesh, just as his disappointment tears at her heart.

It may feel like forever to the girl enduring it but the whipping is soon over. He helps her up, allows her to dress herself, draws her close to him and holds her very tightly whilst she shakes and cries. Tells her that it's over, she's been punished and is forgiven; that he loves her very much. I love you too, daddy, I'm so sorry. He knows that she is, strokes her hair, calms her.

Then she knows that she must swap places with her sister and help Alice to bear the same. Knows exactly what she must go through as Alice takes down her own jeans and knickers, bends over the bed, submits to her strapping as Martha squeezes her hands. As the belt rises and falls, and Alice yelps and kicks in anguish, she hopes desperately that she can convey some strength and support through their clasped hands. For both girls, it is hard to tell exactly who is hanging onto whom as they submit to their thrashings.

Alice finds her punishment and her guilt just as difficult to take. But for all that, she is not spared a single lash less than what she is due, and her cries are as heartfelt as her sister's had been. She in turn is drawn back up afterwards and given all the comfort and reassurance she needs in daddy's love and forgiveness. Finally Martha is called to join them so that all three can embrace and reunite as a family once again. Their bonds are as strong, if not stronger, than ever.

Back downstairs with Abel and Haron afterwards, over that delicious roast lamb, the memories of what has passed also unite we three. This was powerful stuff.

Alice and Martha at school: the final scene

By Martha on 11 April 2007

I have rarely, if ever, played so many intense scenes in such a short space of time! It may have been the final day of my stay with Abel and Haron but we still had one to go before I could be sent on my way. After all, Martha and Alice hadn't yet been to school...

They found themselves, neat in their uniforms, hesitating outside the headmaster's study, longing not to have to knock and announce their presence. Knowing that they had no choice. But knowing also that they had a plan! If they could only pull this off then it would be okay. Or at least, not too bad. They squeezed hands once more, conspiratorially, before Alice tapped.

"Hello?" Mr Jenkins called them forth, always approachable, quite genial even. They shuffled in and closed the door, thoroughly uncomfortable. Gradually he pulled their story from them; why they had been sent to see him by Mr Simmons. We, um, we borrowed a book from him, sir, and we didn't return it on time...well we didn't really ask to borrow it properly at all…and he noticed it was missing and…and he wasn't very pleased. So he sent us to you to…to deal with it, sir.

I see. Hmm. Well it doesn't seem too serious, although Mr Simmons is quite right to be annoyed with you. We can't have girls taking masters' books without permission, can we? No, sir.

Did they understand how the headmaster dealt with matters when pupils were referred by a member of his staff? They did. Not through personal experience, mind, but certainly via the school's jungle lore. He caned them. Always. No wonder they had been so reluctant to approach his study!

Still, he didn't seem too angry. Quite prosaic really. Taking the junior cane from his cupboard without fuss, he asked them who would like to go first? Having failed to be knocked over in the stampede of enthusiasm for this honour, he then asked them again. On the third occasion, a very unwilling Martha, in a very small voice, agreed that she would go first. He told her to lift her skirt and bend over the desk. Slowly she did so, relieved that her knickers were regulation white cotton – for once. She felt the cane lined up across her bottom, then "thwick", brought back down with a sharp flick that made her squeak. And again. Then she was told to get up, go back to her place, swap with her friend. Just two strokes. That was enough; it wasn't a serious offence. Alice similarly pulled her skirt up, prostrated herself and gave two neat little yelps in response to her cuts. Then the matter was done, over, and they were sent on their way. It could have been so much worse!

The scene then paused on cue and domestic science ensued (aka Abel, Haron and I washing up and preparing lunch!), followed by "prep" – the girls working on blog entries under supervision. As the lunchbreak approached, Mr Jenkins advised them that he was returning to his office, whence they were to present themselves again shortly, having been summoned to reappear.

Which they did, puzzled this time, and a little apprehensive. Hadn't they been dealt with already? Why did he wish to see them again? The headmaster's mood was much darker on this occasion, no sign now of that light, reasonable tone. And it soon became apparent why: he had been chatting to Mr Simmons over tea in the staff room, and a very different version of the morning's events had emerged.

Mr Jenkins interrogated the girls remorselessly, and they soon cracked. These weren't hardened criminals, just two girls who had always been well-behaved but had now given in to temptation and landed themselves in deep hot water. Remind me again, what "book" had you borrowed, he demanded, in a voice which brooked no dissent. It...it was the Cambridge Examining Board's 2007 papers in maths, physics and chemistry, sir...

Had they really thought that two strokes each would suffice for cheating? For stealing exam papers and looking at them, trying to gain an unfair advantage over their peers, behaving like criminals? They had no answers, stared instead at the floor, barely offering a protest, knowing none would excuse them. You've had the first two strokes of your canings, you will now be given the remainder, he stated flatly. The carpet pattern swirled and floated in and out of focus.

He repeated the morning's ritual. First Martha, skirt up, flat across the desk and another four strokes delivered. More sharply this time, her gasps louder, but she stuck them, knew she must. Alice squealed this time as rattan struck her smartly across her own white briefs, the momentary imprint shadowing and then fading, whilst Martha stood quietly by, surreptitiously rubbing her sore cheeks. That had been tough! Two visits to the head in one day – and two canings! Not good for the stress levels.

But then the bombshell. As the sorry pair stood once again side by side, Mr Jenkins asked them with a hint of gentle sarcasm if they seriously thought that he had finished with them yet? Martha's heart lurched: she, at least, had. She was very wrong. For of course, not only had they cheated in such a base and appalling manner, causing huge amounts of work for staff and examiners who must now produce fresh papers, but they had also lied. Lied openly, blatantly, calculatedly and repeatedly to him, tried to take him for a fool, even as he had granted them leniency and understanding for their errant behaviour. This he would not tolerate. This meant a second thrashing. And this, despite them being merely fifth formers, could merit only the senior cane for its execution.

Oh Alice, Martha! Cheats never prosper. Surely, surely good, decent girls like you know this? Now you must learn all over again, and it will be a very hard lesson.

Mr Jenkins returned his trusty junior to the cupboard and drew forth its fearsome senior counterpart. At least a third greater in length, visibly thicker, horrifying to behold. Particularly when you are young, scared, your bottom is already striped and you know that none of this will prevent you from being on the receiving end of this new weapon very shortly.

No niceties this time, no asking who'd like to go first or easy explanations of protocol. Alice is simply called forth and told to take her knickers off before going back over the desk. Oh God, no – not bare? She hesitates, trembling...manages somehow to pull them down almost to her knees...attempts to bend over like that and is scathingly asked which part of "knickers off" she has failed to understand? Her silent answer is to slip them the rest of the way down her legs, to step out and leave them in a sad, abandoned puddle of material. Then she bends forth again, skirt lifted high out of the way so that her poor bottom is completely exposed. Traces of faint red lines are apparent from her previous punishment. The next half-dozen will surely glow more brightly than that...

The headmaster draws back his arm and unleashes a scything stroke. The crack as it lands across vulnerable flesh is awesome; Alice's howl in response pure agony. Before the second stroke even falls, a vivid welt has risen up from its predecessor. Martha notes, in an eerily detached manner, that it is pure white, the classic tramlines suffusing in a deepening pink groove. Her thoughts are shattered by the addition of the next; the sheer speed at which the cane is moving; the momentary fear that, despite standing as far back as she can get, she feels much too close to a backswing like that for any comfort. The length and motion of the senior cane, in Mr Jenkins' faithful grip, seems to fill the study. It is, quite simply, terrifying.

There is no mercy from his words either. Pausing in between each stroke, the head leaves neither girl in any doubt as to his anger, his disgust, his enormous disappointment. Alice sounds as though she is crying; the noise which escapes her in response to each stroke is certainly akin to a wracking sob. At one point her knees buckle so badly that she had to be told to straighten her legs and reposition herself. There can be no escaping that this is a very serious caning: to witness, to give and to endure.

The completion of Alice's six strokes frees her from the desk...and in turn condemns Martha to it. Before she is let up, Alice's skirt is hitched into its waistband so that, even standing, her poor backside remains displayed. Six welts stand out luridly against the pale skin, neatly stacked one above the next like some macabre artwork, evenly laid across both cheeks. If one was an admirer of such neatness, such precision, then one would admire this set.

But Martha, at that moment, could only feel sick with apprehension. Having winced her way through her best friend's punishment, she must now somehow survive her own. She took her knickers off without complaint when ordered to do so. She dared offer nothing but complete obedience in the face of this man, this cane. Then she went over the desk, hung onto it for dear life and prayed that she would still be there when six more strokes had been delivered.

The first confirmed all that she had gleaned from Alice's experience. This was nothing like their earlier punishments. No more beginners' strokes, with a starter cane. This was the real thing, and from the very first Martha too was in trouble.

It caught her low down, at the point where buttocks merge into the very tops of thighs, where the skin is so tender and unprotected. She yelped with unseemly volume, clung to the desk. Was reminded that girls are expected to accept their punishments with as much fortitude as they can muster...resolves that she will do so, will try harder on the second stroke, will bite it down...and yelps again as it sears across her cheeks.

These are hard, hard strokes. The sort only given to girls who have done very wrong, who are almost beyond saving but for whom an effort will be made to save them, and which they need to fully appreciate. To actually understand just how lucky they are. Martha *is* so reminded. But it doesn't prevent her knees from sagging under the force of the third, as she cries afresh and is ordered to straighten, as Alice had been, and offer herself properly to receive the remainder.

Martha is good at arithmetic; good at counting. She hasn't been told to count her lashes aloud but she would normally, habitually, count something like this to herself anyway. Somehow, this time, it doesn't work. She remembers three. And she remembers more than three. But it just becomes a haze of pain and cries, hunched over a wooden desk which seems to have become a part of her being. When she is told to tuck her skirt up and stand, it is actually a surprise, for she has no idea where she has got to, what has been given or is still to come. All she knows is that she hurts so, so badly and will never, never do something like cheating again.

Two girls are reunited side by side, their bottoms bare, striped and blazing. Hands that desperately want to cup wounded flesh are ordered back to their sides. What have they got to say for themselves? Oh they are sorry! So very, very sorry! And very, very genuine with it. In an echo of Martha's own thoughts, Mr Jenkins assures them that there will be no repeat, that for as long as they remain at his school and through its sixth form, they will behave. If there is anything, anything at all, which casts them into disgrace like this again, then that's it: I will cane you and expel you. Now get out.

They do. And are still reeling on the stairs, Haron and I struggling back to the surface, when Abel comes to rescue us! We all have some major coming down to do – not to mention bottoms to compare and stripes to inspect! Haron had a seriously impressive set of weals, of which she was extremely proud! They have subsided now, as have my own lines, although they can still be admired when I crane round before the mirror! Abel has caned me quite a few times before but I hazarded to him that I thought this occasion was actually the hardest he has ever done so. "Oh I don't think it was my dear," he replied. "I *know* it was!"

Hot! Seriously hot! Why can't all holidays be like this?! I've had such a good time and hope you've enjoyed sharing some of the memories.

I don't wanna go home!

Abel and Haron are a kinky married couple, living in the UK. Both are published authors of award-winning erotica. Active in the fetish scene, they are both enthusiastic spanking role-players, with kinky thoughts rarely far from their respective imaginations.

She's a student; he's a business writer and consultant. She's in her twenties; he's twelve years older; she frequently gets spanked for pointing out the difference!

The Spanking Writers is well established as one of the web's most highly acclaimed literary spanking sites. Now, for the first time, this "best of" volume brings together the most popular posts from the blog's first two years.

Ideal bedside reading for fans of the cane, tawse, birch and paddle; perfect if your kinky interests embrace punished maids, disciplined schoolgirls and whipped miscreants.

Whether you're interested in historical spankings, fetish fantasies or real-life corporal punishment scenes, "The Spanking Writers" will entertain and stimulate.

"The Spanking Writers" can be found online at www.spankingwriters.com/blog.